"Excellent!"   —*Country Music magazine*

"…a stunning book…"   —*Bone magazine*

"The most lavish book about vintage guitars…"
                —*Vintage Guitar magazine*

"…a welcome addition to any music lover's coffee table."   —*Billboard*

"…remarkably illustrated, wonderfully detailed…an important document in popular music history…"   —*Booklist*

"…a classic history to complement its classic instruments."   —*Playboy*

WALTER CARTER has been a music business professional as an author, songwriter and musician for over 20 years. He is widely recognized as a leading authority on American fretted instruments, having researched and written three books that together provide the most detailed and best illustrated history of important American guitars. He lives in Nashville with his wife, three children and at least 25 lap steel guitars.

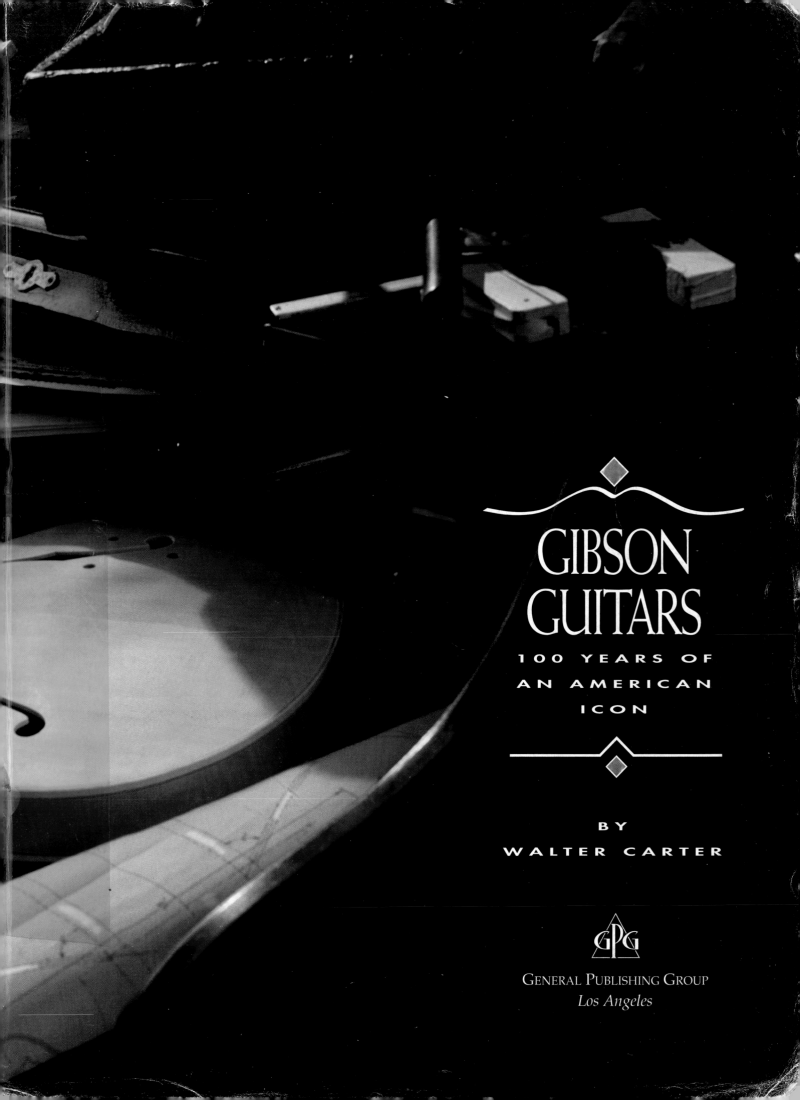

GIBSON GUITARS

100 YEARS OF AN AMERICAN ICON

BY

WALTER CARTER

GENERAL PUBLISHING GROUP

Los Angeles

THE FIRST HUNDRED YEARS

B Y W A L T E R C A R T E R

The first Gibson I ever saw was an A-1 mandolin my aunt bought before World War II. She played a Gibson, I figured, because her mother had played one. A 1917 photo in a family album showed my grandmother with her Gibson K-1 mandocello, standing in the front row of a mandolin orchestra.

FROM ONE LONGTIME GIBSONITE

When the name "Gibson" comes to mind, as it often does, I think first of Orville Gibson himself, his personality and inventiveness, and how 100 years ago he changed the course of the whole guitar family's history.

In England, when I discovered the existence of these guitars through catalogs, it was the late '50s, and Gibson had tremendous mystique. Someone I knew called "Yossell" bought a Les Paul Special, and it knocked us all over. They were rare and scarce. The sales literature and those pictures and photos were all I had until I bought my ES-175D in 1964. The continuity in the range of instruments really appealed to me—their native, classic, smooth, thorough breeding. They shout of American culture. Like the Ultratone lap steel's lift-up flaps—to me, these bear comparison to the Ford Thunderbird of the same period.

Near those railroad tracks in Kalamazoo, Michigan, USA, grew a large factory with a lofty chimney. I visited there several times whilst I was recording and performing on Gibsons such as the ES-175D, ES-5 Switchmaster, ES-345 stereo, Les Paul Junior, Les Paul Custom, and the Les Paul Model. Also in the '80s I played the ES Artist (I had four!), BR-9 lap steel, banjo guitar, various F-5 and F-4 mandolins, doubleneck 6 & 12 guitar as well as 6 & octave, EB-6, and so on. Gibson went hand-in-hand with my musical expansion. Three Custom Shop models, one of which appears on the cover of my book, *The Steve Howe Guitar Collection*, provide evidence of our collaboration.

These instruments are for players to discover themselves on, to decide whether to hammer, bend, dampen, or trill their notes, to have a sound that's natural, clean or dirty, distorted. We touch these instruments, putting fingers on the neck. It must feel right. Then the sound projected can give joy. The craftsmanship aids the musician to go beyond his preconceptions. Gibson will always have an important role to play for those with a compassionate feel for the guitar.

To Gibson and its second hundred years, from one longtime Gibsonite.

Steve Howe

Years later, when I bought my aunt's mandolin from her, my father, who doesn't know an A-style from an F-style from a taterbug, looked at the name on the headstock and said simply, "One of the best?"

For 100 years, that's what the Gibson name has meant—even through times when the instruments were not really the best of their kind. But it's more than that. Like Coca-Cola, Levi's, or Harley-Davidson, Gibson has transcended mere brand-name status to become a presence in life. It seems like Gibson has just always been there, and for all practical musical purposes, that's true. The first Gibsons appeared right along with the first recordings of music, and Gibsons were there through every popular music form of the 20th century: the mandolins that served up sweet orchestral sounds in the early 1900s, the banjos that punctuated the earliest jazz expression, the f-hole jazz guitars that drove the swing rhythms of the big band era, the flattop guitars that laid the foundation for blues, folk, bluegrass, and country music, and, of course, the electric guitars that asserted the dominance of rock & roll. No other instrument maker comes close to having been so profoundly involved in popular music through the past 100 years.

Gibson started in the back room of a musician's apartment in Kalamazoo, Michigan, where Orville Gibson literally carved out a new way to make mandolins. It's a long way from an individual

luthier to a worldwide corporation, and the differences after 100 years are easy to see. For example, the Gibson factory turns out as many

GIBSON GUITARS

100 YEARS OF AN AMERICAN ICON

BY

WALTER CARTER

GENERAL PUBLISHING GROUP
Los Angeles

Gibson: 100 Years of an American Icon

Copyright © 1994 Gibson Guitar Corporation

First Edition

10   9   8   7   6   5   4   3   2   1

Library of Congress Cataloging-in-Publication Data

Carter, Walter -- 1st ed.
        Gibson: 100 Years of an American Icon /
        text by Walter Carter.
        p.   cm.
        ISBN 1-57544-014-8 pbk
        1. Gibson, Inc.--History. 2. Guitar--History.
3. Mandolin--History. 4. Banjo--History. I. Gibson.
ML1000.C37   1994
787.8'1973--dc20   94-33381
                                        CIP
                                        MN

Publisher: W. Quay Hays
Creative Direction: Bill Barnes, Barnes & Company
Art Direction and Design: Karen Cronin
Managing Editor: Colby Allerton
Production Director: Nadeen Torio
Production Assistant: Harry Pierson
Special Photography: Matthew Barnes

THE FIRST HUNDRED YEARS

BY WALTER CARTER

The first Gibson I ever saw was an A-1 mandolin my aunt bought before World War II. She played a Gibson, I figured, because her mother had played one. A 1917 photo in a family album showed my grandmother with her Gibson K-1 mandocello, standing in the front row of a mandolin orchestra.

FROM ONE LONGTIME GIBSONITE

When the name "Gibson" comes to mind, as it often does, I think first of Orville Gibson himself, his personality and inventiveness, and how 100 years ago he changed the course of the whole guitar family's history.

In England, when I discovered the existence of these guitars through catalogs, it was the late '50s, and Gibson had tremendous mystique. Someone I knew called "Yossell" bought a Les Paul Special, and it knocked us all over. They were rare and scarce. The sales literature and those pictures and photos were all I had until I bought my ES-175D in 1964. The continuity in the range of instruments really appealed to me—their native, classic, smooth, thorough breeding. They shout of American culture. Like the Ultratone lap steel's lift-up flaps—to me, these bear comparison to the Ford Thunderbird of the same period.

Near those railroad tracks in Kalamazoo, Michigan, USA, grew a large factory with a lofty chimney. I visited there several times whilst I was recording and performing on Gibsons such as the ES-175D, ES-5 Switchmaster, ES-345 stereo, Les Paul Junior, Les Paul Custom, and the Les Paul Model. Also in the '80s I played the ES Artist (I had four!), BR-9 lap steel, banjo guitar, various F-5 and F-4 mandolins, doubleneck 6 & 12 guitar as well as 6 & octave, EB-6, and so on. Gibson went hand-in-hand with my musical expansion. Three Custom Shop models, one of which appears on the cover of my book, *The Steve Howe Guitar Collection*, provide evidence of our collaboration.

These instruments are for players to discover themselves on, to decide whether to hammer, bend, dampen, or trill their notes, to have a sound that's natural, clean or dirty, distorted. We touch these instruments, putting fingers on the neck. It must feel right. Then the sound projected can give joy. The craftsmanship aids the musician to go beyond his preconceptions. Gibson will always have an important role to play for those with a compassionate feel for the guitar.

To Gibson and its second hundred years, from one longtime Gibsonite.

Steve Howe

Years later, when I bought my aunt's mandolin from her, my father, who doesn't know an A-style from an F-style from a taterbug, looked at the name on the headstock and said simply, "One of the best?"

For 100 years, that's what the Gibson name has meant—even through times when the instruments were not really the best of their kind. But it's more than that. Like Coca-Cola, Levi's, or Harley-Davidson, Gibson has transcended mere brand-name status to become a presence in life. It seems like Gibson has just always been there, and for all practical musical purposes, that's true. The first Gibsons appeared right along with the first recordings of music, and Gibsons were there through every popular music form of the 20th century: the mandolins that served up sweet orchestral sounds in the early 1900s, the banjos that punctuated the earliest jazz expression, the f-hole jazz guitars that drove the swing rhythms of the big band era, the flattop guitars that laid the foundation for blues, folk, bluegrass, and country music, and, of course, the electric guitars that asserted the dominance of rock & roll. No other instrument maker comes close to having been so profoundly involved in popular music through the past 100 years.

Gibson started in the back room of a musician's apartment in Kalamazoo, Michigan, where Orville Gibson literally carved out a new way to make mandolins. It's a long way from an individual luthier to a worldwide corporation, and the differences after 100 years are easy to see. For example, the Gibson factory turns out as many

TABLE OF CONTENTS

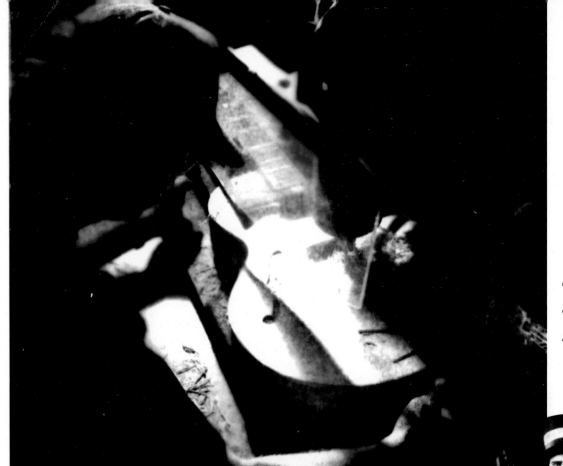

Orville Gibson, 1880s.

Courtesy Roger H.

Siminoff

instruments in a couple of hours as Orville made in his lifetime, and Orville wouldn't know what to do with a computerized routing machine, much less an electric pickup. But where it counts—the ideas—there is not that much difference between 1894 and 1994. Orville would not be surprised to find that someone had figured out new and better ways to make musical instruments. He was, after all, an innovator who lived in a golden age of inventions. Moreover, he would certainly recognize the marriage of innovation and tradition, of technology and craftsmanship, that is still Gibson's calling card.

There is something magical about a musical instrument, and Gibsons, strictly on their own artistic merit, have inspired their own books. The story of Gibson instruments is constantly being told, in ever-greater detail. Names like F-5, L-5, Mastertone, Super 400, SJ-200, Les Paul, ES-335, are well-known, well-studied, and well-photographed. Even the not-so-great ones have been duly chronicled. But there is also something alluring and mystical—if not magical—behind and beyond the instruments, in the stories of those who made them and played them. The images of many

players—Robert Johnson, Maybelle Carter, Charlie Christian, Les Paul, Chuck Berry, B. B. King, Slash, Zakk Wylde, to name but a few—are inseparable from Gibson instruments. But less-familiar names like Williams, Loar, Ferris, Hart, McHugh, Johnstone, McCarty, Berlin, and Juszkiewicz are also inseparable from Gibson's success. Some of their stories are inspirational tales of daring, innovative geniuses who changed the sound of popular music; others are stories of caution, greed, and mediocrity of a sort that make you wonder how Gibson ever survived.

The Gibson mystique has lured many writers into searching for the secrets behind the name. Just as the works of many individuals make up the rich lore of Gibson, the uniquely personal experiences and insights of these writers come together in this book to tell a rich story of music, instruments, and people.

1880s–1902

THE

ORVILLE GIBSON

ERA

KALAMAZOO, 1880s – 1890s

BY WALTER CARTER

Kalamazoo. The name rolls off the tongue like some far-off fairy tale land. In fact, so many people believe Kalamazoo is make-believe that the Chamber of Commerce came up with an official slogan that pervades the city's souvenir shops in the 1990s. "Yes," say the T-shirts and coffee mugs, "there really is a Kalamazoo."

It may have been the unique sound of the name that drew Orville Gibson to Kalamazoo by 1881. It may have been its appealing nickname: The Big Village. Kalamazoo was still incorporated as a village, but with a population of 12,000, it was the largest in the United States. It was a new town, but there were no signs of the pioneers who had settled by the Kalamazoo River just 50 years earlier. "We tend to think of pioneer days as log cabins and guns over shoulders, but that was not true here," explains Catherine Larson, local history specialist at the Kalamazoo Public Library. "People came out from the East because the land had run out. They came here intending to settle and industrialize. They quickly went about doing

what was then referred to as internal improvements: building roads, canals, and actively recruiting business. They established sawmills right away so there were no log cabins. It was a bustling place."

These were progressive-minded Easterners. In the mid 1830s, with the population approaching 1,000, they established a public school system, and the Baptist church founded Kalamazoo College. A state insane asylum was built on the edge of town in the late 1850s.

For Orville Gibson, a young man of about 25, Kalamazoo had a great deal to offer. It was a small town, a college town, but it was not as isolated as his hometown in upstate New York had been. The Michigan Central Railroad had come through in 1846, linking Kalamazoo with Detroit 125 miles to the east and Chicago the same distance to the west. The shore of Lake Michigan, already a resort area, was only 40 miles to the west.

Orville arrived in a thriving town whose

Downtown Kalamazoo as Orville Gibson first saw it, with East Main extending to the left.

1 *Orville's shop and residence from 1899 to 1902 would be on the second floor of 104 East Main, the building with the "Business College" sign. An earlier shop and residence, and the site of the founding of the Gibson company, was one block down the side street, South Burdick. At 118 East*

2 *Main, (under the "Clothing" sign), A. P. Sprague would open the shoe store where Orville worked in the 1880s.*

3 *Two doors back toward the corner, at 114, Benjamin Witwer would open a bakery. The alleyway behind these buildings is East Exchange Place, and the Gibson company's first "factory" was located there, in the back of Witwer's bakery.*

businesses included a foundry, nine carriage makers, a cigar-making industry, an organ company, and a windmill company. The local citizenry was sociable enough to support six photographers and twenty-two saloons.

But Kalamazoo was just hitting its stride, taking two giant steps toward modernization in 1884 when the Big Village was reincorporated as a city and a horse-drawn streetcar line was built. With the streetcar line, the center of town shifted literally overnight as street numbers, which had started at the river, were revised to radiate from the downtown corner of Main and Burdick Streets.

If Kalamazoo was thriving in 1881, it was booming by 1891. A local farmer had planted a celery crop back in

1874, and now there were 150 celery growers. The Big Village was now known as Celery City, with a population pushing 18,000. The streetcar line was electrified in 1893. A year later, electric street lights lit up Main Street. New companies were everywhere, including McCormick Harvesting Machine Co., American Playing Card Co., Upjohn Pill and Granule Co., and S. A. Browne's Kalamazoo Farm (a well-known horse breeding farm). Residents were still sociable, as evidenced by the city directory's listing of two "bands of musicians" and two feather renovators.

Kalamazoo at the end of the 19th century was a progressive town in a progressive time—the perfect place for an aspiring instrument maker to try out his new ideas.

ORVILLE H. GIBSON

BY ROGER H. SIMINOFF

As a young man, Orville Gibson was active in Kalamazoo music affairs. Photos courtesy Roger H. Siminoff

Orville Gibson's talent and imagination are evident in this unusual 10-string guitar, his earliest surviving instrument.

Orville made at least one zither, but the Gibson company never did.

What separates a dream from a vision? While the process may be quite the same, a vision is a thought capsule with a purpose and a destination—an idea begging for truth and reality. Many of us have dreams, but only a handful have visions.

Orville Gibson had a vision.

Over 100 years ago, he began building musical instruments that the world did not know it needed.

Orville H. Gibson was born in 1856 on a farm near the small town of Chateaugay, in upstate New York. Research by Dee Brown and Dick Decosse confirms that he was the youngest child of John W. and Amy Nichols Gibson. He had two sisters, Emma and Pluma, and two brothers, Ozro amd Lovell. Nothing more is known of his early years or how he developed an interest in luthiery.

At some point, Orville headed west and settled in Kalamazoo, where he was first listed in the city directory in 1881. He found menial jobs to support his musical hobby. In 1885, he was working as a clerk at A. P. Sprague's shoe store at 118 East Main, and by 1893 he was listed as a clerk at Butters Restaurant at 216 West Main.

By 1896, Orville had launched his business and was listed in the city directory as "manufacturer musical instruments" at 114 South Burdick. By 1899 he had moved his shop (and residence) to the second floor of 104 East Main three doors down from the corner of Main and Burdick, the center of town.

While Orville's creativity was evident, it is difficult to ascertain if he had the financial resources or business prowess to grow

beyond the capabilities of his workbench. We do know that in early 1902, he was approached by five men from Kalamazoo who were ready to provide the necessary capital to expand on his ideas. A formal agreement was signed on October 10, 1902, in which these men stated their desire to form a "Partnership Association Limited… for the purpose of manufacturing, buying, selling, and dealing in guitars, mandolins, mandolas, violins, lutes, and all other kinds of stringed instruments." Under the terms of a separate contract, Orville Gibson was paid $2,500—a worldly sum in those days—in exchange for which he assigned his vision to these five entrepreneurs.

Although the fuse was lit and Orville's vision was launched, his participation in the future growth of the Gibson Mandolin-Guitar Mfg. Co., Ltd., was coming to an end. It is unclear whether Orville was dissatisfied with this new business relationship, elated with his new wealth, saddened by mass production of instruments, or whether illness forced him to leave the company. The records show, however, that he was in a Kalamazoo hospital in 1909 and returned to New York in early 1911 under the care of a Dr. Madill of Franklin County (the county of his birth). He was treated at the St. Lawrence State Hospital in Ogdensburg (on the St. Lawrence River, about 80 miles west of Chateaugay), and discharged after eight days on August 26, 1911. He returned to the hospital in 1916 and was discharged after another six days of care.

Not long after the company took over Orville's designs, "The Gibson" instruments began to take on a new look, including thinner bodies and arched backs. Around the time of Orville's departure from Kalamazoo, Gibson's sales

emphasis, too, took on a new look. As more artists began to own and love Gibson instruments, their endorsements became heavily publicized in the company's catalogs, and the promotion of Orville's technical attributes took a back seat. But while the chain was broken between the man and his company, somehow everyone who has ever held a Gibson has held a piece of him.

On August 21, 1918, while the vision soared in Kalamazoo, its creator died in Ogdensburg. *The Wednesday,* a local paper, reported, "O. H. Gibson, August 21, 1918, died at Hepburn Hospital after long treatment of five months. He was sixty two. Born in Franklin County, town of Chateaugay."

Orville was buried in his brother Lovell's family plot in Morningside Cemetery in Malone, about 30 miles from his birthplace.

AN AGE OF INVENTION
BY WALTER CARTER

Thomas Edison, June 16, 1888, after 72 hours of continuous work on improvements to his cylinder phonograph.

America in the 1890s was happily caught up in a sweeping modernization plan. Thomas Edison's new light bulbs lit up the World's Fair in Chicago in 1893 (and a year later, the streets of Kalamazoo). With his staff of scientists and tinkerers in Menlo Park, New Jersey, Edison even invented a new way to invent things—a concept known today as research and development. And he wasn't the only one intent on making life more enjoyable. An Atlanta pharmacist had come up with a headache medicine that tasted good, and by the mid 1890s, people all across the country were drinking Coca-Cola, whether they had a headache or not. In 1896, the Barnum & Bailey circus carried an oddity exhibit—a gasoline-powered buggy made by the Duryea brothers. But that same year, Henry Ford and Ransom E. Olds built their first cars (in Detroit and Lansing, Michigan, respectively), and America would soon be on wheels. Women's fashions were on the move, too, with a sleek, smooth-hipped look replacing the shelflike, wire-supported bustle of the Victorian 1880s.

The record business had started in 1887 with Edison's wax cylinders and Emile Berliner's discs. Two years later, on November 23, 1889, a man named Louis Glass put a coin slot on an Edison machine at the Palais Royale in San Francisco, and the jukebox was born. By 1891, the industry was big enough to support its first magazine, *Phonogram.* By the mid 1890s, music lovers could stroll into a phonograph parlor and, for a nickel, listen to their favorite records through a pair of ear tubes.

The new machine created a new kind of entertainer—the recording artist. Len Spencer was the first of the stars. His father had created the Spencerian penmanship method and his mother was a prominent suffragette, but Len took the lowbrow route into the record business with the minstrel classic "Old Folks at Home" and the raucous brass-band imitation "Ta-Ra-Ra-Boom Der E," both hits in 1892.

George J. Gaskin, known as "The Silver-Voiced Irish Tenor," tapped a new source for songs–the Broadway musical. His recording of "After the Ball," from the long-running show *Chinatown,* hit in 1893 and went on to sell five million copies of sheet music.

Spencer and Gaskin shared superstar status with Dan Quinn, who sang some of the era's most enduring songs, including "Daisy Bell" (better known as "Bicycle Built for Two") in 1893 and "The Sidewalks of New York" and "The Band Played On," both in 1895.

In 1896, these three artists had all the Number One records. In 1897, only John Philip Sousa's band cracked their lock on the top spot. Sousa's bombastic march, "The Stars and Stripes Forever," exuded the self-confidence of a nation that in 1898 would free Cuba and annex Hawaii as a territory. The era also produced two songs still familiar to every American almost 100 years later: "Good Morning to You" (better known as "Happy Birthday to You") in 1896 and "America the Beautiful" in 1898.

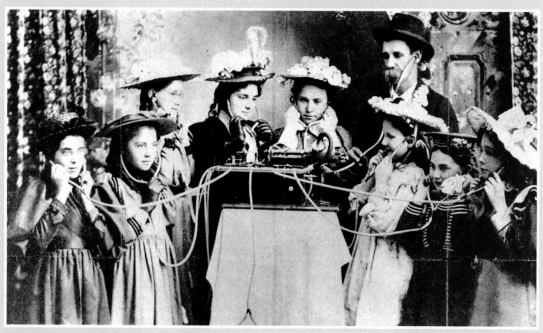

The 1890s had everything, even a Gold Rush. The prospector who rushed to the Alaskan Klondike, however, did not have a "banjo on my knee" like the character in "Oh Susanna," the theme song of the 1849 California Gold Rush. The minstrel banjo had worked its way into high society by the 1890s, with formally outfitted performers and a sophisticated repertoire of pieces arranged for a banjo quartet.

The banjo had been in the limelight for around 50 years, and for young music lovers of the 1890s, that was long enough. From the world of black music, a new style emerged based around the piano. The syncopated rhythms prompted the name "ragtime," and with the publication of Scott Joplin's "Maple Leaf Rag" in 1899, ragtime became the rage. But not everyone approved. The American Federation of Musicians passed a resolution in 1901 declaring ragtime "musical trash."

Fortunately for the genteel crowd, there was another new kind of music. A group called the Spanish Students had hit America in 1880. They dressed like European courtesans and played mandolinlike instruments (actually South American *bandurrías*), and the entire concept caught on. The mandolin proved to be the perfect instrument for a carefree era—a small instrument with a pretty sound that conjured up exotic images of romantic lute players in Renaissance courts. As the century turned, so did America's musical tastes, and the 1900s began with the mandolin foremost among fretted instruments.

It was a time for inventions, for music, and for mandolins. And Orville Gibson was the man for that time.

In an 1890s phonograph parlor, music lovers listen to the earliest recording stars through ear tubes.

By the turn of the century, Edison was in the jukebox business. The backboard advertises a record by the Edison Quartette.

A.O.& E.C. HOWE
MANUFACTURERS, IMPORTERS AND JOBBERS OF
**GUITARS ~ MANDOLINS
BANJOS ~ VIOLINS**
FURNISHINGS AND FIGURE MUSIC INSTRUCTORS.
1609·1610 MASONIC TEMPLE **CHICAGO.**

This Howe company (not related to banjo/sewing machine maker Elias Howe) presaged Gibson's use of women in advertising.

Dobson family members were more interested in performing than in making banjos, and by the time of this ad, 1892, most Dobsons were made by Buckbee.

HENRY C. DOBSON. ONLY MANUFACTURER AND TEACHER OF THE **GREAT PATENT SILVER BELL BANJO.** 1270 BROADWAY, NEW YORK DIAGRAM METHOD WITHOUT NOTES $1.00 UNIVERSAL INSTRUCTOR BY NOTES $1.00 SENT BY MAIL ON RECEIPT OF PRICE.

S. S. Stewart's new invention, the banjeaurine, ca. 1884.

THE S. S. STEWART $50.00 BANJEAURINE

THESE INSTRUMENTS CANNOT BE EQUALLED IN TONE, AND ARE THE FAVORITES WITH ALL WELL ORGANIZED BANJO CLUBS

Ads courtesy Michael Holmes.

BIRTH OF AN INDUSTRY
BY MICHAEL HOLMES

The banjo gave rise not only to a new style of American music in the mid 1800s but also to a new instrument-making industry in America.

Prior to the last quarter of the 19th century, the business was characterized by general merchandise stores that sold mostly European-made instruments. When the banjo hit in the 1840s, however, the only source was local American makers. Still, instrument manufacturers were not able to take full advantage of the banjo boom until the 1870s, when the growth of nationally distributed magazines allowed them to advertise to wide segments of the population. At the same time, improved roads and river transportation allowed larger, centralized companies to produce great numbers of instruments and distribute them economically.

In the middle of the century, there were only a handful of prominent instrument makers, led by William Boucher (a Baltimore drum maker who became the first large-scale banjo maker around 1840), Charles Morrell, Hercules McCord, and William Tilton. By the end of the century, there were more than 1,000 makers, manufacturers, and distributors advertising nationally. Their number was augmented by regional craftsmen whose products were advertised and sold locally. This period saw the first large-scale manufacture and distribution of fretted instruments and the industry's first aggressive advertising and promotion campaigns, but outside of the small circles of instrument collectors and old-time players, virtually none of the great fretted instrument makers of the 1800s is familiar today:

JAMES H. BUCKBEE
Founded in New York in 1863, Buckbee was the largest of all the banjo-making organizations. Buckbee made banjos for many famous performers and teachers who claimed to have factories of their own, including Farland, Mather, and Dobson. Two employees, William L. Lange and William P. Rettberg, purchased the company in 1897. As Rettberg & Lange, they produced such popular brands as Orpheum and Paramount through the 1920s.

ELIAS HOWE
Howe began making banjos in Boston in 1840, but he got out of the banjo business by the turn of the century to manufacture and market his new invention, the sewing machine.

OLIVER DITSON
Ditson is best-known today in the guitar world as the company for which Martin first made dreadnought-size flattops, but in the 1800s, Ditson was one of the largest music publishers, distributors, and instrument manufacturers. Founded in Boston in 1834, Ditson also started the Lyon & Healy Company in Chicago, the John Church Company in Cincinnati, and the John C. Haynes Company in Boston.

LYON & HEALY
Ditson established this Chicago branch in 1864 and later sold to the two founders, George Washburn Lyon and Patrick J. Healy. Initially, Lyon & Healy contracted for most fretted instruments, which were sold under the George Washburn brand, but the company began making its own guitars in 1885 and mandolins in 1886 (and later zithers, accordions, band instruments, and harps).

Lyon & Healy pioneered in the use of advertising and promotion campaigns, and by its own account (which is likely exaggerated) its Washburn brand showed a phenomenal growth in the 1890s. The

Sears, Roebuck was among the "makers" who didn't really make instruments. This 1902 catalog spread illustrates the transition in popularity from banjos to mandolins at the turn of the century.

Lack of roads or rails posed no delivery problems for the aggressive Lyon & Healy company. The company mule is loaded with a piano headed for a South American customer.

1889 catalog indicated annual sales of around 1,000 fretted instruments; by 1897, the claim was 100,000 Washburns a year.

S. S. STEWART

The promotional techniques of Lyon & Healy were only a primer for Philadelphia banjoist Samuel Swaim Stewart. In addition to performing, Stewart pushed his banjos by publishing music, writing prolifically, even inventing new banjos—such as the banjeaurine in 1885—so he could invent the banjo club in 1887.

FAIRBANKS & COLE

A. C. Fairbanks and W. A. Cole were the most prominent of many Boston makers. They started independently, joined forces around 1880, and split in 1890. Fairbanks sold out to Vega and went into the bicycle business.

AND MORE...

Bruno & Son in New York, J. W. Jenkins in Kansas City, H. A. Weymann in Philadelphia, Wulschner & Son in Indianapolis, Morrison in New York, Regal in Indianapolis (later sold and moved to Chicago), and Gatcomb and Luscomb in Boston made instruments in the 1800s. Additionally, many stores, teachers, and performers claimed to manufacture instruments themselves, but these were most often supplied by someone else.

Few of these great names of the 1800s lasted through the 1920s. Today, Lyon & Healy still makes harps. The Washburn brand has been through several owners, died and revived overseas, and recently brought back to the United States by a new Washburn company. The Regal name also relocated to a foreign country after the Chicago company went out of business.

Some of the great names of the 20th century were in business in the late 19th century. They just weren't great names yet:

C. F. MARTIN

Christian Friedrich Martin founded the company in New York in 1833 and moved to Nazareth, Pennsylvania, in 1839, although guitars continued to be stamped "New York" until 1898. In the late 1800s the Martin company was very small and its product was small "parlor" guitars, produced at a rate of only 200 to 400 a year. Martin didn't make banjos.

THE OTHER MARTIN

The Martin Brothers company began making guitars in New York by the 1850s. Martin brother G. Robert Martin was happy to have his instruments confused with C. F. Martin's (which also bore a "New York" stamp), and he encouraged the confusion by advertising his company as "Manufacturers of the Celebrated Martin Guitars." C. F. Martin & Co. retaliated in ad slogans with "The Old Standard," "The Only Reliable," and "No Connection With Any Other House Of The Same Name."

GRETSCH

Founded in Brooklyn in 1883,

Gretsch would be a major guitar and drum maker from the 1930s through the '60s. In the 1890s, however, founder Friedrich Gretsch was still making tambourines.

KAY

Before Kay folded in 1969, it was one of the most successful makers of low-priced instruments. Kay started as the Groehsl company in Chicago in 1890 and became Stromberg-Voisinet in 1921. Stromberg-Voisinet executive Henry Kay Kuhrmeyer lent his company his own middle name in 1929–and it stuck.

HARMONY

Harmony, Kay's rival in the low-end market, was founded in 1892 but was a wholesaler exclusively until the late 1920s.

EPIPHONE

Epaminodas Stathopoulo, the "Epi" of Epiphone, was only 10 years old when the century turned. His father, Anastasios, and probably his grandfather, too, were making violins and lutes in the late 1800s—but in their hometown of Sparta, Greece. The family wouldn't arrive in New York until 1903.

The Washburn Babies were used in print ads, and one set of miniature Viennese bronzes has been seen. Courtesy Michael Holmes

THE MANDOLIN COMES TO AMERICA

BY SCOTT HAMBLY, PH.D.

Mandolins began to evolve from the lute family of instruments in southern Europe during the Renaissance. In Italy there were several forms of mandolin with varying paired "courses" of strings: from the regions of Lombardy/Milan (six courses), Rome, Florence (five courses and a relatively long neck), and Naples (four courses). The Neapolitan style, known today as "bowlback," was standardized in the 18th century and became preeminent in the 19th century. It was almondine in shape, with a round soundhole, a deeply vaulted belly of 15 to 20 narrow, fluted ribs, about 12 total frets on the fingerboard, and four courses of gut strings tuned in fifths (to the pitch of a violin). It was played with a plectrum.

As early as 1755 in Stuttgart, the mandolin was used in orchestras and was the favorite small,

Mandolin by Antonio Vinaccia, 1780s. When the mandolin craze hit, Vinaccia was the biggest name in the mandolin world. Courtesy Smithsonian Institution

portable instrument of nobility and fashionable society, with sonatas for mandolin and cello, etc., in vogue. By the commencement of the 19th century, members of the royal family of Italy were students of the mandolin. Players of rank and title emulated the royal family, and consequently the mandolin became very popular with the Italian musical public.

The most prized Neapolitan mandolins were made by the Vinaccia family of Naples. Pasquale Vinaccia is recognized as the perfecter of the Neapolitan mandolin. He extended the fingerboard, gave it steel strings and machine heads (ca. 1850), extended the compass of the fingerboard, improved the tone quality, and added to its carrying power. His sons Gennaro and Ahille Vinaccia continued their father's artistry after his death in 1882 and received royal appointment as mandolin makers to the court of Italy.

Classical composers Mozart, Beethoven, Handel, Paisiello, Vivaldi, and Verdi wrote music for the mandolin. Its popularity in fine art music subsided in Italy after about 1830, not to emerge again until the end of the century, but by this time mandolins had been embraced by folk and popular musicians.

Neapolitan mandolins were brought to the United States by Italian immigrants by 1769. That year, John (Giovanni) Gualdo, an Italian resident of Philadelphia, played "a solo upon the Mandolino," according to a concert program. But in the mid 19th century, fashionable disdain for the mandolin in the United States paralleled that of Europe. For example, Lydia M. (Francis) Child's *Fact and Fiction: A Collection of Stories,* published in 1846,

indicates the mandolin was banished along with a spinet.

The mandolin vogue in America was begun, ironically, by Spaniards playing *bandurrías*. The bandurría is a southern Spanish instrument, formerly played outdoors in small ensembles that included the lute and guitar. It has a pyriform (pear-shaped) outline, flat back and soundboard, a depth of about three inches, round soundhole, relatively short neck with less than a dozen frets, five (old form) or six (newer form) pairs of strings tuned in fourths, and is played with a plectrum. The bandurría consort includes the higher-pitched *bandurrilla* and the lower-pitched *bandolón.*

On New Year's Day, 1880, the Estudiantina Figaro arrived in New York City. They were called the Figaro Spanish Students in the United States. These Madrileños featured about 12 bandurríasts, a guitarist, and a cellist. They created a "furor" among the concert-going set, as they apparently had in 1878 at the Paris Exposition and in the capitals and principal cities of seven other European countries. They wore costumes unique to the students of Spanish colleges and played unique instruments, as reported in *The New York Times* the day after their arrival:

Originally a banjo club, the Boston Ideals were covering all the bases— banjo, guitar, and mandolin—by the time of this 1897 Washburn catalog.

"Their costume is knee-breeches and stockings, the velvet cloak of the brigand thrown over their shoulders, and a hat resembling the three-cornered affair worn by Washington and his aides. Fastened to the front of this hat is the distinctive badge of the Spanish Students, an ivory spoon. Their instruments comprise five guitars, nine mandolins, and a violin, all of which have double the number of strings of the ordinary instruments, the guitars having 14 and 16 strings, and the mandolins 12."

A month later, on February 4, *The Times* reported on the group's performance at Booth's Theatre, noting "their darkly picturesque attire, performing melodies in which the true soul of music was perceivable."

A longer review appeared in *The Times* on February 16, written by a hardened music critic whose skepticism had been overcome:

"They played an arrangement of the overture to Flotow's 'Marta,' which was remarkably well done, and, considering the resources of the mandolin and guitar, was effective… The unity and finish which these gentlemen show is worthy of praise, though the nature of the instruments they use makes it impossible that they should do more than light and trivial work. The novelty and originality of the music they offered are, however, sufficiently attractive to please an audience, and their proficiency in all they undertake disarms any criticism as to its character."

More than 20 years later, in the September 1901 issue of *The Cadenza* magazine, G. Henri Picard commented on their musicianship: "…The students numbered 22 men, and of these only two could read music; which argues seriously against those who are continually condemning what they term 'playing by ear.'

"When playing in public they had no director to mark time, crescendos, ritards, etc. All these details were thoroughly memorized; each player knew when and where to use the shadings, and every note was picked uniformly, which, apart from the beautiful smoothness thus imparted to the playing of the Students, was pleasing to the eye, all movements being in unison. One member did not play with a flat wrist, but all played alike, producing the tremolo from the wrist entirely, and not from the elbow, which is the case with many mandolin players, and especially those using the trio and quartet movements."

"The repertoire of the Students consisted of one hundred and fifty selections, including many famous Spanish and Polka dances, Mozart's and Beethoven's sonatas and principal overtures, all of which were thoroughly memorized and played without the use of printed music. Their success was due entirely to this method of right-hand training, memorizing everything, and the extreme respect held by the members for their teacher and director…"

Although it appears that the original Figaro Spanish Students disbanded in about 1885, they made a significant impact on those fortunate enough to have enjoyed their performance. In the June 1906 issue of *American Music Journal,* F. O. Gutman wrote, "I doubt if ever there was or will be, a better organized mandolin combination producing better results than the original Spanish Students did. The soft sweet tone of those gut string bandurrías, and gut string guitars will never leave the memory of those who had the pleasure of hearing them."

Emulators of the Figaros may have begun within a month of their first New York appearance; an advertisment in *The Times* on March 1, 1880, for Booth's Theatre touts the "only and original Spanish Students who only appear at this theater." The first documented imitative group was formed by Carlos Curti with talent readily available in New York City: Italian immigrants. Many were violinists who now employed their own culturally familiar instrument, the mandolin, rather than the bandurría.

The many emulative Spanish Students ensembles were successful, partly because they boldly adopted the Figaros' exotic appearance and approach and contributed their own appealing musical skills, which combined to produce satisfying if not

sensational entertainment. Another reason for the emulators' success was that their audiences were unable to differentiate between specific details of small wooden, fretted, double-strung instruments, making them susceptible to clever marketing and consequent mistaken identity. Within a year or two, "Spanish Students" had become a generic term, usually implying use of the mandolin, and the bandurría had been nicknamed the "Spanish mandolin."

The Boston Ideals, originally an ensemble of five-string banjo players, performed American music in a mandolin ensemble setting from 1883 until the early 1900s. They often played preliminary musicales preceding John Philip Sousa's concerts, and it was they who completed the mandolin's progressive assimilation from Spanish music through Hispano-Italian music and finally in American popular music.

The Noss Jollity Company would become one of the first "name" acts to use Gibsons, but in the late 1890s, they played Washburns.

ORVILLE'S INSTRUMENTS

BY ROGER H. SIMINOFF

In the stringed instrument world, Orville Gibson's contributions are typically ranked with C. F. Martin's flattop guitars, the Vinaccia family's mandolins, Antonio de Torres's classic guitars, and Antonio Stradivarius's violins. But Orville stands alone and apart from these legends of luthiery. Whereas their instruments represented innovative refinements and the perfection of existing styles, Orville's were an abrupt departure from accepted styles and the beginning of a new type of instrument (the refinements would come later). Moreover, he came up with *two* new styles—the "A" and "F" mandolins—that are the standards of the mandolin industry today.

Orville's revolutionary idea was an instrument with a violin-style carved soundboard and backboard (although his backs were flatter than those of violins), and he applied it successfully to guitars as well as mandolins. But that was just one of many integrated elements of his instruments.

Orville's artistry featured rims that were sawn from a solid block rather than bent from thin strips. His only patent was issued on February 1, 1898. This document, U.S. Patent 598,245, describes an oval-hole mandolin with a pear-shaped body, a deeply-carved top and back rather than the traditional multi-pieced back of the Venetian mandolins, and sawn rims which "are carved out of a single piece of wood integral with each other in a manner to leave the layer grains of the wood in the same position they occupied in the natural growth."

In the patent drawing, the neck joined the body at the seventh fret, but the narrow upper body shape was able to provide "up the neck" playability. Another interesting feature was a partially hollowed neck which, although structurally unfavorable, provided the instrument with an integral tuned cavity. It seems obvious that Orville was fascinated by the addition of this secondary space to the instrument's air chamber. His earliest lyre-shaped mandolin boasted two such horns, and just after the turn of the century, these cavities evolved to the scrolls which have become the trademark of the Gibson company's top-of-the-line mandolin family of instruments.

Orville further experimented with the graduated "plates," an attribute of the violin family where the soundboard and backboard are carved increasingly thinner near their edges (the transition to violin-like f-holes was not made until several years after Orville's death in 1918).

The first Gibson catalogs spoke of these "distinctive features" and further discussed the absence of

Body scrolls and points are closely identified with Orville Gibson, but they may have been inspired by earlier European designs, such as this 1850s "guitarpa."

Orville put his name inside his instruments, but even without the labels, his "trademarks" are boldly stated with peghead and pickguard inlays: star-and-crescent, butterfly, and lyre.

THE PECULIAR EXCELLENCY
BY WALTER CARTER

Orville Gibson filed his mandolin patent in 1895, when he was still working in a restaurant. In contrast to the dry, stilted language typical of patent text, his application is vibrant with emotion, a first triumphal shout from an inventor who nurtured his vision until it blossomed into an instrument that makes beautiful music.

He begins by dismissing all others but his own. *Heretofore, mandolins and like instruments have been constructed of too many separate parts...*

All other mandolins lack *that degree of sensitive resonance... to produce the power and quality of tone and melody.*

Orville's imposing stare, photographed ca. 1898, became the centerpiece of his instrument labels. Courtesy Roger H. Siminoff

These are not just problems or drawbacks, they are *objections* that his invention corrects.

Orville's mandolin is an instrument of natural oneness, with components carved *to leave the layer-grains of the wood in the same position they occupied in natural growth.*

It is free of internal *braces, splices, blocks, or bridges... which, if employed, would rob the instrument of much of its volume of tone and the peculiar excellency thereof.*

After describing his newborn child, Orville can barely control his excitement. [E]very portion *of the woody structure seems to be alive with emphatic sound at every touch of the instrument—a character and quality of sound entirely new to this class of musical instruments, and which cannot be imparted to others by a description in words.*

In closing, Orville finds himself again at a loss for words as he attempts to describe the dedication and artistry required to make such a mandolin. *Just the degree and the graduation of the thickness of parts comes to an expert almost intuitively by long practice and cannot be communicated to another in words.*

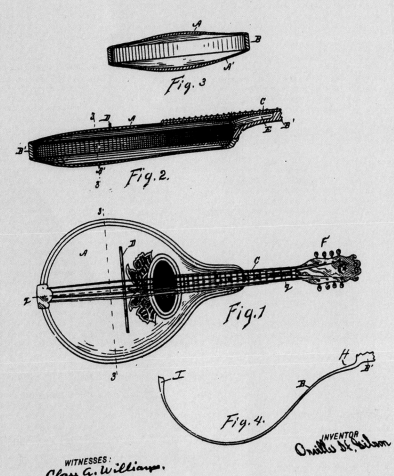

(No Model.)

O. H. GIBSON.
MANDOLIN.

No. 598,245.   Patented Feb. 1, 1898.

Fig. 3.

Fig. 2.

Fig. 1

Fig. 4.

INVENTOR
Orville H. Gibson

WITNESSES:
Clara A. Williams.
W. S. Wood

Stanley Jay

Orville Gibson F-style mandolin, ca. 1898.

Orville experimented with several styles of fretted instruments, including the harp guitar.

"braces, blocks or cleats to impede vibrations." While we attribute the development of advanced structural tuning to the company's acoustical engineer Lloyd Loar in the early 1920s, it is interesting to note that Orville promoted a "special relatedness and agreement of parts" to his construction techniques at the very outset of Gibson's development.

All of his early instruments had an oval soundhole, and all boasted pickguards wide enough to be positioned equally under the strings. Whether this was done to make his instruments cosmetically pleasing or easily swappable from right- to left-handed instruments, we will never know. But we do know that Orville, the seed and creator of millions of right-hand instruments, was left-handed, a trait considered unacceptable for making instruments by some superstitious crafts people.

Since it was difficult to re-saw large logs and boards at that time, his earliest materials came from old furniture where the lumber was already worked to manageable sizes. From these findings he sought seasoned walnut and maple as his primary rim, neck, and backboard woods. The majority of his early soundboards appear to be Adirondack spruce with occasional findings of cedar and fir.

THE INSTRUMENT ON THE LABEL

BY ROGER H. SIMINOFF

Thousands of early Gibsons featured the "lyre-label," which boasted a lyre-like instrument with an inset photo of Orville Gibson. For many years, the history and cataloguing of such an instrument was uncertain. The only telltale signs of this model were to be found in a photo of Orville's workbench in which the body patterns can be seen hanging on the wall over his bench.

Intrigued by this unique instrument, I built one in 1975 to get a better appreciation of what Orville might have been thinking 80 years before. I enlarged the label to lifesize (using scale length and distance between tuner holes as parameters) and then built the instrument using the concepts Orville used: cutting the frail rim out of a single piece of mahogany, hand-carving the spruce top and mahogany back, and trying to match the decoration and finish as I imaged he would have. The instrument took about 100 hours to make, and it was time well-spent, even though it didn't have the greatest tone.

In 1976, the real thing appeared in Kalamazoo. Under the helpful guidance of J. P. Jenks of Homespun Music, a former music dealer in Kalamazoo, and the watchful eye of former employee and Gibson historian Julius Bellson, the owner of an original lyre mandolin instrument brought it back to Gibson to be restored (although it had not been made at the 225 Parsons Street factory). For this historic moment, Gibson consulted me regarding the constructional properties of the instrument and to discuss the owner's request for refinishing it to its original black surface (we recommended that the instrument not be refinished and the owner agreed).

In keeping with Orville's patented concept, the instrument had a rim cut out of one piece of wood rather than being heated and bent, and it was about three inches deep. The neck was fully hollowed out and was constructed in two halves sideways—a strong contrast to the typical centerline splice. The backboard of the mandolin was deeply carved and had a long center extension that continued onto the neck for added strength. It differed some from the one I had built—especially in its deeper body—but like mine, it did have poor tone, power, and sustain.

Aside from the removal of the black finish at some point in its life, the most striking difference between this instrument and the one pictured on the lyre-label was the addition of a pickguard, adorned with cherub and vine art. Closer inspection revealed that the soundhole was a bit more oval-shaped than on the label instrument, and there were eleven pieces of half-round pearl around the soundhole on the label instrument compared to nine on the instrument in our possession. It was not long before we concluded that Orville made at least two of these very unusual mandolins.

Inside the soundhole, we found evidence to suggest that this was not the first of Orville's lyre mandolins. Glued to the backboard was the early square O. H. Gibson label. In the middle of the label, framing Orville's portrait, was the "other" traditional, black-faced, pickguard-less lyre mandolin.

Orville Gibson made the lyre mandolin pictured on labels (top) and a second one with the first one on its label (center). A third lyre mandolin was made and played by Roger Siminoff. © Roger H. Siminoff

According to the model, soundboards were finished in either a "beautiful orange" or an "ebonized" black finish. The sides, back, and neck usually sported a walnut color. The earliest finishes were hand-rubbed French polish, a shellac and linseed-oil compound typically used for violins. Although his first instruments were made of a wide variety of easily available woods, the production line instruments were specified with Michigan maple backs (although many early examples were of walnut and later ones were of birch), Norwegian spruce soundboards, and ebony fretboards.

Orville's diversity of musical interests was obvious. The first official Gibson product line featured five different instrument groups: mandolins, mandolas, mando-cellos, guitars, and harp guitars. Each group had two distinctively different styles: A and F mandolins, L (round-hole) and O (oval-hole) guitars, and R (12 strings) and U (18 strings) harp guitars. Several degrees of ornamentation were available: the F-style mandolin, for example, was available as an F, F-2, F-3, F-4, with the F-4 being the fanciest. By the time the Gibson company made its first instruments, Orville's concept had blossomed into 27 different models.

Though refinished, this guitar shows Orville's concept of a one-piece back (carved out of a huge piece of walnut) and his patented one-piece carved sides. Courtesy Gruhn Guitars

1902–1916

THE
SYLVO REAMS
ERA

ORVILLE AND THE BOARD OF MANAGERS

BY WALTER CARTER

JOHN W. ADAMS
President

Judge John Adams

presided over Gibson's

board for 42 years but

was photographed

only once for Gibson

catalogs.

Orville Gibson in his last

years in Kalamazoo.

Courtesy Roger H.

Siminoff

Five men from Kalamazoo deserve the credit for turning a few mandolins into a successful company—a feat that Orville Gibson alone would never have been able to accomplish—but did they have to destroy poor Orville in the process? They took his ideas, his one and only patent, and put him out to pasture. Or so the story goes.

First of all, the original five on the Board of Managers:

JOHN W. ADAMS

Chairman (title later changed to president). As a newly elected judge, the Hon. John W. Adams was an important—and maybe a bit self-important— figure in Kalamazoo in 1902. He was born in 1859 in Salona, Pennsylvania, the son of a prominent physician. After graduating from Union College in Schenectady, New York, he spent a few years helping his father on a family farm in Iowa and also served as postmaster, apparently deciding what he wanted to do with his life. At 28, he made that decision, and his inner drive shifted into high gear. He arrived in Kalamazoo in 1887 to study law, but he listed his occupation in the city directory as "with Dallas Boudeman," a prominent lawyer. He was admitted to the bar on January 1, 1890; before the year was out, the law firm of Boudeman and Adams had been formed. As the city directory of 1899 was going to press, he had been elected but not yet sworn in as circuit court judge, but he wanted everyone to know about it. His entry read "ADAMS JOHN W. HON. lawyer and judge-elect." He stayed on the bench into the 1940s, and remained president of Gibson until the company was sold to CMI in 1944. Although Adams

no doubt wielded a great deal of influence in board meetings, he is remembered as the owner who visited the factory only once a year, when it was time to divvy up the profits.

SAMUEL A. VAN HORN

Treasurer. Like Adams, Van Horn was a Kalamazoo lawyer, and he, too, was headed toward a judgeship. He was a newcomer to Kalamazoo, having arrived in 1901, and for a time he supplemented his law income by selling insurance. He took care of the Gibson company's legal business and later went into partnership with Adams. His office was at 112 South Burdick.

LEROY HORNBECK

How many lawyers does it take to start a business? LeRoy Hornbeck made three. His office was at 120 South Burdick, four doors down from Van Horn's.

SYLVO REAMS

Secretary and general manager. Somebody had to run the business, and Sylvo Reams knew how to sell instruments. He and his brother Arthur had opened Reams Bros. music store in 1899 to sell pianos, organs, and musical merchandise. It was the fourth music store in a town of just 25,000, and their competitors included Grinnell Bros., a well-known chain based in Detroit, so they had to be aggressive. Their success could not have gone unnoticed by the principals-to-be of the Gibson company, since Reams Bros. was located at 143 South Burdick, within a block of Van Horn, Hornbeck, Adams, and Orville Gibson. At Gibson, Reams had a broad base of consultants available within his immediate family. Brother Arthur continued to operate the store, providing Sylvo with a direct line to consumer reactions. A third brother,

Andrew Jay Reams, was a musician who could give Sylvo a consumer's professional opinion on the product. Sylvo died in January 1917, and a few months later, after a squabble with the board, Jay became treasurer (but he did not succeed his brother as general manager).

LEWIS ALFRED WILLIAMS

Sales manager. After Orville Gibson and Lloyd Loar, Lew Williams is the most intriguing figure of the early Gibson years. He holds the singular distinction of having been a business partner of both Orville and Loar. Williams was a music teacher in New York state who found he could sell every mandolin Orville Gibson could send him. A story in Gibson lore tells of a dealer who asked Orville for a price quote and delivery date for 500 mandolins. Orville's answer: $100 per instrument, 500 years for delivery. Williams may well have been that dealer, for in the summer of 1902, he made a personal trip to see Orville, intent on getting more instruments. His timing couldn't have been better. Williams was likely Orville's strongest supporter among the original investors. He became secretary and general manager after Sylvo Reams died.

These five men signed Articles of Association forming the "Gibson Mandolin-Guitar Manufacturing Co., Limited" on October 10, 1902 ("Manufacturing" was inadvertently left out and written in by hand). The agreement was recorded by the county Register of Deeds the next day at 2:55 p.m. Stock was priced at $10 per share and each man started with 100 shares. Each chipped in an additional $500, a total of $2,500, to buy the rights to Orville Gibson's name and patent.

Every written account of the origin of the Gibson company has stopped right there, and for the better part of a century, the original five have been portrayed as sharpies who duped poor Orville out of his own name. The fact is, Orville wasn't duped at all. Orville Gibson was one of the original stockholders.

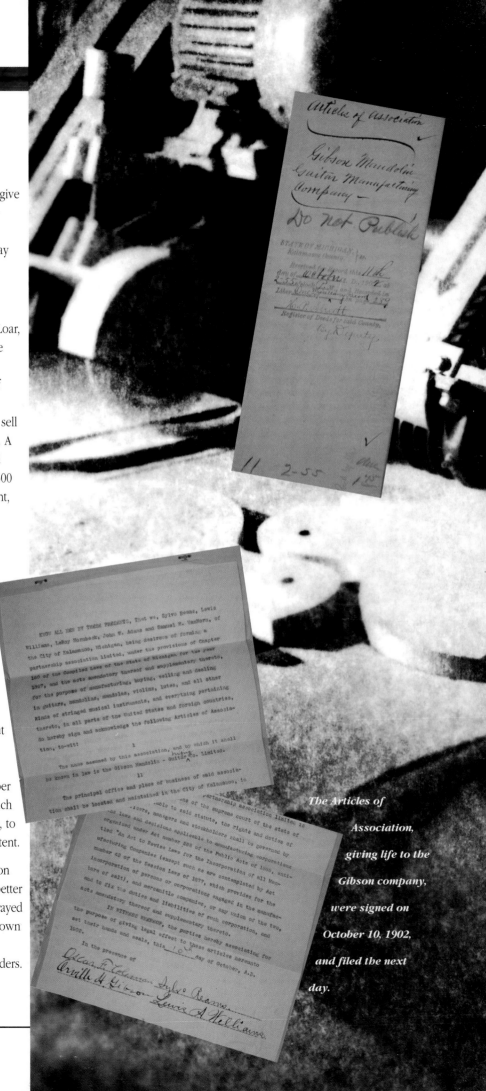

The Articles of Association, giving life to the Gibson company, were signed on October 10, 1902, and filed the next day.

The five founders were the five principal stockholders—but not the only stockholders. Their agreement stipulated that before they commenced business they would have to raise an additional $5,000 from the sale of stock. The very first person to sign up for Gibson company stock was Orville H. Gibson. He bought 60 shares for $600, and it was recorded in the stock ledger on November 1, 1902 (although the actual certificate was apparently not issued until July 6, 1903).

Orville was obviously enthusiastic about the Gibson company—but not for long. His $2,500 agreement called for him to work as a consultant, but showing others how he made his instruments did not sit well with him. On May 25, 1903, only seven months after the company's founding, the board passed a motion "that O. H. Gibson be paid only for the actual time he works for the Company."

The only other action at that board meeting was equally shocking: to elect a new board member to fill the vacancy caused by L. A. Williams's resignation. They elected George H. Broesamle, an insurance agent who had been the fifth subscriber to the initial Gibson offering.

It seems a surprising move, but it was no surprise to Broesamle. He was waiting outside the room, and he joined the board for the remainder of the meeting. Then, after being on the board for all of one minute, he made the motion, seconded by Hornbeck, that was intended to bring Orville into line.

Williams's resignation is curious in light of the fact that at the previous meeting (April 30, 1903) the board offered him an employment contract—then accepted his resignation. Minutes from later meetings detail his compensation—$20 a week, or $25 if he were on the road—which may explain his resignation. Road trips might conflict with board meetings, so it would have been impractical for him to remain on the board.

Minutes from April 30 also provide fuel for speculation as to why Orville's attitude had soured. The board voted to call in $2,000 in treasury stock, a reserve fund beyond the original operating capital of $10,000. Despite their careful budgeting they had found out the hard way what any instrument maker—whether large corporation or individual luthier—could have told them: Good wood is hard to come by. They had figured wood costs according to prices of standard-cut lumber, but Orville's instruments required unusual sizes, and wood costs were coming in over budget. It's not hard to imagine Orville laughing and saying "I told you so."

On July 6, three days before the final 25 percent payment on the original stock subscription was due, Orville Gibson bailed out of the Gibson Mandolin-Guitar Mfg. Co., Ltd. He sold his 60 shares for the original price of $600 to Charles H. Rickard, who owned a saloon at 105 East Main—directly across the street from Orville's residence. (Rickard bought out another early investor, then got either cold feet or cash poor; by the end of the year he sold all his 77 shares to LeRoy Hornbeck.)

What happened to the board after that? For the most part, they went about their business and eventually died doing what they had been doing in 1903. Broesamle acquired a substantial amount of Gibson stock before he died in 1924, but his son lost everything in the crash of 1929, relegating the father to an obscure place in Gibson lore. His grandson, John R. Broesamle, was contacted in 1993, still living in Kalamazoo. He had a connection to Gibson—until recently he had been the owner of a rare, ca. 1940 Gibson electric violin—but he was surprised to learn that his grandfather had ever had any association with Gibson.

And Orville? Either Orville was a better businessman than he is given credit, or he had a lawyer as sharp as the lawyers on the board. Instead of working as a consultant, he took a royalty arrangement. He sat at home in 1904 and collected $375. In 1905, his royalties totalled $750, which was almost as much as Lew Williams made working 40 hours a week as sales manager.

The company's success may have gone to Orville's head, for in 1906, he upped his professional status in the city directory from manufacturer of musical instruments to "inventor." But he didn't invent anything of note, and his 1909 listing—"music teacher"—reveals how he may have filled his idle hours.

In 1909, Orville turned 53. He had seen the company that bore his name grow into one of America's prominent instrument makers. Mandolins with "The Gibson" on the headstock were well on their way to becoming the standard to which all makers aspired. If he felt any pride, however, it was offset by the many changes the company had made in his original designs and the undeniable fact that "The Gibson" of 1909 was a better instrument than those he had made. And the company had done it all without his help.

Orville's royalty agreement apparently had a five-year term, expiring in 1908. By then, the board members had forgiven and forgotten the troubles of the early days, and in December 1908, they granted him a modest but stable income of $500 a year. They sent him a monthly check of $41.66 until he died in 1918.

The honeymoon with the company over, Orville sold his stock to his local saloon keeper.

The resignation of founder L. A. Williams was probably not connected with trouble brewing on the board for Orville.

After assigning his name and idea to the company, Orville Gibson was the first to sign up for Gibson stock.

NEW MUSIC FOR A NEW CENTURY

BY MICHAEL McCALL

At the turn of the century, instrumental and vocal ensembles sprang up across America. Center for Popular Music, Middle Tennessee State University

As the new century began, America reeled forward with rampant prosperity, advancing technology, and expanding forms of mass communication, and music reflected the exhilarating tone of the times. Thanks to the rapid proliferation of sheet music and the introduction of the gramophone, nearly everyone in America had access to the most popular songs of the day, and they wanted to learn to play, sing, and dance to the latest ragtime or vaudeville tune.

No matter that the rest of the world seemed locked into turbulent times beset by border struggles and political upheavals. The Russo-Japanese War, the Turkish-Italian War, and the Balkan Wars had given new shape to major parts of the world. In 1911, the Republic of China was formed after a revolution, and an armed insurrection resulted in a new government in Mexico. In 1917, Lenin and Trotsky led the Bolshevik revolution that would overturn Russia and create a new communist system of government.

In America, however, the new century brought immense discovery and progress. Orville and Wilbur Wright pushed the first powered airplane off the ground, Henry Ford organized his motor car company, the New York City subway was opened, and the first skyscraper, the Flatiron Building, towered above the rest of

Olympia Ladies Quartette

Manhattan. Nickelodeon theaters drew immense crowds to see crude "flickers" which turned into silent movies and led to D. W. Griffith's cinematic masterpiece, *Birth of a Nation,* in 1915.

The recording industry came of age in the early years of the century. In 1900, Eldridge Johnson's Consolidated Talking Machine Company illustrated his product with a logo featuring a dog with his head cocked toward a gramophone horn, listening to "His Master's Voice." A year later, Consolidated became the Victor Talking Machine Co. In 1902, Enrico Caruso's glorious tenor voice first soared from the grooves of a Victor recording and sent the record business soaring as well.

The mandolin rose dramatically in popularity, especially in urban areas. On college campuses, mandolin societies were born, as well as clubs touting the banjo and guitar. Mandolin orchestras provided concerts that mixed songs of a semi-classical air with popular melodies. Smaller string combos performed with barbershop quartets or strummed out the newly rhythmic popular music coming from the songwriting establishments of New York City.

A stretch of 28th Street in Manhattan was christened Tin Pan Alley in 1903 by Monroe Rosenfield, a songwriter and journalist who wrote about popular music for *The New York Herald.* He coined the term after an interview with Harry Von Tilzer, the highly successful songwriter and music publisher who wrapped paper between the strings of his piano to get a tinny sound. It inspired the perfect name for the brisk syncopated music that would be the hallmark of Tin Pan Alley.

The smooth sounds of barbershop quartets were popular in the early years of the century. The

Empire City Quartet introduced "Sweet Adeline" in 1903; the Haydn Quartet had a huge hit with the same song on Victor (they also recorded for Edison as the Edison Male Quartet) in 1904. The Haydns' chief rival group, the Peerless Quartet, made their recording debut on Columbia that same year with the same song and the same success. The Haydn Quartet later hit with "In the Shade of the Old Apple Tree" (1905) and "Take Me Out to the Ballgame" (1908), while the Peerless hit with "Let Me Call You Sweetheart" (1911).

The sweet barbershop harmonies were challenged when the emergence of Broadway musicals and the spread of vaudeville road shows brought out a brasher, bawdier style that simulated the energy rippling through this age of discovery. George M. Cohan dazzled the musical theater with songs like "Yankee Doodle Boy," "Give My Regards to Broadway," and "You're a Grand Old Flag"—all three huge hits in 1905 and 1906 for recording sensation Billy Murray. Comedy singer Arthur Collins had the first million-selling record (two million, actually) in 1905 with "The Preacher and the Bear." He and his partner Byron Harlan gave songwriter Irving Berlin his first of many hits with their 1911 recording of "Alexander's Ragtime Band." Though not a true representation of the syncopated piano music created by Scott Joplin and other turn-of-the-century composers, it nonetheless popularized the term and tuned America into a rhythmically more aggressive style of music.

It wasn't just the novelty of recordings. Americans were genuinely music-mad. Between 1900 and 1910 they bought more than a billion copies of sheet music. The new upbeat songs of the era made dancing easier and more fun, and the tango, an Argentine import that arrived in America in 1910, added a new erotic element to the romance of dancing. Upscale hotels and restaurants added

dance floors, and the demand for after-theater dancing led to the opening of the first American nightclubs. *The Ziegfeld Follies* and similar vaudeville-style shows created stars of Al Jolson, Fanny Brice, Sophie Tucker, Blaze Starr, and W. C. Fields.

The onset of World War I turned Tin Pan Alley into a propaganda machine. Cohan wrote his wartime classic, "Over There." There were melancholy ballads like "I May Be Gone for a Long, Long Time," "Till We Meet Again," and "Bring Back My Soldier Boy to Me." There were aggressively pointed rousers like "We Will Make the Kaiser Wiser" and "We Don't Want the Bacon, What We Want Is a Piece of the Rhine," as well as social commentaries like "How Ya Gonna Keep 'Em Down on the Farm (After They've Seen Paree)."

In the meantime, two other important styles of music had been born, and they would profoundly influence the music of the 1920s. W. C. Handy had published the first nationally popular blues songs, "Memphis Blues" and "St. Louis Blues," in 1914. And the Original Dixieland Jazz Band introduced the country to jazz (in name, at least, if not quite in full-fledged jazz style) with their popular recordings of "Livery Stable Blues" and "Darktown Strutters' Ball" in 1917. A new, more wide-open style of music born in the Deep South was beginning to start another cultural revolution.

Mandolins dominated in the early 1900s. By this time, the large five-string bass banjo in the center was a relic.

The erotic moves of the tango arrived in America from Argentina in 1910.

THE ARGENTINE
(TANGO-DANCE)

In the Musical Play
"THE SUNSHINE GIRL"

THE MANDOLIN MAKERS
BY MICHAEL HOLMES

It was not easy to get a mandolin in the United States in the early 1800s, but following the success of the Spanish Students tour in 1880, guitar makers turned to the smaller instrument.

Joseph Bohmann of Chicago, who had already won medals for his guitars, was, if not the first, certainly the first to attain fame as a mandolin maker. One of the largest makers was Angelo Mannello, who came to New York in 1886 and established a guitar factory. Mannello had won medals in world competition in 1893, '94, and '97, and by 1900, he employed 61 craftsmen in a five-story factory turning out 4,000 instruments a month, most of them mandolins and mandolas.

Orville Gibson was not the only one with new ideas for mandolins. In 1886, a decade before Orville opened shop, Neil Merrill of New York took advantage of a new technology—an economical way to extract aluminum from ore—and advertised mandolins, guitars, and banjos with aluminum backs and sides, but with wooden tops and necks. Those made by C. W. Hutchins had aluminum tops as well; the only wooden parts were the necks and bridges.

The f-holes that would be touted as one of many innovations introduced with Gibson's F-5 mandolin in 1922 were in fact a 19th-century idea. In the late 1890s, Barrows Music Company of Saginaw, Michigan, made mandolins and guitars with f-holes. By 1902, the company had been renamed Waldo Manufacturing and was claiming 51 employees turning

out 500 instruments per month. Waldo also claimed to have one of the largest instrument factories in the country, but the company appears to have gone out of business a year later.

Besides Barrows, Dallas makers Roy B. Simpson and Walter E. Kaye patented an f-hole bowlback model in 1898 and were marketing instruments under the Salos brand in 1900 as "the original, perfected, 'F-hole' instruments." Albert Shutt of Topeka, Kansas, also patented f-hole mandolins and guitars, and his instruments, available by about 1912, had Gibson-style carved tops. Shutt was awarded several patents between 1906 and 1926 for instrument designs, accessories, and parts. He made many, if not all, of the Shutt-brand instruments in his basement, and he remained active as a performer, teacher, and composer until his death in 1963.

Lyon & Healy, the aggressive Chicago-based company that claimed sales of 100,000 Washburn instruments a year, continued to produce fancy bowlback mandolins until 1911, when they began distributing mandolin family instruments made by L. H. Leland of Chicago. Leland surfaced around 1905 with mandolins modeled after the *mandore,* a Spanish instrument with a flat back and bent top. Lyon & Healy didn't offer a carved-top mandolin until about 1915.

The mandolin craze caused a major rift between C. F. Martin & Co. and its exclusive distributor, the Zoebisch company of New York. F. H. Martin, grandson of the founder, wanted to add mandolins to Martin's production, but Zoebisch was opposed. Martin went ahead with mandolins, severed its relationship with Zoebisch, and began distributing instruments from the Martin factory in Nazareth, Pennsylvania.

Martin was never influential as a mandolin maker— the 1895 models were bowlbacks, the most popular

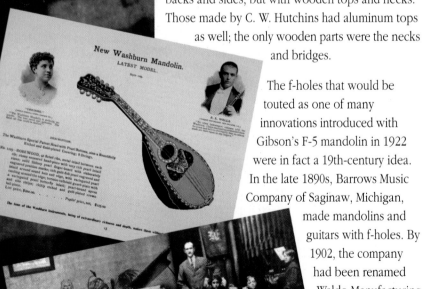

models had a flat back and first appeared in 1914, and Martin didn't make a mandolin with a carved top until 1929. Martin sold around 200 mandolins a year at the turn of the century—a modest amount by Washburn or Mannello standards but an unqualified success for a company whose annual guitar production was only about 400.

Factory fires had a dramatic effect on the instrument business in the mandolin era. Boston banjo maker A. C. Fairbanks sold to Vega (which had been a mandolin and guitar company) after a fire in 1904. Mannello's New York factory was destroyed by fire in 1905, and although he started up again, it was on a different scale. Two other New York City companies—both with the name Favilla—suffered fires. Joseph, Nicholas, and Pasquale Favilla, who had been making guitars and mandolins as N. Favilla & Son from 1890, suffered a serious fire in 1904 but reopened later that year and continued in business until 1973. The other Favillas, Antonio and John (doing business as Favilla Brothers), made violins and were advertising mandolins and guitars by 1900; their shop was destroyed by fire in 1907. They reopened shortly thereafter directly across the street—as a bank.

Gibson, with a superior product and aggressive advertising and promotion, dominated the mandolin market for as long as the market boomed. None of the guitar makers who ventured into mandolin production seriously challenged Gibson, and, with the exception of some hybrid instruments, the banjo makers typically did not attempt to make mandolins. Instead, they bided their time, hoping for the return of the banjo. Indeed, the banjo would soon rise again—in a different form, but as a banjo nevertheless—and all of the prominent mandolin makers except for Gibson would be left behind.

The first Gibson catalog, 1903.

Slotted pegheads made a brief appearance on guitars around 1907. Courtesy Gruhn Guitars

THE GIBSON COMPANY'S FIRST MODELS

BY ROGER H. SIMINOFF

Our instruments are an exclusive line of original, artistic models, producing wonderfully brilliant tone of great carrying power, yet peculiarly sweet and sympathetic.

With this statement in the 1903 catalog, Gibson launched a robust program of articulating its new technology to the world of acoustic stringed music. Gibson didn't rest on the laurels of these new concepts, however, but immediately began improving and refining Orville's ideas.

The very existence of a catalog represented a change. Whereas Orville had built instruments as a free artisan, experimenting and venturing into any creative avenue that stimulated him at the moment, the investors who came on board in 1902 realized the need for standardization, for a formal product line of regular cataloguable instruments with model and price variations.

The first catalog contained 32 pages and boasted several variations of four instrument styles: mandolins, mandolas, guitars, and harp guitars. The rationale behind these new-design instruments was explained in a list of "distinctive features," many terms of which were consistent with Orville's patent, while others were the first gems of prosaic, semi-scientific arguments from the pen of founding partner Lewis Williams:

◆ No braces, blocks, or cleats to impede vibrations.

◆ Special relatedness and agreement of parts.

◆ Front and back made in swelled shape by being carved, leaving the layer grain of the wood in the same position as in its natural growth, thus insuring strength, free vibration, and unusual sympathetic resonance.

◆ The Gibson acoustic rim, to which is glued face and back, performing the office of redistributor of vibrations, which greatly enhances the tone.

◆ Unity attained by carving rim, neck, and head all from a single piece of wood, …inducing instantaneous and continuous sound waves.

◆ Neck hollow beneath the finger-board, …giving in the upper registers a beautiful flute-like tone.

◆ Body made of finest selected and thoroughly air-seasoned woods of most durable, elastic, and sonorous qualities. Maple, mahogany, vermilion, and other suitable woods, all in beautiful figures, finished in natural colors, and selected from a stock varying in age from six to twenty-six years.

◆ Scale as near perfection as it is possible to make same according to the laws of "equal temperament."

◆ Any piece of suitable wood or furniture which may be highly prized because of its associations, we will make into an instrument, if so desired.

Elevated pickguards and three-point bodies date this group to 1907–10. © Roger H. Siminoff

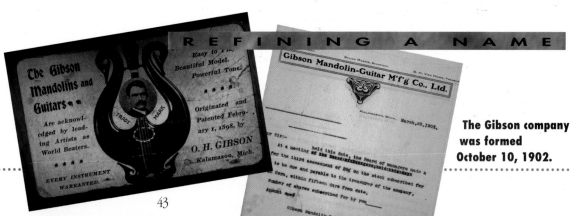

Before the Gibson company, labels on Gibson instruments attributed them to O. H. Gibson.

The Gibson company was formed October 10, 1902.

Orville had stated in his patent application that fashioning the rims, neck, and peghead out of a single piece of wood was the ideal way to implement his concepts. While this was an innovative concept, and the very basis of his patent, it wasn't practical from a manufacturing standpoint and did not become a feature of production instruments. In addition, maple, mahogany, and vermilion have virtually never been seen in the rims or backs of early Gibson instruments; instead, they were made from the mysterious "other suitable woods," which in practice was walnut, a chosen favorite of woodcrafters of that era due to its color, grain, abundance, and ease of carving.

One improvement had already been made by the time of the first catalog. Orville's original pickguard design—wide, ornate, symmetrical in shape, and centrally placed under the strings—was replaced by a smaller guard, inlaid "on the E side only." The new style was more practical and more economical, even if it was to be short-lived. Lewis Williams invented a pickguard that was elevated above the top, and it debuted on the F-style mandolins in 1908.

Orville's mandolins were intended to provide more physical strength and acoustical power, and his instruments were louder and structurally stronger than the conventional bowlbacks. His instruments also had a bassier tone than the bowlbacks. In an effort to reduce some of the manufacturing snags and to improve the mandolin's treble qualities, the Gibson company undid some of Orville's work. First, the hollow neck area was eliminated—a move to increase structural stability at the neck joint and reduce the size of the "air chamber" (body). The air chamber was further reduced by making the bodies smaller—thinner in depth at first, then slightly narrower in width, and almost two inches shorter in length. While Orville's backs were carved, they were essentially flat across the middle; the company carved them in a rounder shape with improved graduations and arching. The company also switched from sawed sides to bent sides, thus abandoning the essence of Orville's only patent. These changes occurred by 1907.

Orville applied similar design criteria to the acoustic guitar, providing it with a carved soundboard and backboard and a one-piece rim. While Orville didn't conceive the cutaway body style, he was acutely aware of the fingering problems up the neck, and he notched away the upper treble bout of his guitars to provide better access to the fretboard over the body.

"The Gibson" name, while fully developed as a company logo in 1903 and used graphically throughout the first catalog, did not appear on pegheads until 1905.

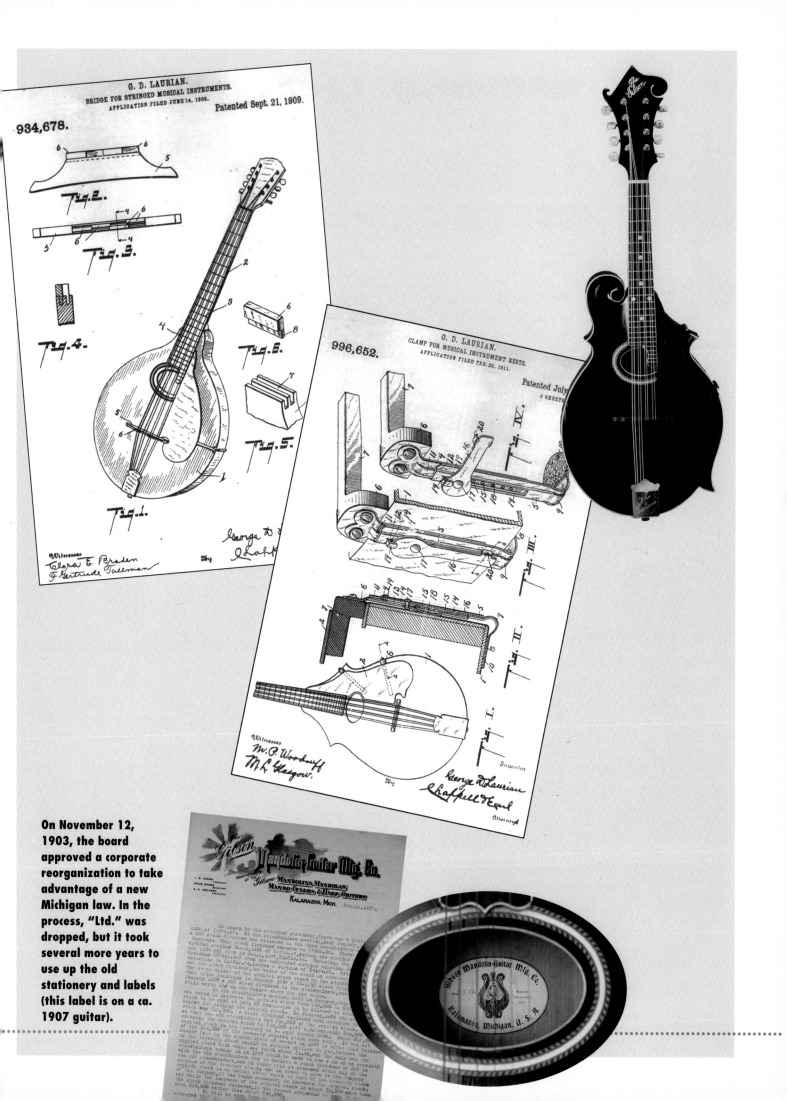

G. D. LAURIAN.
BRIDGE FOR STRINGED MUSICAL INSTRUMENTS.
APPLICATION FILED JUNE 14, 1909.

934,678.

Patented Sept. 21, 1909.

G. D. LAURIAN.
CLAMP FOR MUSICAL INSTRUMENT RESTS.
APPLICATION FILED FEB. 25, 1911.

996,652.

Patented July

2 SHEETS

On November 12, 1903, the board approved a corporate reorganization to take advantage of a new Michigan law. In the process, "Ltd." was dropped, but it took several more years to use up the old stationery and labels (this label is on a ca. 1907 guitar).

Oddly, the less expensive models had geared machines and the Artist models had friction pegs fitted with leather shims—quite a juxtaposition by today's standards. The company switched over to right-angle tuners within a few years. By 1907, the round paddle-shaped pegheads on A-style mandolins and guitars were gone. The top of the A mandolin pegheads received a modified scalloped shape; the guitar pegheads got the "moustache" shape, with the dip in the center that still graces the top of today's Gibson guitar pegheads. Guitars had slotted, classical-type pegheads in 1907, but by 1908, all Gibson pegheads were solid.

By 1907, the company had begun to live up to its catalog specs with regards to the family of wood for each model. The higher mandolin models had maple backs and rims; the lower mandolins and all the guitars were made of wood that looked like lower-grade maple but was actually birch.

On Orville's instruments the bridge was very low, with the strings close to the body. By about 1909, the company began setting the neck at a more severe angle, necessitating a higher bridge. This increased the string pressure on the soundboard, enhancing the amplitude and the tone of the instrument. Orville's F-model mandolins had three

body points. The two points or "little flanges," as Gibson called them, along the treble side were intended to eliminate slippage when the instrument was rested on the leg. With the elimination of the third point, on the bass side, in 1910, the F-style mandolin assumed the heralded shape that would survive to today's models.

Orvillle Gibson's contact with the company ended soon after its formation, but his spirit of innovation was picked up by others. The first of the shining stars of Gibson's engineering staff was George D. Laurian. In 1909, Laurian invented a bridge with two saddle slots to compensate for differences in string gauges. He patented a trapeze-and-pin tailpiece and an improved bracing pattern for guitars in 1910. In 1911, he improved the metal clamp for the elevated pickguard. (Gibson employees assigned their patents to the company in exchange for a flat fee, but they received no additional royalties.)

Laurian was Gibson's plant superintendent until 1915, when he may have seen greener pastures and greater mechanical interests in another company. He resigned to become president of United Garage and Machine Co. in Kalamazoo and was with the company for four years. After 1919, he spent his later years in the auto shop business, as a machinist, painter, and mechanic.

The spirit of invention and improvement continued at Gibson after Laurian. Ted McHugh picked up the momentum with the adjustable truss-rod neck and height-adjustable bridge, and Lloyd Loar finally brought mandolin, mandola, guitar, and banjo designs to a peak with the Style 5 models in the early '20s.

On January 9, 1905, the board approved another shortening of the name, dropping "Mfg."

The Gibson

The Five Nosses, formerly the Noss Jollity Company (page 25), were early converts to Gibson instruments.

Catalog E, ca. 1907, illustrated the Gibson company's thinner mandolin bodies and a new peghead logo. Courtesy Roger H. Siminoff

By 1923, the banjo was more popular than either the mandolin or guitar, so in December of 1923, the board voted to drop the passé instruments from the company name. However, "Gibson, Inc." labels didn't appear on instruments until 1933. Gibson, Inc. lasted 55 years, finally ending when Gibson, Inc. was merged into Norlin Industries in June 1979.

Gibson Inc
Mastertone String Instruments
KALAMAZOO, MICH.
June 25, 1926

Miss Gwendolyn Walters
Seaton Bldg.
Uniontown, Pennsylvania

Dear Miss Walters:

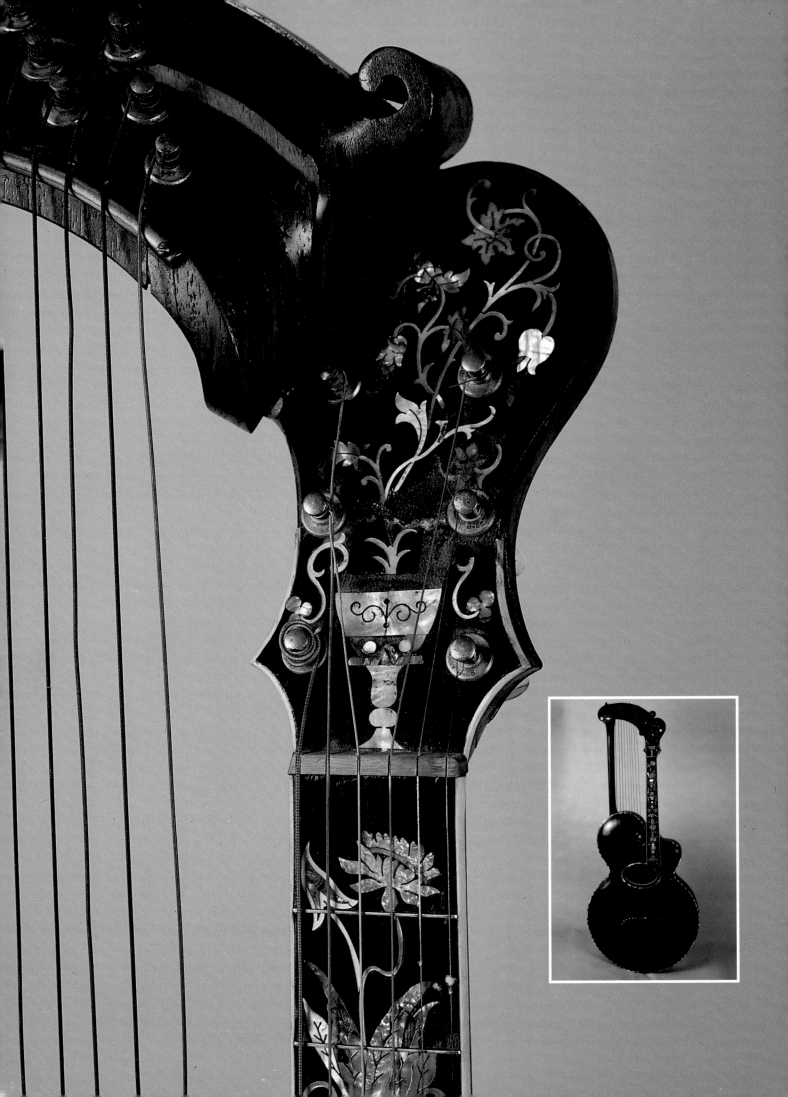

THE GIBSON TEACHER-AGENT

BY WALTER CARTER

Gibson stockholders divvied up $7,865.53 at the end of 1906—a tidy profit for a company whose capital stock at the beginning of the year had been $12,000. The business was growing so fast that the board voted to increase the capital stock to $40,000 in 1906, then to push it to $50,000 in January 1907.

What was the secret of Gibson's success? A good mandolin and a very good market for the mandolin were obvious factors. Sales were up $6,000 over the previous year, the report for 1910 said, despite a month-long strike in the finishing department. And the credit department was operating so efficiently that bad debts totaled only $152.36 for the year. But the real key to Gibson's success lay between the lines of this statement: "During 1906 the Company had no travelling man on the road."

There was a good reason why Gibson needed no traveling sales representatives. The company had *de facto* sales reps all over the country. They didn't travel—at least not at company expense—and they weren't on commission. Like a dealer with a music store, they bought instruments at a "net" price and sold at a markup. Unlike the typical dealer, they worked out of their homes or music studios. They were the Gibson teacher-agents.

There were plenty of stores selling musical instruments in the early 1900s. Gibson's general manager Sylvo Reams had himself been a music store owner, and perhaps he was the one who sought a better way to market instruments—a more direct avenue to the customer where the dealer did not have to lure the customer into a store, a system where the Gibson mandolin did not have to sit in a store window competing with a piano, a cornet,

Gibson got the girl in many early ad campaigns (although the "girls" were questionable in one Hawaiian group). An intimate moment between a couple and their instruments adorned the cover of many a **Sounding Board Salesman.**

and a bass drum, a system that bypassed the distributor and retailer altogether.

Who had the strongest link to the mandolin player, especially the beginning player? Who would be the most trusted person to recommend a Gibson over a less expensive brand? Who could really use the extra income?

The answer: the music teacher. Call the teacher an "agent"—a title that suggested a closer, more exclusive tie to the company than "dealer"—and *voilà,* a sales rep and dealer system.

For the average mandolin teacher, it was a golden opportunity. Gibson armed teacher-agents with heavy ammunition, including the Gibson catalog, with its 100 pages of text and photos, and a special publication just for teacher-agents: *The Sounding Board Salesman.*

Furthermore, Gibson made it sound painless to buy a fine instrument. Time payments were available with no finance charges. The teacher-agent did not even have to calculate payments. It was right there in the catalog—a list price, a monthly payment, and even a pennies-per-day figure. The top-of-the-line guitar, the scroll-body Style O, for example, listed at $150.72, but it could be had for $3.00 down and $3.00 a month. That came out to only *"ten cents a day,"* the catalog pointed out. The low-end Style A mandolin could be had for a mere five cents a day.

In addition, Gibson offered bonus incentives. Various levels of net sales earned a free instrument. Older-style and shopworn instruments were discounted. Gibson even took non-Gibson instruments in trade.

More support for the teacher-agent came from Gibson's heavy promotion of mandolin clubs and orchestras. Groups with all the players using Gibsons were featured in catalogs and advertisements above the caption "Every One a

Gibson-ite." Gibson literature pushed the "tenor" mandola (tuned a fifth below the mandolin) rather than the "octave" mandola, which was a controversial issue in the mandolin world. To help the club or orchestra leader, Gibson catalogs included a list of music publishers with arrangements available for tenor mandola.

The teacher-agents had one of their own in the home office in the person of sales manager L. A. Williams. He had been a Gibson teacher-agent back when "Gibson" was only Orville Gibson. As a founding partner of the company, he was living proof of the good things that can happen to a true believer in "The Gibson."

Williams answered inquiries about instruments with an inspired form letter (one from 1912 is addressed to a Miss Frapwell, but the salutation remains "Dear Sir"). He comes directly to the point in the first sentence of the letter: "Instruments that smack of parrotness rather than superlativeness do not interest you."

He spends the entire first page softening up the customer. Then on the second page begins the hard sell: "The payments are spread out thin over enough months so you won't miss the money.

"A free trial is yours for the asking.

"Price can not longer [sic] stand in the way.

"Have the instrument to use and enjoy now. Just a postal card from you will 'turn the trick'...

"May we hear from you within the next ten days?"

In addition to teacher-agents, Gibson used beautiful women to sell instruments. The 1903 catalog opened with a racy, revealing photograph of a woman relaxing with her mandolin in a garden. A few years later, silent film star Priscilla Dean perched on a rock with her Gibson.

The exquisite Style O listed for $150.72. Too expensive? What if a Gibson agent said you could have this guitar for only ten cents a day? Dan Loftin, courtesy Gruhn Guitars

Tongue-tied Gibson agents had only to look at the back of a Sounding Board Salesman for the perfect words.

A TOUR OF CATALOG H

BY WALTER CARTER

Mandolin virtuoso and Gibson legend-to-be Lloyd Loar testified that the Gibson "has added 50 per cent to the artistic value of my work."

Well, not quite every one is a Gibson-ite, but in the years before Gibson made a banjo, a few five-stringers on the back row were nothing to quibble about.

The first instrument doesn't appear until page 43. One can imagine the layout man being so enthralled by the text that he reversed the first two photos. This is an A-1 rather than a model A.

Step right up, ladies and gentlemen, and witness The Most Exhaustive Treatise on Instrument Architecture Ever Issued by Any Manufacturer.

That's how Gibson's Catalog H of 1912 was billed, and it lived up to its billing, with 100 pages of technical data, formal arguments, testimonials, photographs of musicians, and, oh yes, pictures of Gibson's latest instruments.

A Gibson catalog was a valuable sales tool for a teacher-agent. He had a ready source of logical arguments to convince the reasonable person to buy a Gibson. And if gentle persuasion didn't work, he could find a fire-and-brimstone sermon to save the musical soul of any Gibson skeptic.

The catalog copy, though uncredited, was written by L. A. Williams. His later, signed sales pitches for the Vivi-Tone company had the same style and flair. In a time before radio and television, a time when skillful and imaginative use of language was appreciated by the reading public, a time when "attention span" was not an issue, the Gibson catalog was more than a listing of instruments. It was an entertaining read.

DON'T BE A POTATO BUGGIST

The catalog gets right to the point, debunking old theories of mandolin construction and ridiculing the "Potato-buggist" (the player of a bowlback mandolin) and his "love of tonal diminutiveness."

"EVERY ONE A 'GIBSON'-ITE"

POTTER MANDOLIN ORCHESTRA, OMAHA, NEB.

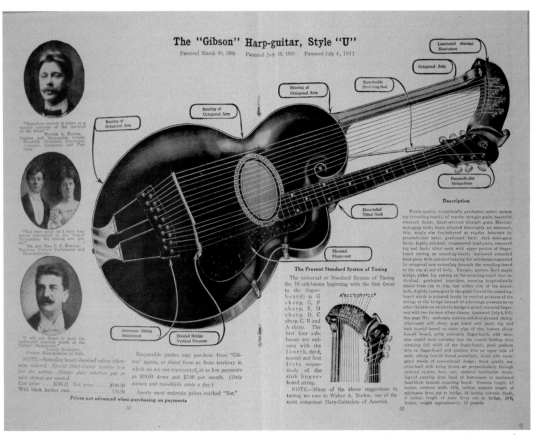

[a skin disease known as St. Anthony's fire] to get recognition, get an instrument to recognize."

A LITTLE HARP GUITAR TALK

"When gray hairs applaud, progress may well ask, what have I done amiss?" The catalog advises to be wary when old-timers like your style. "The mighty Bach" made the mistake of sticking with the old-timey harpsichord rather than embracing the modern piano. "Only death saved Bach from ridicule." It could happen to you if you don't put down that guitar and pick up a harp guitar.

PHANTOM OF THE IMAGINATION

Another debate: the elevated pickguard vs. the pickguard inlaid into the top (whose proponents had included Orville Gibson himself). "Those who without knowing enough of the merits of the elevated guard-plate think ill of it do it no wrong; for they attack not it, but the phantom of their own imagination."

THE GREATEST INJUSTICE

Near the end of Catalog H, back amongst the strings, picks, and parts, and ordering information, lies a request for teachers to let Gibson know about their problems. Furthermore, dissatisfied customers are requested to tell Gibson first before "informing your musical friends of our freckled (?) goods or business methods. To be dropped like a hot coal without earnest endeavor to place the matter squarely up to the Gibson Company to its complete understanding is the greatest injustice both to you and me."

The inside back cover shows scenes from the Gibson factory on Harrison Court.

Philosophy of tonal ideality and fashionable hair styles, all on the same page.

The harp guitar was double-trucked across the middle of early Gibson catalogs. Walter A. Boehm's endorsement is not surprising. He was one of Gibson's biggest stockholders.

JAS. H. JOHNSTONE

BY WALTER CARTER

By 1915, Gibson had a strong sales organization, a factory full of fine craftsmen, and many professional musicians playing Gibson mandolins. That year, the company upped its image another step by hiring James H. Johnstone.

Jimmie Johnstone needed no introduction to the thousands of people across America who had seen him on vaudeville stages. Born in New York City and raised in Albany, he was orphaned as a teenager, and he and his younger brothers Robert and Albert put together an act by 1910, performing as The Johnstones: Musical to the Fingertips. (A later version of The Johnstones consisted of Jimmie and an unrelated partner.)

Jimmie soon went solo, billed as The Musical Johnstone: The Man With the Mandolins. He even signed his contracts "Musical Johnstone." A typical program from 1914 would have him sharing the bill with a "novelty pickaniny" act and a Charlie Chaplin movie. He was an accomplished mandolinist, but he also knew the value of entertainment. He told audiences he would play "Yankee Doodle" backwards, and then he played the tune (forward) with his mandolin held behind his back. In later years, 90 percent of his repertoire was classical, according to his son Jim, but the remaining 10 percent included popular tunes like "Beer Barrel Polka." "Dad never drank, but he loved that 'Beer Barrel Polka,'" Jim recalls.

Although he was on the Gibson payroll, Johnstone's personal testimonial for the new Gibson banjo in 1918 was a seal of approval that no amount of Lewis Williams's catalog prose could equal. In a flyer entitled "A Professional Player's Opinion," he spoke directly to his fellow musicians. "In a nutshell,—boys—it's in a class by itself…" he began. In a dramatic scenario, he told how he secretly switched banjos in the middle of a fox-trot, and how the "more musical tone" of the new Gibson caused heads to turn on the bandstand.

Given Johnstone's high profile in the music world, it might seem surprising that his position at Gibson was supervisor of the stringing department. He was certainly overqualified for the job of putting strings on instruments. In addition, he was blind in one eye, so he would not have had an easy time with any task that required depth perception, such as threading a string through the small hole in a tuner post. He may have strung up some instruments, but Gibson's real purpose in hiring him was to have a

Gibson's first banjo, the TB. Courtesy Gruhn Guitars

The portrait of JHJ—not FDR—hangs on the wall, along with mementos of his career, in his house in Kalamazoo. His son Jim still lives in the family home.

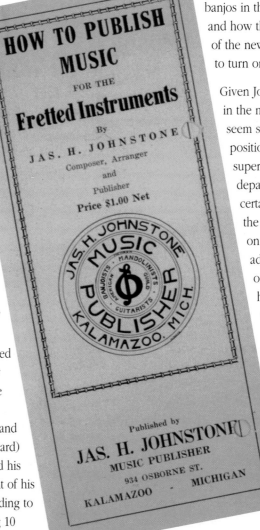

HOW TO PUBLISH MUSIC

FOR THE

Fretted Instruments

By

J A S. H. JOHNSTONE

Composer, Arranger

and

Publisher

Price $1.00 Net

JAS. H. JOHNSTONE MUSIC PUBLISHER KALAMAZOO. MICH.
BANJOISTS · MANDOLINISTS · GUITARISTS
AMERICAN GUILD

Published by

JAS. H. JOHNSTONE

MUSIC PUBLISHER

934 OSBORNE ST.

KALAMAZOO - MICHIGAN

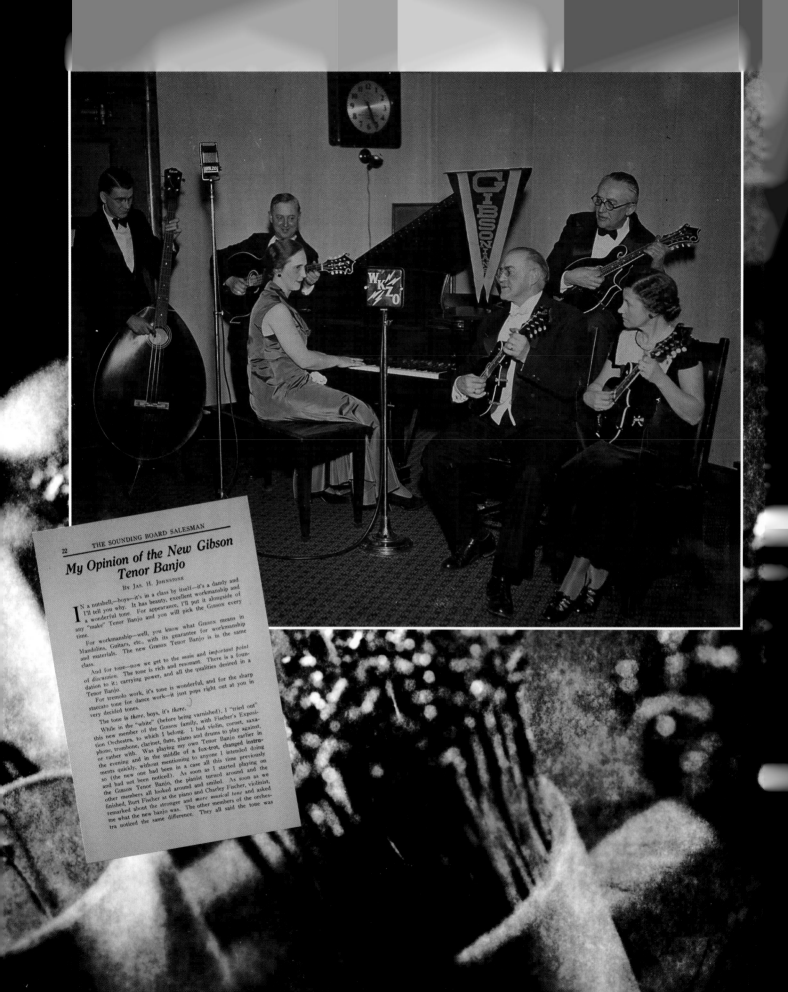

My Opinion of the New Gibson Tenor Banjo

By Jas. H. Johnstone

IN a nutshell,—boys—it's in a class by itself—it's a dandy and I'll tell you why. It has beauty, excellent workmanship and a wonderful tone. For appearance, I'll put it alongside of any "make" Tenor Banjo and you will pick the Gibson every time.

For workmanship—well, you know what Gibson means in Mandolins, Guitars, etc., with its guarantee for workmanship and materials. The new Gibson Tenor Banjo is in the same class.

And for tone—now we get to the *main* and *important point* of *discussion*. The tone is rich and resonant. There is a foundation to it; carrying power, and all the qualities desired in a Tenor Banjo.

For tremolo work, it's tone is wonderful, and for the sharp staccato tone for dance work—it just pops right out at you in very decided tones.

The tone *is there*, boys, it's *there*.

While in the "white" (before being varnished), I "tried out" this new member of the Gibson family, with Fischer's Exposition Orchestra, to which I belong. I had violin, cornet, saxaphone, trombone, clarinet, flute, piano and drums to play against, or rather with. Was playing my own Tenor Banjo earlier in the evening and in the middle of a fox-trot, changed instruments quickly, without mentioning to anyone I intended doing so (the new one had been in a case all this time previously and had not been noticed). As soon as I started playing on the Gibson Tenor Banjo, the pianist turned around and the other members all looked around and smiled. As soon as we finished, Burt Fischer at the piano and Charley Fischer, violinist, remarked about the stronger and *more musical tone* and asked me what the new banjo was. The other members of the orchestra noticed the same difference. They all said the tone was

professional musician there to test the sound and playability of every finished instrument—the ultimate in quality control. (If Johnstone had put his signature on the instruments he inspected, he might be as well-known today as Lloyd Loar.)

Johnstone's starting pay was 31.5 cents per hour, or $17.01 a week for six nine-hour shifts. By comparison, the highest-paid plant worker, Ted McHugh, made 44.5 cents an hour, other department heads made 40 cents, and the lowest-paid worker made 15 cents per hour. It seems like a better deal for Gibson than for Johnstone, who was probably accustomed to making as much in one night on the road as he made in a week at Gibson, but the Gibson job allowed him to stay home. He met his wife Ethyle in Kalamazoo, and he set up a publishing base there, offering a variety of products, including his own compositions and arrangements, a book of mandolin solos by fellow mandolin virtuoso Lloyd Loar, a ukulele tuning guide by Loar, and even a how-to book for music publishers.

Johnstone's son recalls him as a stern man, and with his Franklin D. Roosevelt-style pince-nez glasses he appears quite serious, but he also had a lively streak in his personality. He concocted a photograph of a mandolin quartet with the head of Walter K. Bauer pasted onto the body of every member, and he placed the gag photograph of the Bauer Quartet in *The Cadenza* magazine. The photo was humorous, but it also scored a publicity coup for Johnstone's employer. Every "member" of the Bauer Quartet was holding a Gibson.

Johnstone maintained a high profile as a musician through the 1920s and '30s. He founded the Kalamazoo chapter of the American Guild of Mandolinists, Banjoists and Guitarists and was the organization's

vice president and field secretary. He led a group that performed as the Gibsonians. His wife performed with him and with her own group, the Gibson Mandolin Girls.

He developed glaucoma in his good eye, and when his sight began to fail Gibson general manager Guy Hart fired him, giving him a $100 severance check. An operation around 1940 restored some of his sight, and after taking an inspector's course at Western Michigan University in Kalamazoo, he was hired by the Bauer cigarette lighter company.

Jas. H. Johnstone, as he usually referred to himself in literature and publishing contexts, continued to be an energetic performer, as shown by a commendation he received for organizing a show for wartime troops, not long before his death in 1945. The commendation was dedicated to "Jumpin' Jimmie Johnstone's Jazz Orchestra."

In the '30s, the Gibsonians, directed by James H. Johnstone, performed every Sunday on Kalamazoo's WKZO. Johnstone is seated next to his wife Ethyle. The group includes Henry Dornbush on mandola, pianist Elizabeth Otten, mandocellist Lester Skilling, and an unknown mando-bassist. Courtesy Jim Johnstone

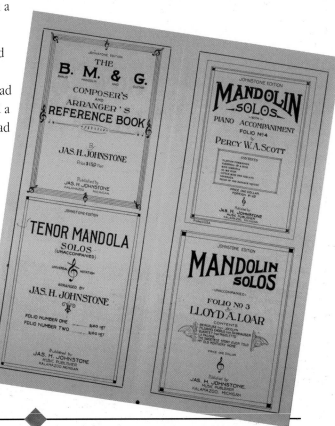

59

KALAMAZOO, 1993

B Y   W A L T E R   C A R T E R

If you're looking for traces of Gibson—Orville or the company—Kalamazoo will break your heart.

On paper, on a city map, Kalamazoo promises the world if you've come to town searching for the wellspring, the genesis, something in the air, whatever combination of cosmic forces that came together in this small town to change the world of musical instruments. You know almost by heart the street addresses where a lone luthier built a new kind of mandolin, where a young company nurtured one innovation after another to become the leading maker of fretted instruments for the better part of the 20th century.

112 South Burdick (by turn-of-the-century street numbers), now part of a pedestrian mall. Gibson stockholders had their first meeting in the corner building in 1902. Orville Gibson's first shop was next door.

South Burdick St., Lovell St., East Exchange Place, East Main—they're all in downtown Kalamazoo. In fact, Burdick hits Main at the dead center of town and is the dividing street between east and west. Just looking at the map, your image of Orville Gibson has to be revised. His lifelong bachelorhood, his lack of participation in the Gibson company, his later years in and out of psychiatric hospitals—all this suggests he was an odd, antisocial sort. But the man lived and worked for more than 20 years right in the heart of the business district. He was a salesman for the better part of 20 years—selling shoes and then selling his mandolins before the company was formed. And

Dave Patrick

he was a performing musician. He had to have been a sociable person, at least in his professional life, and he was probably acquainted with most of the 20,000 people who lived in Kalamazoo in the 1890s.

Kalamazoo in the 1990s has 100,000 people, but it's still in many ways the Big Village that it was when Orville arrived. A visiting driver, needing to check his map, can slow his car almost to a stop without fear of someone plowing into his rear end. Driving in from the airport, south of town, a few turns put you on South Burdick, aimed like an arrow straight at the heart of the Gibson mystique. The older homes along the way build up hope that 114 South Burdick, where Orville Gibson first declared himself a "manufacturer of musical instruments," where he lived and built "The Gibson" instruments in 1896, might still be there. If not 114, then maybe next door at 112, the corner of Burdick and West Exchange Place. There, in Samuel Van Horn's law offices, Gibson's board of managers had their first meeting on October 18, 1902, followed by the first stockholders meeting on October 31. Half a block from the corner, at 114 East Exchange Place, the newly formed company manufactured its first guitars and mandolins.

The feeling of anticipation takes a hard blow along about the 400 block of South Burdick, when the end of the street comes into sight. Burdick stops at Lovell St. (another street where Orville lived). It was closed to traffic and turned into a pedestrian mall in 1959—one of the first pedestrian malls in the country, a travel brochure proudly states.

Gibson buffs will not be the only ones disappointed by Kalamazoo's progress. Pharmaceutical historians looking for the origins of aspirin or "friar pills" will find only a marker in the middle of the Burdick Mall, noting that the Upjohn company (which is still based in Kalamazoo) was founded in a building that once stood near this spot.

Not all of the buildings along the mall are new. A stone pediment at 226 says "Boudeman, 1904," which has to be Dallas Boudeman, mentor and later partner of old Judge Adams, one of Gibson's founders. Maybe the building at 114 has an 1890s date carved into stone.

But no. The buildings at the corner of South Burdick and East Exchange (the numbers are different now than they were in 1900) are old, but not old enough. Nevertheless, this is a sacred spot, where Orville Gibson opened shop and where the Gibson company started. Orville's place is now a hair salon; Van Horn's is a shoe repair business. No plaque, no marker.

Turn around and you're looking down East Exchange Place, where the company was located until 1911. It's an alley. Nothing more.

One block farther down Burdick, Main St. (now Michigan Ave.) crosses. Two blocks to the left, at 215 West Main, was the restaurant owned by Frank Butters, Orville's last employer. To the right, most of what was the 100 block of East Main is occupied by a shiny new bank building. The buildings across the street, dating from the turn of the century, reflect on the face of the modern glass-and-concrete structure, providing an eerie mirage where once was the second floor of 104 East Main, where Orville lived and worked from 1899 to 1902. The pride he took in his work was shown by his all-caps entry in the 1899 city directory: "GIBSON ORVILLE H., mnfr. musical instruments, The Gibson Mandolin a specialty, office and r. [residence] 104 E. Main, 2d fl." (Next door, at 106 East Main, had stood the Michigan State Bank building, where a 1925 article in *The Kalamazoo Gazette* erroneously placed Orville's business on the third floor.)

Benjamin Witwer's bakery was located a few doors down, at 114 East Main. The Gibson company's board of managers resolved in their very first meeting in Van Horn's office to secure a lease from Mr. Witwer. The unnamed, roach-infested, former bakery that general manager L. A. Williams, in an address to Gibson agents in 1919, referred to as Gibson's first home was almost surely the back of Witwer's Bakery. In 1906, Gibson

The 100 block of East Exchange Place. The Gibson company made its first instruments down this alley on the left side, then moved to larger quarters on the right.

expanded into two of Witwer's buildings across the alley (Exchange Place) from the back of the bakery. Land for the company's next location, on Harrison Court, was also bought from Witwer.

Farther down East Main, at 118, was A. P. Sprague's shoe store, where Orville worked for at least five years in the 1880s. In 1889, he lived next door to his work, at 120 East Main.

The beast of progress in Kalamazoo, embodied in the new bank building, devoured 20 years of Orville Gibson's life in a single gulp.

Moving back up the South Burdick Mall two blocks, a right turn puts you near 108 West South St., where many of the early board meetings were held in the law office of John W. Adams, company president from its founding until its sale to CMI in 1944. Ironically, the source of all this information, the Kalamazoo Public Library, occupies the spot where Judge Adams's office building once stood. In the library, a microfilm copy of *The Kalamazoo Gazette* reveals that Adams was a prominent, highly respected citizen—much more prominent, apparently, than the Gibson company. When Adams died at age 89 in 1949, his funeral service was the lead story on the front page of *The Gazette*. So many lawyers and judges attended the service that circuit court was closed for the day. His

lengthy obit chronicled his various law partners, his family members, his civic activities, even his hobbies of fishing and small game hunting. Gibson—the only name among all his associations that would have been recognized outside of Kalamazoo—was not mentioned.

The last chance for a glimpse at Orville Gibson's life is on Lovell St. It's a one-way street running west, so you have to keep backtracking to find 414 East Lovell, where he lived and took his meals for his last six years in Kalamazoo. It hardly seems worth the trouble to find that most of the 400 block, including 414, is a parking lot.

The last chance to touch the company's early years is at 521–523 Harrison Court, Gibson's home from 1911 to 1917. Harrison St. is easy enough to find, and a lot of "Courts" extend a half-block off Harrison, but it takes an old map to locate Harrison Court. Harrison Alley, as it was called in the 1920s, is now literally that—an alley running between a fast food business and the railroad tracks. A concrete slab in a vacant lot is all that's left of the building at 521.

It's a good thing you saved Parsons St. for last, because you know it's still there. You've

Harrison Court. Site of the Gibson factory from 1911 to 1917.

Corner of East Main (now Michigan Ave.) and South Burdick, same view as the photograph on pages 12–13.

Dave Patrick

seen the aerial view of an entire block of buildings devoted to the manufacture of Gibson instruments, and the brick smokestack with the letters G-I-B-S-O-N inlaid in white brick. In these buildings Ted McHugh invented the adjustable truss rod that set Gibsons apart from all other instruments of their day. Lloyd Loar personally inspected and put his signature on the first F-5 mandolins and L-5 guitars. Guy Hart's staff created the overpowering Super 400 and J-200 guitars. Ted McCarty and his designers conceived the Les Paul, Explorer, ES-335, and the Firebird. A proud workforce turned these ideas into instruments that represented the ultimate combination of modern design and traditional craftsmanship for generations of musicians.

The Parsons St. building was opened with a housewarming party and dance on July 10, 1917. The land was in the middle of a strong, working-class Dutch neighborhood, and the work ethic of Gibson employees became a vital part of the Gibson tradition. But the neighborhood is no longer Dutch, and vacant lots are as numerous as houses. The smokestack still stands proudly, but alone in its pride. The original building is painted a dark red, possibly meant to match the red bricks of the newer buildings. In bright sunlight the peeling paint gives it the aura of a rusting old car. Heritage Guitars, a company founded by ex-Gibson employees after Gibson left Kalamazoo in 1984, rents space in the original building. The newer structures house a variety of businesses, including the Black Arts and Cultural Center, Lakeview Plastics, and Richard Allan Medical Industries.

At this point, it looks like no one in Kalamazoo cares that Gibson guitars were made here. You can't blame the city, of course. Gibson abandoned Kalamazoo—not the other way around. Despite the feelings of Gibson buffs, who are sure Kalamazoo owes its worldwide name-recognition to Gibson, the fact is that the town has always courted industries. In the 1930s, *The Gazette* ran a series profiling local industries, and Gibson was featured

in the 36th of more than 60 articles. At the end of 1936, the Chamber of Commerce proudly announced that Kalamazoo's industrial production had totaled $70 million that year; by comparison, New York City's total was $71 million.

The only place you can find Gibson in Kalamazoo is in the memories of former employees. For them, too, the relic on Parsons St.—the only company home many of them knew—is a heartbreaking sight. Some are understandably bitter, having lost not only their jobs but their pensions when Gibson left town. But most, when they remember Gibson, remember Gibson fondly.

Ted McCarty, president of Gibson from 1948 to 1966, owner of Bigsby Accessories (located in Kalamazoo) since 1966: "I loved it right down to the last minute I was there. I feel like crying every time I go by that thing. That was the finest guitar factory in the world."

J. P. Moats started in final sanding in 1957, was quality control manager when the Kalamazoo plant closed in 1984, then formed Heritage Guitars with three other ex-employees. "They paid well, had good insurance, good vacation. It was a real good place for people to work."

Maudie Moore started in 1964 in routing and buffing, later moved to engraving, left in 1980, but still does engraving and inlay work for Gibson and other companies. "I loved it. I love Gibson instruments. I loved it when you'd see an instrument on TV, and you know you did the work on that particular instrument.

"We all thought we would be there for the rest of our lives."

225 Parsons St., Gibson's home from 1917 to 1984.

The only Gibson work in Kalamazoo in 1993 is not in a factory, but in Maudie Moore's home workshop.

1917–1923

THE
L. A. WILLIAMS
ERA

THE JAZZ AGE

BY MICHAEL McCALL

Duke Ellington's Washingtonians, with Fred Guy on a Gibson L-4 guitar, brought a new sophistication to dance music. Center for Popular Music, Middle Tennessee State University

As World War I ended, America celebrated by loosening up and letting it all hang out. It was as if freedom had taken on a whole new meaning: Suddenly, it seemed, American society became more impulsive and impetuous. A country once defined by temperance and morality now reveled in indulgence and hedonism.

Everything about the American lifestyle opened up and grew bawdier. People began kissing freely and flagrantly in the streets as sexuality began to be exalted in media and music. The passage of the 18th Amendment, starting Prohibition, only made carousing more fashionable and fun, as drinking, smoking, gambling, and dancing increased abundantly.

The women's suffrage movement led to the passage of the 19th Amendment, and the so-called "second sex" responded by flaunting a more provocative style. Cosmetic sales soared. Women bobbed their hair and dressed more alluringly, shortening hemlines and baring shoulders. They dared to smoke and even curse in public.

Along with this new boldness, a smart cynicism flourished. H. L. Mencken spewed literary venom in his *American Mercury* magazine, Dorothy Parker flashed her sharp wit in *The New Yorker*, and F. Scott Fitzgerald's novels seductively and insightfully summed up what Gertrude Stein later called "The Lost Generation."

Music took on a similarly sophisticated gaiety. The sweet, sentimental vocal tunes of Tin Pan Alley were displaced by a brasher, more urbane style of brassy instrumental dance music. Everyone fell in love with dancing, as the shimmy, the hoochie-koochie, the black bottom, and especially the Charleston became the rage.

Bix Beiderbecke proved how sublime a cornet could sound. Eddie Lang proved that the guitar could create sounds just as refined and advanced as any other orchestra instrument. Paul Whiteman and His Orchestra, the decade's most popular dance band, presented elegantly polished pop tunes featuring pleasing arrangements that borrowed instrumental, harmonic, and rhythmic elements from the harder-swinging jazz bands of New Orleans, Chicago, and Kansas City.

Chicago was a hotbed of stunningly creative jazz players. Louis Armstrong moved to town from New Orleans to join Joe Oliver and eventually formed his Hot Five with such famed bandmates as trombonist Kid Ory and banjoist Johnny St. Cyr. Other Chicago heavyweights included saxophonist Coleman Hawkins, pianist Earl "Fatha" Hines, drummer Gene Krupa, and clarinetist Mezz Mezzrow. In addition to Hines's inventive expansion of jazz piano, Chicago also spawned many boogie-woogie specialists, including Pinetop Smith, Jimmy Yancey, Albert Ammons, and Meade Lux Lewis.

In New York, another renowned jazz patriarch was beginning to create music that would change the sound of America. Duke Ellington took up residence as the leader of a band at Manhattan's eminent Cotton Club, and his intense, ambitious

In 1923, a one-tube, battery-operated radio required earphones. By the end of the decade most of America was tuned in. Courtesy **The Tennessean**

Adrian Rollini's band of 1927 spawned some of the most influential musicians of the Jazz Age, including Eddie Lang, who would soon put down his banjo and pick up his Gibson L-4, cornetist Bix Beiderbecke (seated behind guitar), and violinist Joe Venuti (standing at far right). **Frank Driggs Collection**

arrangements elevated jazz to a new level of sophistication.

On Broadway, the musical leaped from light entertainment into a medium capable of telling touching, complex stories of substance. Nearly all of the revered musical writers either made their debut or greatly expanded their repertoire, including George Gershwin, Cole Porter, Jerome Kern, Oscar Hammerstein II, Rodgers and Hart, Irving Berlin, and Vincent Youmans.

In 1920, Broadway revue singer Mamie Smith recorded "Crazy Blues." Regarded as the first authentic blues recording, it sold more than 100,000 copies, mostly in the black community, thereby indicating a market that record companies had previously ignored. All of the other record labels responded with their own acts, giving voice to such outstanding stylists as Bessie Smith, Alberta

Hunter, Ma Rainey, Ethel Waters, Ida Cox, and Lucille Hegamin.

Country music—then known as "hillbilly"—traces its commercial origins to the Jazz Age. The first live radio broadcast of *The Grand Ole Opry* occurred in 1925. That same year, a New York light opera singer named Vernon Dalhart recorded a country-style ballad, "The Prisoner's Song," which hit Number One and eventually sold more than seven million copies.

In 1927, Victor Records executive Ralph Peer ventured south in search of new hillbilly talent. In one recording session in Bristol, Tennessee, Peer discovered country music's first two nationally famous acts, the Carter Family and Jimmie Rodgers. Both acts featured the acoustic guitar as a primary component of their sound. The long-neglected instrument, considered too quiet to compete with

Country music gained popularity in the '20s, spurred by radio shows like The National Barndance *on Chicago's* WLS. Country Music Foundation

the brassy sound of most popular bands, suddenly saw its influence begin to rise. Still, even in most country string bands, the banjo reigned supreme.

The first radio station signed on the air in 1919, and radio quickly became a national phenomenon, spreading from state to state faster than an influenza outbreak. By 1922, there were 500 stations in the United States; three years later, the number had doubled. Live broadcasts of urban dance bands in the North and hillbilly string bands in the South ruled the airwaves, giving musicians more work and greater popularity than ever. Paul Whiteman, Ted Weems, Fred Waring, Jimmie Rodgers, and Uncle Dave Macon were as well-known as such movie stars as Gloria Swanson and John Barrymore.

The decade ended with the stock market crash and the beginning of the Depression, which put a firm cap on the reckless attitudes that had flowered in the Jazz Age. In popular music, however, the age of unabashed creativity and growth was only beginning.

Benny Goodman had just moved to New York, as had Cab Calloway, Guy Lombardo, and Glen Gray. Glenn Miller was performing as a pit orchestra trombonist on Broadway, Count Basie marked time as a pianist and organist in a Kansas City movie theater, and Jimmie Lunceford formed his first band in Memphis. Meanwhile, Charlie Christian and Django Reinhardt were developing their six-string skills in Oklahoma and Paris, respectively.

While America was preparing to weather one of its roughest decades, music was ready to expand its vocabulary and its cultural impact.

Maybelle Carter played a Gibson L-1 when she, A. P., and Sara made the first Carter Family recordings in 1927. Courtesy Gruhn Guitars

EVOLUTION OF THE BANJO

BY DR. ELIAS J. KAUFMAN

For more than a hundred years the banjo has been called the only American instrument—because it developed here and because its music reflects the American spirit. Even today the banjo remains a vernacular instrument, an outsider compared to the "legitimate" instruments of orchestras and bands, but a true instrument of the people, used in folk music, country, bluegrass, jazz, and even classic style.

There is little question that the banjo developed from African-American slave instruments of the 17th and 18th centuries. Though constructed from gourds, boxes, animal shells, and the like, and strung with three or four horse hair, thread, gut, or plant-fiber strings, these early folk instruments often displayed a simple elegance.

In the early 19th century we begin to find sporadic mention of banjos being played by white Americans. They were usually imitating blacks—often in a mean way. Thomas "Daddy" Rice's "Jump Jim Crow" routine, begun about 1828, gave a great impetus to blackface minstrelsy on stage, and it was during this period that the unique American five-string banjo, a fretless instrument with four long strings and a short thumb string, was developed. Virginia-born minstrel Joel Walker Sweeney (1813–60) is often credited for this, and Sweeney may have been responsible for adding the low, fourth bass string (not the short thumb string). Certainly Sweeney was playing such a banjo of his own construction in public by 1835 or '36.

Early minstrel players used what is now referred to as the "frailing" or "old-time" style, with the thumb playing the high-pitched fifth string on the off-beat, giving the "ring" and an added eccentric character to the banjo. This rhythmic stroke style is clearly closer to African rhythmic, polyphonic music than to European music.

In the late 1830s, blackface Negro imitators performed in circuses and theaters, singing and dancing. But it was not until Februrary 1843, when Dan Emmett (fiddle), William Whitlock (banjo), Dick Pelham (tambourine), and Frank Brower (bones) formed the Virginia Minstrels in New York City, that the true American minstrel show was born. Their "Ethiopian" or "African" entertainment—a complete program of music, skits, speeches, and jokes—was a great success, and the minstrel show rapidly became *the* American entertainment.

Through minstrel shows, the banjo reached a wider audience. It went west with the Forty-Niners and into the remotest hamlets via traveling shows, fairs, and itinerant performers. It was picked up by people from all walks of life, and in 1850 the first tutorial was published. Although city dwellers could buy banjos, backwoodsmen, farmers, and homesteaders made their own. The Civil War helped the spread of the banjo, bringing people out of isolated enclaves and exposing them to minstrel shows, which were a popular form of entertainment for the troops.

Fred Van Eps, recording for Victor, ca. 1918. Van Eps made hundreds of commercial recordings from 1897 through the late 1920s. Courtesy Elias J. Kaufman

Joel Walker Sweeney, ca. 1844, pioneer and popularizer of the five-string banjo. Courtesy Elias J. Kaufman

About the time of the Civil War, a different playing style emerged, with the individual fingers plucking the strings. The "guitar style," as it was called in an 1865 method, became the predominant urban banjo form for the rest of the century. In the 1870s and '80s, "genteel" people learned chords to accompany singing, and they played waltzes, schottishes, marches, and popular tunes of the day, as well as breakdowns, reels, and jigs. The instrument itself underwent improvements, with frets common in the 1880s.

Also in the 1880s, various small banjo bands began to form. They were given a boost by the invention of the banjeaurine, an instrument with a shorter neck but a full-size head. This was the idea of Samuel S. Stewart of Philadelphia, a major manufacturer of high-grade banjos, and Thomas Armstrong, a teacher and composer. They designed the banjeaurine to play the lead part in banjo orchestras, and they supported their invention by publishing banjo orchestra music. Two other instruments were also used in banjo groups: the piccolo banjo and the cello or bass five-string. By the mid 1890s, most major colleges and universities had banjo clubs playing popular airs, marches, or special compositions for banjo, as well as light classics.

Banjo virtuosos began to emerge in the 1890s, both on the concert stage and on the newly invented phonograph recordings. Alfred A. Farland excelled at what was called "sostenuto" or "tremolo" playing (tremolo with the fingers on the higher strings, countermelody with the thumb on the lower strings). He toured for over 40 years, playing the music of Bach, Beethoven, Chopin, Haydn, Shubert, etc. Sylvester "Vess" L. Ossman made his recording debut in 1893. With a strong, robust tone and a wonderful sense of rhythm, Ossman was well-known for characteristic banjo music and for some very fine ragtime.

By 1900, however, the classic five-string's popularity was waning. As early as 1885, mandoline-banjos—small banjos strung like a mandolin—were in use, and it wasn't long before players started using plectrums on regular banjos. This style made the short string of little use, and soon players began using "plectrum" banjos: four-string instruments which dropped the short string but kept the long neck and tuning of the five-string.

About 1907, the first tenor banjo appeared. It had a shorter neck, four strings, and was tuned in fifths (to the pitch of a viola). It was strung with heavy steel strings, but was less shrill than a mandolin. The tenor came into its own with the dance band craze that began about 1911. These bands wanted banjos to provide a chord rhythm, and violinists and mandolinists, being familiar with the tuning pattern, could adapt to it readily. The five-string banjo declined (although it did not entirely disappear), and tenor banjos were the choice of players in early jazz bands of the post-World War I years.

STANDARD COMPOSITIONS

----- ARRANGED FOR THE BANJO BY -----

A. A. FARLAND.

HAYDN-Gypsy Rondo, with Piano Acc., $1.00
SCHUBERT-Serenade, with P. Acc., .75
POPPER-Gavotte (No. 2), with B. Acc., .60
YRADIER-La Paloma, with B. & G. Acc. .50
THOMAS-Gavotte from Mignon, with
     B. & G. Acc., - - - .60
——La Castenara, with B. & G. Acc., 50
DUSSEK-"La Matlnee" Rondo, with B.
     & P. Acc., - - - - 1.00
SCHUBERT-Military March, with P.
     Acc., - - - - - 1.00
ROSSINI-Overture, "Wm. Tell" (Last
     Movement) with P. Acc., 1.00
CHOPIN-Choral Nocturne. Solo only, .50
HAUSER-Wiegenlied. (Cradle Song)
     with P. Acc., - - - .50
WIENIAWSKI-2d Mazurka. "Kuiawiak"
     with P. Acc., - - - .60
PADEREWSKI-Minuet, Op. 14, with
     P. Acc., - - - - 1.00
CHOPIN-Funeral March, with G. Acc., .60
DANCLA-5th Air. Varied, with P. Acc., .75
SCHUMANN-Traumerei and Romanze,
     with P. Acc., - - - .60
SCHUBERT-Hark, Hark the Lark.
     Trans. solo only - - .50
MOSZKOWSKI-Serenata, solo only .50

Boston: Cincinnati: NEW YORK: San Francisco: Chicago:
Oliver Ditson Co.   John Church Co.   Published by A. A. FARLAND.   Sherman, Clay & Co.   Lyon & Healy

REVENGE OF THE BANJO MAKERS

B Y   M I C H A E L   H O L M E S

Banjo makers endured the mandolin orchestras that rose at the turn of the century, faithfully waiting for the second coming of the banjo. They didn't have to wait long for a sign. J. B. Schall of Chicago, in an attempt to lure mandolin players to the banjo, introduced a four-string banjo in 1907. "Tuned like a mandolin and plays with a pick," read Schall's first ad for his "banjorine," which in actuality was the first tenor banjo.

Next, the tango dance craze arrived in America from Argentina in 1910, providing such a perfect setting for the new instrument that it became known as the "tango banjo." By the end of World War I, the banjo was back, and so were many of the makers from the classic era, albeit with different names:

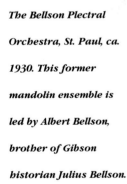

The Bellson Plectral Orchestra, St. Paul, ca. 1930. This former mandolin ensemble is led by Albert Bellson, brother of Gibson historian Julius Bellson.

◆ Vega of Boston carried on the legacy of prominent 19th-century maker A. C. Fairbanks, whose business Vega had acquired after a factory fire in 1904.

◆ H. A. Weymann and Sons of Philadelphia had only been making banjos since 1900 but had been a well-known distributor since 1864. Weymann introduced a screw-on resonator by 1920.

◆ Orpheum and Paramount were new brands, but their maker was William Lange, who (with William Rettberg) had bought the New York-based Buckbee company in 1897. Lange's Paramount banjos debuted in 1921, sporting the first modern flange-and-resonator system.

◆ Fred Bacon's name was familiar as a leading player in the classic banjo style. He began marketing his own instruments (with necks and rims by Vega and a tone ring of his own design) in 1905 and actually making them himself in 1912. He enlisted former Vega employee David Day in September 1922, and together they produced the famous B&D brand banjos, highlighted by the fancy Silver Bell line.

Other banjo makers arrived on the scene in the mid '20s and made an immediate impact. In 1925, a small New York mandolin maker, Epaminodas "Epi" Stathopoulo, acquired the Favoran banjo plant in Long Island City for production of his newly introduced Epiphone banjos. The Epiphone Recording models were among the fanciest of the Jazz Age.

Ludwig & Ludwig, founded in Chicago in 1907, was one of several drum makers who took advantage of the similarities between banjos and drums. Ludwig banjos, introduced in 1924, sported geared "Planetary" tuners.

U. G. Leedy of Indianapolis started making drum equipment in his boardinghouse room in 1896 and became the largest drum company in the world by the 1920s. Leedy hired banjoist Mike Pangatori of Paul Whiteman's orchestra to help develop a banjo line, and the new Leedys debuted in 1926.

A third maker closely associated today with drums—Slingerland—was a familiar name in the banjo market of the '20s, but unlike Leedy and Ludwig, Slingerland did not start out with drums. H. H. Slingerland was reportedly a riverboat gambler. About 1912, in a card game, he won a Chicago-based company that sold correspondence courses for the ukulele. Hawaiian music had been growing in popularity since the turn of the century; when the territory of Hawaii featured music in its exhibit at the 1915 Pan-Pacific Exposition in San Francisco, Hawaiian music swept the mainland. Slingerland's customers wanted ukes as well as uke instruction, and he began making them, adding banjos around 1918. When Ludwig added banjos to its drum line in 1924, Slingerland was reportedly irked by the invasion of his market, and he retaliated by adding drums to his line in 1927.

Although Slingerland was a minor player in the drum field until 1930, the total production of drums, banjos, and other instruments led the company to advertise in 1929 as the largest instrument maker in America.

The major mandolin makers were overpowered by the banjo. Washburn began to fade and was sold for the first of several times in 1927. Gibson made a nominal entry into the banjo market in 1918 and then counterattacked the banjo makers in 1922 with new and improved mandolins—a bold but

Boalsburg Banjo Band, Boalsberg, Pennsylvania, 1930. Gibson was able to apply the large-ensemble philosophy of the bygone mandolin era to the banjo by 1930.

The big banjo names in the 1920s were holdovers from the classic banjo era.

Mandolin Players

TAKE NOTICE

This Banjorine was designed by Prof. Stepner, the celebrated mandolin soloist, and is played by him in his concert work. It is the only Banjorine on the market that retains the true banjo tone. It has four strings, and is tuned like a mandolin, and plays with a pick. To play this instrument it is not necessary for the mandolinist to learn a new system of fingering. The mandolin or violin score can be played. These instruments are now played by the following artists in their concert work: Prof. Louis Stepner, Aubrey Stauffer, J. J. Hill, F. J. Brooks, Frank Ryan and many others.

unsuccessful move that almost bankrupted the company. Martin made a total of 96 tenor banjos before turning its back on the banjo market.

(Martin did not ignore ukes and Hawaiian guitars; these bolstered Martin's sales considerably through the '20s and into the Depression.)

Banjo styles reflected the spirit of the Roaring '20s, with prices of fancy models passing $500. High-end guitars and mandolins, by comparison, could be had for half that. By the end of the decade, musicians had begun putting down their banjos and picking up guitars, but even if they had stayed with the banjo, the Depression would have killed off the demand for all but the cheapest instruments.

Just as the rise of the tenor banjo had been rough on mandolin makers, the rise of the guitar in the late '20s put many banjo makers out of business. In 1929, Leedy sold to Conn, which probably sold off existing stock without making any more banjos (Conn's Leedy banjo sales totaled only $1,800 in 1930, and the figures went down from there). Later in 1929, Ludwig sold to Conn, but since the Leedy acquisition had taken all of Conn's available cash, Ludwig was paid off in Conn stock, making the deal

in effect a merger. Both brands eventually became best-known again for drums.

Bacon and Paramount continued to concentrate on banjos and faded quickly. Slingerland became a player in the mid- to low-end guitar market of the '30s but eventually settled into success as a drum maker. Epiphone was the most successful—initially even more so than Gibson—in recognizing and capitalizing on the rise of the guitar.

When the folk boom of the 1960s hit, only Vega and Gibson were still showing banjos in their catalogs, and of the more than 200 makers in business at the turn of the century, only Vega had them in regular production.

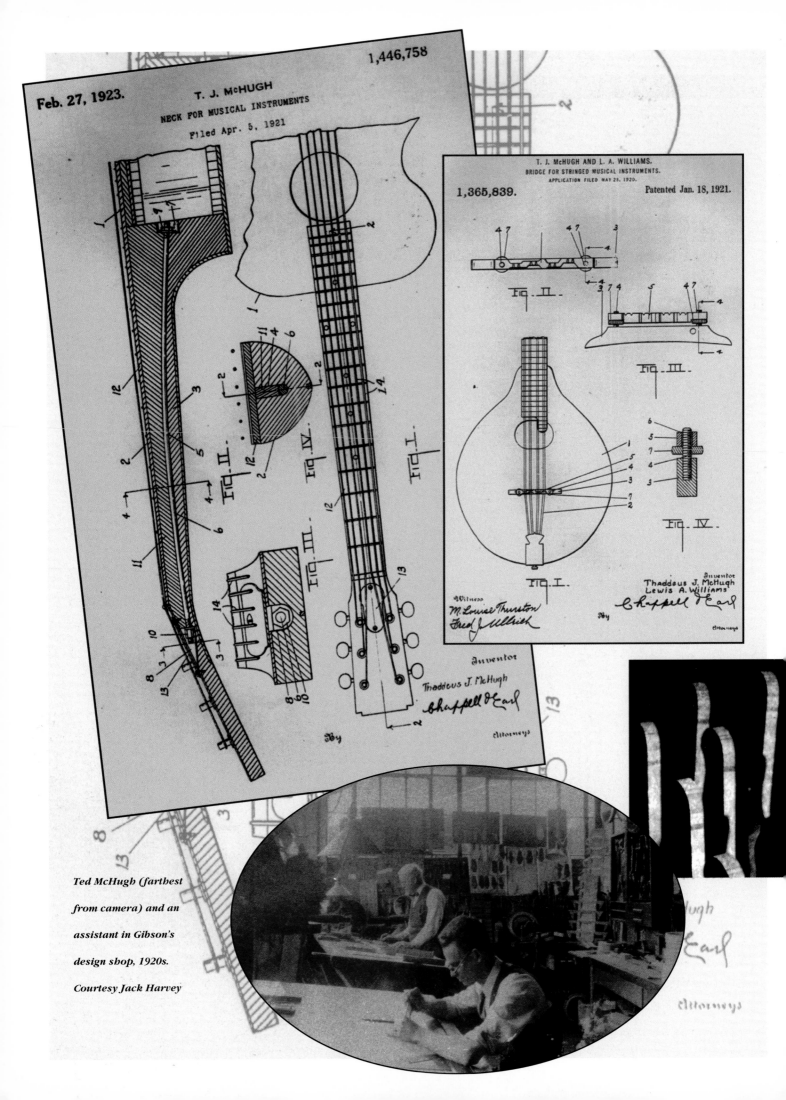

Feb. 27, 1923.

T. J. McHUGH

NECK FOR MUSICAL INSTRUMENTS

Filed Apr. 5, 1921

1,446,758

T. J. McHUGH AND L. A. WILLIAMS.
BRIDGE FOR STRINGED MUSICAL INSTRUMENTS.
APPLICATION FILED MAY 28, 1920.

1,365,839.

Patented Jan. 18, 1921.

Ted McHugh (farthest from camera) and an assistant in Gibson's design shop, 1920s. Courtesy Jack Harvey

TED McHUGH

BY WALTER CARTER

Ted McHugh, ca. 1940.
Courtesy Jack Harvey

Ted McHugh's legacy:
Today, an adjustable
truss rod reinforces the
neck of virtually every
steel-string guitar, a
height-adjustable bridge
is standard equipment
on carved-top guitars
and mandolins, and the
adjustable tension rod is
still a feature of Gibson
banjos.

Between 1920 and 1922, Gibson introduced three major innovations that are still standard equipment on many fretted instruments: the adjustable truss rod, an adjustable tension rod for banjos, and the height-adjustable bridge. The inventor of these metal devices, ironically, was not a machinist or even a musician but a 60-year-old woodworker. And even though he didn't join Gibson until five years after its founding, he had been a friend and musical partner of Orville Gibson, and through him, the company maintained a personal link to Orville into the 1940s.

His name was Thaddeus Joseph McHugh, but his friends called him Ted or T. J. His father, an Irish immigrant, had contracted to clear the right-of-way for the Michigan Central Railroad, and when he reached Kalamazoo in 1844, he stayed. Ted was born there in 1859.

Ted McHugh never learned how to play guitar, but he had a beautiful Irish tenor voice. In the early 1880s, he was invited by a local guitar player to help out on a show sponsored by the Ladies Library Club for the Children's Home in Kalamazoo. The guitarist's name was Orville Gibson.

Like his friend Orville, McHugh kept his performance career as a hobby. He sang first tenor in a quartet, and he performed at church and social functions for many years, but he made his living in the late 1880s as a woodworker. If Orville Gibson ever needed any tips on carving mandolin bodies and necks, he likely would have asked Ted McHugh. According to his granddaughter Alice Hughes of Kalamazoo, "He believed in human hands doing the work. The house that he lived in, he had hand-carved the woodwork. I know. I dusted it."

Also like Orville, McHugh had ambitions for his handiwork. In 1899, three years after Orville opened his own instrument-making business, McHugh had his own business: Everett, McHugh & Co. He was not as successful as Orville, however, and by 1901 was working for a boat-building company. In 1907 he began working for Gibson, and he never worked for another company. He started as foreman of the woodworking shop, became factory superintendent in 1915, and moved in the 1920s into a position of designing, drafting, and experimental work.

McHugh's grandson Jack Harvey of Manton, Michigan, recalls visiting his grandfather's workplace—an office full of instrument parts and drawings. He has one memory that may represent yet another McHugh innovation. "Performers from Europe used to come to Kalamazoo to see my granddad," Harvey said. "He would make casts of their hands. A lot of them had hands too small for the necks on Gibson guitars." Perhaps McHugh's plaster casts were the first step in the development of the three-quarter-size guitars Gibson began making in the late 1930s.

McHugh worked for Gibson into his 80s. Gibson's "retirement plan" was to keep old-timers on the payroll as long as they could make it to the factory. Some ended up as night watchmen; McHugh ended up in the stockroom. He was standing on a box one day, reaching to hang up a spare bandsaw blade, when he lost his balance and grabbed the blade as he fell. His hand was badly damaged, and he had to wear a glove from then on to help the circulation.

Ted McHugh died in 1945, and with him went the last personal link to the spirit of Orville.

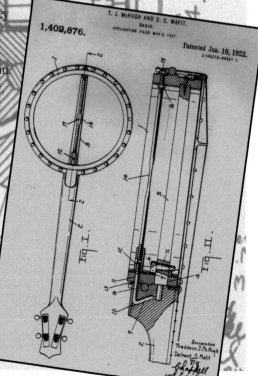

MR. LOAR'S MASTER MODELS

BY   R O G E R   H .   S I M I N O F F

Loar's Style 5 family

rated color treatment in

Gibson catalogs.

Gibson entered a difficult period after World War I. Secretary and general manager Sylvo Reams died in January 1917. Lewis Williams, sales manager nonpareil and one of the founding partners with Reams, moved up to head the company, but he proved to be less capable as a general manager than as a sales manager. World War I hurt instrument sales, and the sudden rise of the tenor banjo (and demise of the mandolin) threw Gibson into the unfamiliar position of a company without a product to meet the new demand.

Gibson's banjos, introduced in 1918, did not turn the company around, nor did the introduction of the height-adjustable bridge in 1921 and the adjustable truss rod in 1922. By early 1923, however, Williams had found new hope for the future. He reassured a worried group of stockholders that Gibson's new Master Model instruments were so superior to the competition that they would bring back the mandolin orchestra. Indeed, if quality alone had been the determining factor, the 1920s might well be known today as the Second Coming of the Mandolin, for the instruments Williams described— Lloyd Loar's Style 5 Master Model mandolin family— really were better than their predecessors.

Loar's F-5 mandolin, H-5 mandola, K-5 mandocello, and L-5 guitar were obviously different. They sported violin-style f-holes rather than the round or oval holes of conventional instruments. But the f-holes were just one of

many features that made Loar's instruments outstanding. Among his specific contributions were: graduated soundboards (tops) and backboards (backs), longitudinal tone bars, f-holes, longer playable necks, sizing of air chambers (resonance tuning), classic finishes, and hand "tuning" of tone bars and f-holes. He also developed a new banjo design with the tone chamber supported by ball bearings.

Loar's major contribution was "tuning"—*not* adjusting the string pitches, but the art of tuning the various structural components of the instrument to specific pitches so that the whole instrument worked as a coupled system (acoustically speaking), producing the best tone possible from the sum of its parts. In this regard, soundboards,

backboards, tone bars, f-holes, and air chamber sizes were adjusted so that each element was tuned to a specific note that resided on a scale that used A-440 as its calibration point (historically, A has not always been 440 vibrations per second). With the entire instrument assembled and strings tuned to A-440, the parts of the instrument responded harmonically rather than discordantly to the strings' energy, avoiding any unwanted "beats" or overtones and bringing forth the best dynamics and tonal qualities of the instrument.

The specific techniques Loar employed were:

◆ Graduated soundboards and backboards were initially carved to .100 inches around the perimeter and .250 inches at the center. Since these components were "tuned," the thicknesses differ from instrument to instrument, depending on the stiffness of the wood, grain distribution, etc. This carving technique, often called "Stradivarius arching," allowed the soundboard and backboard to "pump" like the paper cone in a common speaker, generating greater "compression" within the instrument to produce the maximum amplitude.

◆ Longitudinal tone bars were thinned ("tuned") to adjust the stiffness and tuning of the soundboard. The bass bar and treble bar were positioned and sized differently so that the treble side and bass side of the soundboard could be separately adjusted (the two tone bars were not structurally symmetrical). By removing wood from the tone bar, the soundboard would become less stiff, resulting in the pitch being lowered. The tuning process is so controllable that a whole-tone difference could be attained between the two tone bars. Examination of many Master

In his factory workshop, Loar holds his one and only 10-string "mando-viola." Gibson catalogs captioned this photo "Corner of the Experimental Lab." Courtesy Roger Siminoff

Loar played his F-5 with the Gibsonians. This ca. 1923 version of the group includes, from left, Loar, Dorothy Crane, Fisher Shipp (Loar's first wife), James H. Johnstone, Nell VerCies, and Lucille Campbell.

Model instruments shows a wide variety of tone bar sizes, proving that the independent and labor-intensive hand-tuning concept was aggressively employed.

◆ The f-holes were adjusted in size to achieve the final tuning of the instrument's body once the entire instrument was assembled. By enlarging the f-hole (since wood could only be removed, the opening could not be made smaller), the pitch of the air chamber was raised. This adjustment provided the most noticeable change in pitch. It is interesting to note that the original Master Model instruments were not heavily finished with varnish, as the addition of varnish to the tuned body would alter its adjusted pitch.

◆ Following the developments of Hermann L. F. Helmholz (1821–94), who studied sensations of tone and defined sizes of air chambers and their relative resonant frequencies, Loar carefully sized the air chambers on his instruments to provide a correctly tuned space for the type of instrument (mandolin, mandola, or guitar).

Since an adjustment to one part of the instrument affects the tuning of another part, one can appreciate the hours of trial and error that preceded the development and subsequent finalization of the dimensions of Gibson's Master Model instruments. As final proof of the hand-tuning process, Loar put his signature on a label inside the instrument, attesting that "The top, back, tone-bars, and air-chamber of this instrument were tested, tuned and the assembled instrument tried and approved ___(date)___." This and a sister signature label became the famous "Loar-signed" labels.

◆ Another Loar contribution (though not of his invention) to the tonal characteristics of Gibson's mandolins was the Virzi Tone Producer affixed to the soundboard inside some Master Model

Gibson owned exclusive rights to the Virzi Tone Producer, and it was installed in many of the instruments signed by Loar. © 1993 Roger H. Siminoff

instruments. The Tone Producer was a spruce disc with two f-hole-like apertures, affixed to the underside of the soundboard. It was the intention of the Virzi brothers, who patented the design, that it would impart a better overtone series to the instrument. While the Tone Producer did not survive to today's instruments, it gained popularity during the 1920s and '30s with classical players and was heavily promoted to performers on violin family instruments.

In addition to acoustical adjustments, Loar also provided some cosmetic and performance benefits:

◆ Departing from the common black and mahogany red sunburst models, Master Model instruments boasted a hand-rubbed "Cremona" finish (a reference to the Italian city where Stradivarius made his violins): shaded sunbursts in rich dark-chocolate browns which sometimes ventured almost to black.

◆ To extend the playable area of the neck, and to move the bridge closer to the center of the soundboard, Loar lengthened the neck so that it joined the body binding at the 15th fret (on the F-4, the neck joined the body binding at the 12th fret). This move retained the popular playing scales, provided extended playability "up the neck," and moved the bridge to a position where it could be more effective as a soundboard "driver."

◆ While it is interesting to note that most of the Master Model instruments had flat-grained necks rather than vertical-grained—a feature that provided greater strength and stability—one can only surmise that the flat-grained neck was one of Loar's great contributions to Gibson and to players worldwide.

What Loar did not do: Loar is often credited with the development of the elevated fretboard (rising above the soundboard), the elevated pickguard, and the adjustable truss rod. However, these contributions came from other designers at Gibson.

This family of Loar instruments, owned by Santa Cruz collector Hank Risan, includes an F-5 mandolin, H-5 mandola, K-5 mandocello, and L-5 guitar, all signed by Loar, plus Loar's personal electric viola and his 10-string mando-viola.

Paul Haggard, courtesy *Guitar Player*

THE STRAD OF MANDOLINS

B Y   W A L T E R   C A R T E R

David Grisman with his '22 F-5, "the best sounding mandolin I've ever owned, hands-down."

Only one issue of *The F-5 Journal* has been published so far—not as strong a statement as *The Strad* magazine makes for the superiority of Stradivari violins, but evidence nonetheless of the reverence many mandolinists hold for the Loar F-5.

Like the world's finest violins, some of the world's finest mandolins have come to be known individually by an owner's name. Among the listings in *The F-5 Journal* are "The Griffith," "The Wm. Place, Jr.," "The Bellson," and, of course, "The Bill Monroe."

The serial numbers and the dates Lloyd Loar signed these instruments are recorded, as are details of construction, ornamentation, and finish, including repairs and refinishes. The Bellson, for example, marks the first appearance of a logo pattern "cut in the open style." No. 73014, signed on April 25, 1923, has the labels

VOL. 1, 1987 $10.00

The **F5** Journal

DEDICATED TO THE FURTHERANCE OF GIBSON F5 MANDOLINS

DARRYL G. WOLFE

reversed—the signature label is under the treble-side f-hole; the Master Model label is under the bass-side f-hole. Bill Monroe's, as every bluegrass mandolin player knows, is "triple-bound on sides"—meaning that the white-black-white layering of the binding is visible from the side rather than from the front of the instrument.

Darryl Wolfe, who published *The F-5 Journal,* began compiling notes on every Loar-signed and Loar-related (late 1920s and early 1930s) instrument he saw. He explained his purpose in solemn prose: "Most of these instruments have already outlived their original owners. Most should survive their present owner and several future ones. Many of these future owners are going to wish their mandolin could tell its life story."

Jazz-bluegrass player David Grisman, whose name appears several times in the F-5 Journal, believes that the Loar F-5's combination of sound, playability, and quality of workmanship makes it "the pinnacle of mandolin construction."

"It's a refinement of what Gibson was doing in the first 20 years," he explains. "Gibson was onto a great thing before the F-5 came around and I think that just finished it off. What they were shooting for is a more contained sound. It's better suited for playing over a microphone—I don't know if they realized that at the time."

Grisman came by his opinion honestly, unprejudiced by the high prices Loar-signed instruments command on today's vintage market. "When I bought my first Lloyd Loar F-5 they were not called 'Lloyd Loar F-5s,'" he recalls. "It was 1964. I looked at four mandolins. I didn't care about the model or the history. I just picked the one that sounded the best to me that day."

"Side binding" on Darryl Wolfe's '23 Loar F-5.

THE LOAR F-5: OH, HORRIBLE!
BY WALTER CARTER

Not all mandolin players embraced the F-5. Jimmie Johnstone was one who stayed with the F-2 (page 58). Julius Bellson also preferred the brighter tone of an oval-hole F model to Loar's f-hole model. Probably the most vocal of those who disdained the F-5 is noted mandolinist Walter K. Bauer.

Ironically, Bauer may have been the first to be pictured with a Style 5 instrument—several times, in fact, in a photograph of the "Bauer Quintet." Seventy-one years after the gag appeared in *The Cadenza,* a 94-year-old Walter K. Bauer remembered the photo much more fondly than he did the F-5 mandolin or its inventor.

For starters, the F-5 was an expensive instrument—$250.00 list, around $140.00 dealer net—and Gibson did *not* give one to Bauer for promotional purposes. "Gibson never gave anything away," he said.

Furthermore, Bauer was anything but impressed with the F-5. "I detested that mandolin. Oh, horrible! It was the most blown-up advertised thing, and it had a very cheap tone producer [Virzi] which worked the opposite way—reducer. The f-holes were in the wrong place. I helped design a mandolin the following year made by Bill Nelson. It had the f-holes closer to neck."

Before the F-5, Bauer played a stock Maurer model (the brand name of the Chicago-based Larson Brothers), and he compared the two in no uncertain terms: "A $50 Maurer was better than that F-5 creation."

Bauer knew Lloyd Loar personally but did not offer Loar a critique of the F-5. "You couldn't tell him anything—a very opinionated man," Bauer recalled. "He was the same way about everything, his playing and his instruments."

The Bauer Quintet, created by Gibson's Jimmie Johnstone, in the December 1922 issue of The Cadenza.

LEWIS A. WILLIAMS

B Y   W A L T E R   C A R T E R

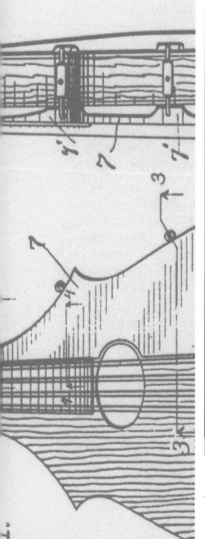

The house that Lew built, 2500 Parsons St., 1916. On the strength of Williams's sales success, Gibson built a new factory. Williams became secretary and general manager six months before the factory's formal opening on July 20, 1917. Courtesy Jim Johnstone

Trivia question: Who was the only man to be a business partner of both Orville Gibson and Lloyd Loar?

HINT:
He is the inventor of the Mysterio.

HINT:
He is the author of "When Gray Hairs Applaud…" and "Is the Absolute of Present Day Tonal Ideality Know-able?"

HINT:
His son played the part of Mary Pickford's son in a Hollywood movie.

ANSWER:
Lewis A. Williams—not exactly an obscure figure in Gibson history but not as well-known as he deserves to be. He was one of the five principals who founded the company, he was the first sales manager and the man who wrote the classic Gibson catalog prose of the early years, he and Ted McHugh patented the height-adjustable bridge, he was the general manager who hired Lloyd Loar. But that is only the beginning of his story.

The five original board members might be described as three lawyers, one piano salesman, and one visionary. Lew Williams was that visionary. He was the one in 1902 who saw how bright the future could be for Orville Gibson's new mandolins. He was the one in 1919 who recognized a similar talent for innovation in a concert mandolinist by the name of Lloyd Loar. He was the one in 1923 who saw that the future of the music industry was in

electrical amplification—particularly the electric instruments Loar was working on.

Williams was a man of integrity and conviction. Although his resignation from Gibson has been attributed in most historical accounts to a disagreement over electric instruments, Gibson's faltering financial position under his leadership from 1920 to '23 was no doubt a mitigating factor. Ten years later, he still believed Loar was another Orville Gibson, and he formed the Vivi-Tone company with Loar to market Loar's ideas, envisioning another success like the Gibson company.

Williams left Gibson in late 1923, a year before Loar resigned, and went straight into the electronics business. He opened Specialized Radio in Kalamazoo, a store that sold radios and phonographs. When the Depression hit, he expanded his inventory to include electrical appliances such as refrigerators.

He did not sit idly and wait for customers to buy radios. In the tradition that he helped create at Gibson, he set to work immediately on a new product that would be better than anything on the market at the time. *The Kalamazoo Gazette* trumpeted the news with this headline on May 4, 1925:

Kalamazooan Invents New Broadcaster

Says 'Mysterio' Gives Ideal Tone Production and Interpretation.

Williams gave public demonstrations of the Mysterio for three days at Gilmore Brothers, a dry goods store established in the 1800s that had become Kalamazoo's leading department store. (Donald Gilmore would eventually become a

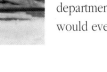

business partner of Williams and Loar.) Coincidentally, Gilmore Brothers was (and still is) located on South Burdick in a building that extends back into the space occupied by Gibson's first factory at 114 East Exchange.

Williams described the Mysterio in appropriately mysterious terms as a "new electrically controlled musical instrument" that was "neither phonograph nor radio." He made it sound like the most incredible instrument ever invented. "It includes all voices, all instruments, all ensembles," he said. "It has an unusual beauty of tone, seldom ever surpassed."

The best thing about it: "No knowledge of music is required to play the 'Mysterio.'"

Whatever this Mysterio was, it was loud. "Its volume is great enough to supply music from one central control to every home in Kalamazoo," the article said.

Halfway through the article, an image of this "instrument" finally comes into focus: "The amplifying system permits talking, playing, singing to one or thousands of listeners.

"'The Mysterio' may be used to announce through an entire department store, hourly sales, important events, special bargains and the advertising manager does not need to leave his desk...

"'The Mysterio' furnishes dance music of wonderful volume and tonal beauty, perfectly diffused."

The Mysterio was, in fact, a public address system. According to a later *Gazette* article, Williams's

Inside 2500 Parsons St., late 1910s.

In his 20 years with Gibson, L. A. Williams was pictured only once, in a 1919 issue of The Sounding Board Salesman.

Shortly after Williams became general manager, Gibson introduced the flashy, white-topped A-3 mandolin. It only lasted until 1922.

VIVI-TONE PERSONNEL

Lloyd Loar   Walter Moon   L. A. Williams

PAT.MAR.30,'09

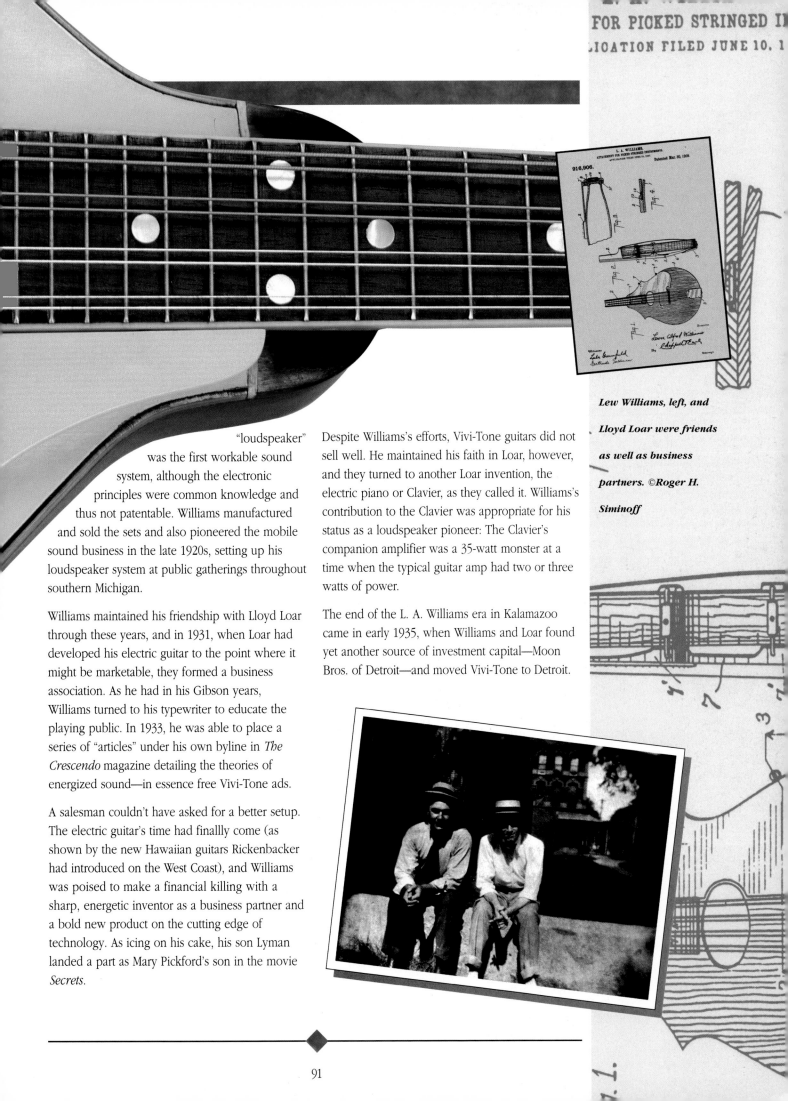

Lew Williams, left, and Lloyd Loar were friends as well as business partners. ©Roger H. Siminoff

"loudspeaker" was the first workable sound system, although the electronic principles were common knowledge and thus not patentable. Williams manufactured and sold the sets and also pioneered the mobile sound business in the late 1920s, setting up his loudspeaker system at public gatherings throughout southern Michigan.

Williams maintained his friendship with Lloyd Loar through these years, and in 1931, when Loar had developed his electric guitar to the point where it might be marketable, they formed a business association. As he had in his Gibson years, Williams turned to his typewriter to educate the playing public. In 1933, he was able to place a series of "articles" under his own byline in *The Crescendo* magazine detailing the theories of energized sound—in essence free Vivi-Tone ads.

A salesman couldn't have asked for a better setup. The electric guitar's time had finallly come (as shown by the new Hawaiian guitars Rickenbacker had introduced on the West Coast), and Williams was poised to make a financial killing with a sharp, energetic inventor as a business partner and a bold new product on the cutting edge of technology. As icing on his cake, his son Lyman landed a part as Mary Pickford's son in the movie *Secrets*.

Despite Williams's efforts, Vivi-Tone guitars did not sell well. He maintained his faith in Loar, however, and they turned to another Loar invention, the electric piano or Clavier, as they called it. Williams's contribution to the Clavier was appropriate for his status as a loudspeaker pioneer: The Clavier's companion amplifier was a 35-watt monster at a time when the typical guitar amp had two or three watts of power.

The end of the L. A. Williams era in Kalamazoo came in early 1935, when Williams and Loar found yet another source of investment capital—Moon Bros. of Detroit—and moved Vivi-Tone to Detroit.

LLOYD ALLAYRE LOAR

BY ROGER H. SIMINOFF

Only a handful of artisans conjure up such greatness that their names circumscribe the whole of an art form. One might typically ask, "Is that a clarinet?" but in the world of stringed instruments, the question is more likely to be "Is that a Gibson?" or "Is that a Loar?"

The names of Gibson and Loar belong in the company of Stradivarius and Martin. The legacy of their craft and their contributions to the art of luthiery has exceeded the merits perceived in their time and established precedents by which today's instruments are measured.

But unlike Gibson, Stradivarius, or Martin, Lloyd Loar saw little evidence of his genius in his lifetime. His f-hole mandolins of 1922 weren't considered to be great until bluegrass music began to find a wider audience in the 1960s and '70s. His concept of an electric piano, an outgrowth of the clavier, wasn't successfully marketed until the Fender Rhodes and Wurlitzer instruments of the 1960s. He invented the f-hole "jazz" guitar and wound his first electric pickup in the early 1920s, but when these innovations finally found a home in the big bands of the '30s, he received no credit, much less any financial reward.

Fortunately, Loar's interests were always directed toward expanding the art form first and his wallet second. He focused purposefully on bringing his designs to the forefront and to his fellow musicians. A man of modest means, his financial sucess was never commensurate with his great contributions. For Lloyd, his great reward was a good cigar.

Lloyd Loar was born on January 9, 1886, in Cropsey, Illinois. He attended high school in Lewiston, Illinois, from 1899 to 1903 and showed excellent grades with special interests in physics and geometry. While in high school, he performed in local music programs. His interest in physics and music came together in the early 1900s when he made his first mandolin. In 1904, he entered the Oberlin Conservatory where he studied harmony, orchestration, canon, counterpoint, fugue, music theory, and piano. He was the leader of the Oberlin Mandolin Club for two years. Gibson's mandolin work caught his attention, and he later purchased a three-point Gibson F-3. By 1906, when he was just 20 years of age, he was performing professionally on Gibson mandolins in both concert and solo settings. From 1906 to 1910 he performed in concert under the management of the Chicago Musical Bureau.

In 1908, Lloyd met a female singer named Fisher Shipp, the leader of the well-known Fisher Shipp Concert Company. They performed on numerous concert tours, occasionally billing themselves as The

Gibsonians (a name used by various groups organized and sponsored by Gibson). Photos of their ensemble show Shipp and Loar with a wide array of Gibson instruments, including a 10-string mando-viola. In 1926, Lloyd and Fisher were married, a union that lasted eight years.

Lloyd was employed by Gibson in June 1919, working mainly as a design consultant but also taking on various business management responsibilities. By 1921, he had constructed his unique mando-viola, which had five pairs of strings tuned in fifths except for a minor third between the highest pairs: (treble to bass) Eb, C, F, Bb, Eb. While he did enjoy building instruments as a hobby, his primary contribution to Gibson was the design and development of the Master Model instruments: F-5 mandolin, H-5 mandola, K-5 mandocello, L-5 guitar, and Style 5 banjos.

Loar's unique arrangement with Gibson gave him July and August free each year to perform concert tours. Consequently, we find very few Master Model instruments signed and dated by him in late July or August. Furthermore, since there were no hand-tuning properties that could then be attributed to the banjo body, none of the Mastertone banjo models bore a Lloyd Loar signature label.

While at Gibson, Loar wore many hats: credit manager, factory production manager, purchasing agent, and repair manager. When general manager L. A. Williams resigned in late 1923, Loar was one

Loar may have been frustrated by the commercial failure of his inventions, but he found personal happiness with Bertha Snyder, whom he married in 1938.
© 1993 Roger H. Siminoff

of two executives authorized to sign checks. But his most important position was design consultant, and as an accomplished musician, Loar could lend an ear as well as a hand in the development of the prized Master Models.

In December 1924, after more than five years as an employee and two decades as a performer on Gibson instruments, Lloyd Loar left Gibson to pursue several other interests in musical instruments. In 1925, he became Professor of Acoustics in the Music School at Northwestern University in Evanston, Illinois. He began developing several musical designs and was eventually granted nine patents.

While Loar's achievements gained him great fame in the area of acoustics, he is little-known for his pioneering contributions to electric instruments, specifically the coil-wound pickup. His earliest instrument that featured this pickup was a solidbody electric violin he built in 1923. His patent also shows a pedal device with volume controls and an on-off switch.

Although Loar's legend rests on his Gibson mandolins, his nine patents were granted for guitars and keyboard instruments—all post-Gibson.

On November 1, 1933, Loar and Lewis A. Williams, his close friend and fellow ex-Gibsonite, along with five other local businessmen founded the Vivi-Tone Company in Kalamazoo. The new company's stated purpose was the "manufacture and sale of wholesale and retail musical instruments, acoustic and electric products, including research, consulting services and financing such business." In addition to guitars (available with Spanish, Hawaiian, tenor, or plectrum neck), the Vivi-Tone line included mandolins, mandolas, mandocellos, mandobasses, violins, violas, cellos, double-basses, and Claviers. Most of these were electric instruments, amplified with Loar's coil-wound pickup. The acoustic instruments were unusual in that both the soundboard and backboard were made of spruce, and they had a thick maple rim which extended beyond the back so that the back would vibrate freely. In addition, Vivi-Tones had "fairy" frets—frets so high that the strings did not come into contact with the fingerboard.

On January 23, 1935, 15 months after the incorporation of Vivi-Tone, Loar and Williams pursued a second round of financing. To accomplish this, they founded the Acousti-Lectric Company, also in Kalamazoo, with an identical charter to that of Vivi-Tone, raising an additional $33,000 from the same seven stockholders.

By the end of 1935, Vivi-Tone/Acousti-Lectric was in trouble again, and a new partner was added to the ranks. Walter Moon, of the powerful Moon Bros. music store chain, bought into the company, and it was moved to Moon's facility in Detroit.

By 1938, Loar was teaching again at Northwestern University. That year, he met his second wife, Bertha Snyder, then a student in the school of music. After Lloyd's death on September 14, 1943, Bertha continued his memory by protecting many of his instruments, music, and writings. And, through the most unusual circumstances, Bertha also preserved Lloyd's ashes, which as of early 1994 were still not laid to rest.

The memory of Lloyd Allayre Loar lives on through the contributions of his widow. In 1985, I brought her to the National Association of Music Merchants (NAMM) trade show in Anaheim, California, where she visited the Gibson booth and took a minute to inspect the great Gibson instruments that grew from Lloyd's genius some 60 years before.

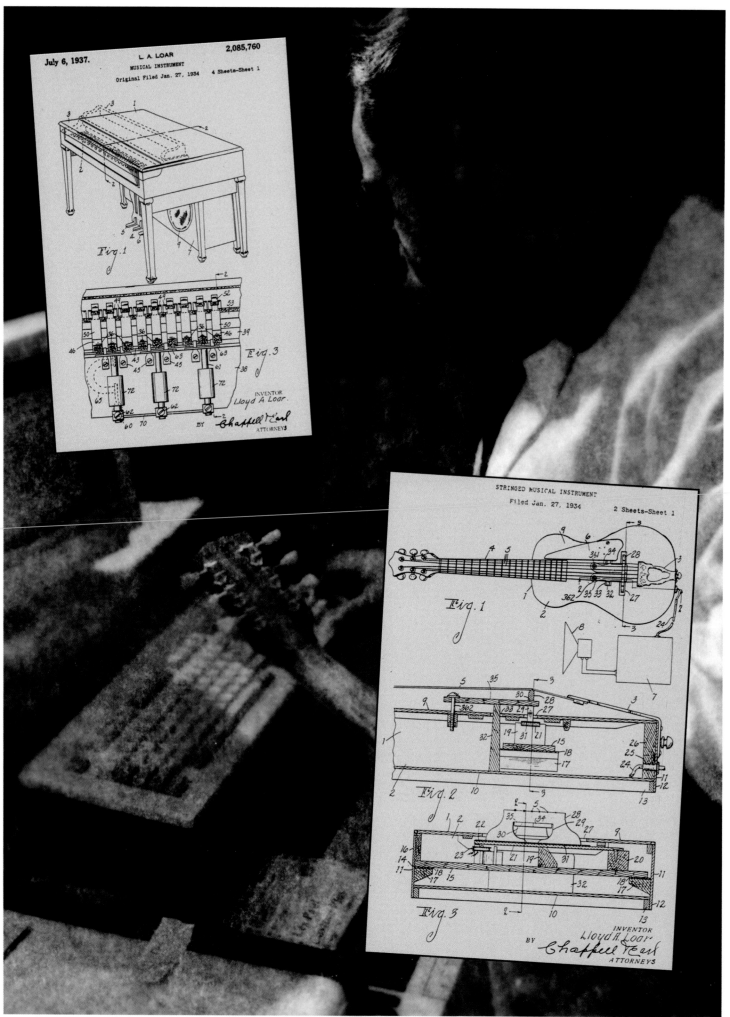

1924-WWII

THE
GUY HART
ERA

THE BRIEF REIGN OF HARRY L. FERRIS

BY WALTER CARTER

Lightning struck and cracked the Gibson smokestack in 1918—an omen if ever there was one that hard times lay ahead.

In Gibson lore, the years 1923 and 1924 are a period of great controversy. These are the years when key men L. A. Williams, C. V. Buttleman, and Lloyd Loar resigned. The issue, as the story has often been told, was electric instruments. But in reality, these three men may well have jumped ship not because the ship was heading on the wrong course, but because the ship was sinking.

Gibson was in severe financial trouble in 1923, on its way to losing $26,000, which would make three straight years in the red. Williams, as secretary and general manager, wrote a letter to stockholders in early 1923 blaming the company's bad fortune on the war (which had ended in 1919). Gibson's 43 foreign distribution agents had "practically done nothing" since the war, according to the letter. Furthermore, the 23 mandolin "symphony" orchestras in existence before the war had all been decimated by the draft, and not one major orchestra survived.

The war had an accomplice in this dirty deed, according to Williams, and the villain's name was Jazz: "Mandolin orchestra members returning from the war discovered that the 'jazz' instruments were typically saxaphone [sic], trombone, banjo, xylophone, traps [drum sets], etc., all of which are instruments of other than our manufacture with the exception of the banjo."

Williams predicted Gibson's new Style 5 mandolins and banjo would bring the company back to prosperity. But to get to that point, all stockholders were asked to return their last dividend.

Williams's points had some merit, but by the latter part of 1923, Gibson was still foundering, and he resigned on October 2, along with his sales manager Clifford V. Buttleman. He left the meeting as the board discussed securing one Harry Ferris as the new secretary and "business" manager.

Harry L. Ferris is a mystery man. He did not live in Kalamazoo until hired by Gibson, and he left town immediately after his employment ended. He ran Gibson for a little less than a year—not long enough for employees to remember his name. Kate Harris, who began her 51-year career at Gibson as a telephone operator in 1920, remembered his first name as Guy; Julius Bellson, in his 1973 book *The Gibson Story*, afforded him one sentence in passing and called him G. Ferris.

A letter from Ferris to C. F. Martin III of Martin guitars, dated November 16, 1923, left no doubt about his experience in the mandolin-guitar business. He had written to ask about a formal association of manufacturers. His letter opened with a startling admission: "The present manager of this company assumed his position on October 1 [!] of this year and so is quite an ignoramus in the field of fretted instrument manufacturing."

Candor was one of Ferris's dominant personality traits. A week after he was hired, he issued a terse four-paragraph statement to the stockholders that included this indictment of management: "There has been no coordination between and seemingly

The slick cover and illustrated foldouts of Catalog O disguised Gibson's dire financial position in 1923, but the truth was told by the size of the catalog: forty pages shorter than the tomes of the previous decade.

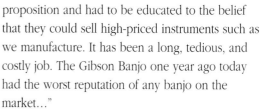

no understanding of the relation between production, sales and financing. The affairs of the Company indicate the greatest proficiency in spending money, tying up capital and withdrawing dividends, but no appreciation of the business necessity of using money wisely, or conserving resources."

Ferris found Gibson to be an archaic company in every aspect of its business, and he set about bringing Gibson into the modern age. By year end, he removed the words "mandolin" and "guitar"— instruments which made Gibson sound like an old-time company in the era of the jazz banjo—from the corporate name. The mandolin-guitar company was now simply Gibson, Inc. In his first and only annual report to the stockholders, dated February 18, 1924, he laid out plans for a sweeping reorganization. Among his goals:

◆ Reduce the number of models.

◆ Follow a production budget with a carefully planned schedule of purchases in order to maintain uninterrupted production.

◆ Increase efficiency by "centralizing responsibility in two foremen and a superintendent, instead of having this responsibility scattered among several men."

◆ Further increase efficiency by firing inefficient men and giving everyone else a raise.

◆ Broaden the dealership base to include music stores.

◆ Establish five regional sales areas, with managers on commission.

◆ Initiate a $50,000 promotional campaign to include ads in 50 magazines, direct mail, placing instruments in nationally known dance orchestras, and providing sales reps with material for newspaper use.

◆ Reduce debt.

◆ Declare no dividends for at least two years.

Ferris's most important modernization move—and one that has always been credited to his successor—was to replace Gibson's teacher-agents with a network of music store dealers. In this case, Gibson's reputation worked against it, as Ferris would explain to the board on September 8, 1924: "The music dealers in the country were not receptive to the Gibson proposition and had to be educated to the belief that they could sell high-priced instruments such as we manufacture. It has been a long, tedious, and costly job. The Gibson Banjo one year ago today had the worst reputation of any banjo on the market…"

Ferris never got his $50,000 promotional budget—it was more like $15,000—but his plan worked anyway. He had projected sales of $400,000, a 30 percent increase over the $278,000 for 1923, and by September, sales had increased 25 percent. He had succeeded in getting Gibsons into music stores and had more than doubled Gibson's accounts, from 226 to 500. He showed a profit of $2,000, versus a $20,000 loss for the same period in 1923. And he had given everyone a raise.

All this he had done in the middle of a recession. He contrasted Gibson's success with the closed cotton mills in New England, closed steel mills in Pennsylvania, hoof and mouth disease that had curtailed commerce in California, as well as sales

The banjo was the culprit—the killer of the mandolin orchestra—in the years after World War I. Even renowned mandolinists like Lloyd Loar, left, and James H. Johnstone doubled on banjo. Despite their use of Gibsons, Gibson banjos were not well-respected. ©Roger H. Siminoff

drops experienced by larger instrument makers such as Buescher, Conn, and Wurlitzer.

In the meantime, though, Ferris had done the unthinkable. He had insulted and embarrassed Judge Adams, Gibson's president. In a stinging statement to the board, he put the blame for the company's current problems squarely on their management from 1916 to 1920, when they had issued bonds to raise enough money to pay dividends. Ferris told them Gibson needed an infusion of $50,000 but that the company was already so overcapitalized that no investor in his right mind would touch them. In addition, state banking officials had started asking questions about Gibson's solvency, so another bank loan was out of the question. He suggested that to keep the banks from calling in their notes, the board of directors should turn over all their stock to a trustee from the Kalamazoo Savings Bank, which held Gibson's largest note.

Hon. John W. Adams, 30-year veteran of the circuit court bench, was not accustomed to being spoken to so bluntly, but Ferris didn't stop with the insult. He followed it with embarrassment when, without consulting the board, he discussed Gibson's problems with a banker, effectively letting the Kalamazoo business community know what a mess Adams had let his company fall into. Adams had had enough. He summoned Ferris to his office for a private meeting, where he called Ferris incompetent and told him to resign.

A board meeting was called on September 8, at which Ferris read a lengthy statement refuting the charge of incompetency by recapping his accomplishments. "If such results as these in the face of a period of depression do not show good managerial ability," he told the board, "then I would like to know what would indicate managerial ability." Within the statement was his resignation, effective January 1, 1925. Judge Adams was hearing none of it, and he asked for a resignation that would be effective immediately. After some discussion, Ferris wrote it out by hand. Having turned Gibson around in less than a year and brought it into the modern business world, he then turned himself around and walked out of Gibson history.

The board promptly appointed the company's new auditor—the most conservative and least threatening individual on the payroll—to be secretary and general manager, and he lasted 24 years in the job.

Instrument shop, early 1920s. The diversity of Gibson's line was an asset in good times but a problem in the eyes of new general manager Harry Ferris.

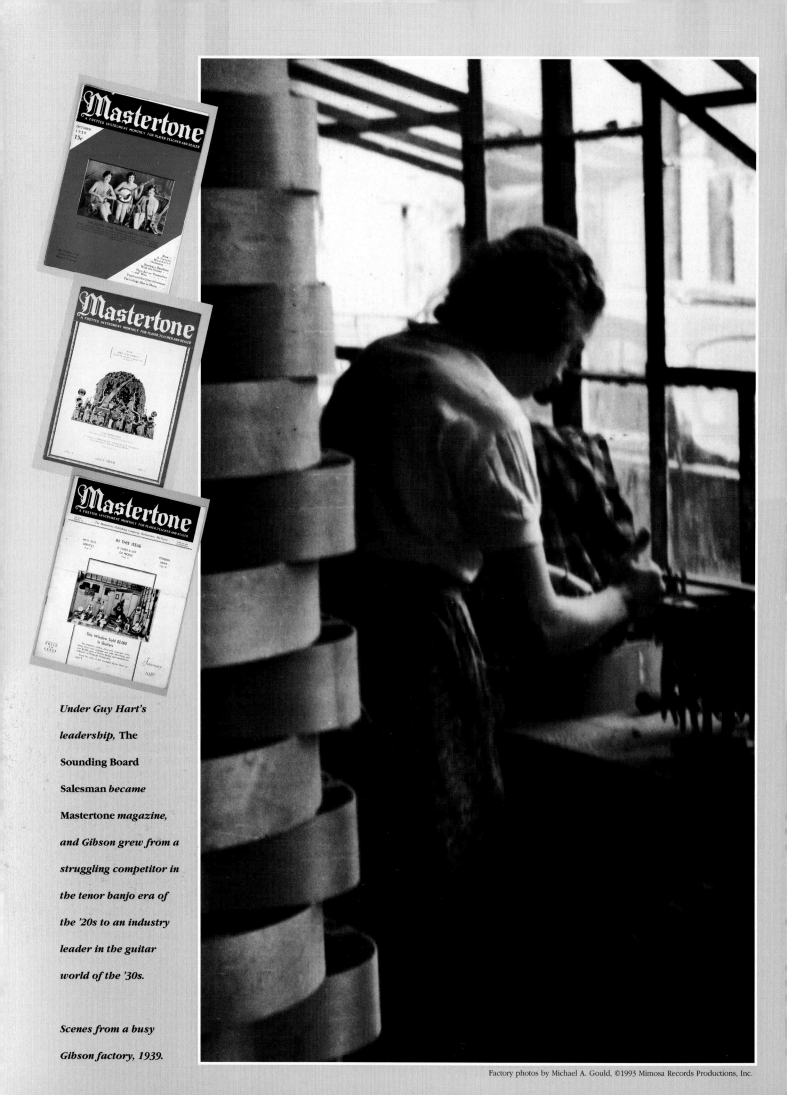

Under Guy Hart's leadership, The Sounding Board Salesman *became* **Mastertone** *magazine,* **and Gibson grew from a** *struggling competitor in the tenor banjo era of the '20s to an industry leader in the guitar world of the '30s.*

Scenes from a busy Gibson factory, 1939.

GUY HART

BY WALTER CARTER

Guy Hart, 1920s.

After guiding Gibson through one of its most glorious eras in the 1930s, Hart's career peaked in 1944 with his acceptance of an award for Gibson's contributions to World War II.

Guy Hart ran Gibson from 1924 to 1948—the most important period in company history since the debut of Gibson instruments at the turn of the century and, moreover, the period of greatest innovation for the guitar since the emergence of the six-string guitar in the late 1700s. As the guitar rose to prominence, so did Gibson. Under Hart's management, Gibson developed the Super 400, the SJ-200, the ES-150—models that returned Gibson to a position of respect and success the company hadn't enjoyed since before World War I.

One would expect Guy Hart to have been a charismatic, revered, visionary leader. He was none of those things. In fact, he was the exact opposite of the men who had guided Gibson from 1902 to 1923. The first general manager, Sylvo Reams (1902–17), was an entrepreneur who owned a music store. Lew Williams had been the heart and soul of Gibson sales before he ascended to the general managership (1917–23). He had also contributed to innovations in instrument design and had brought in an aggressive sales manager, C. V. Buttleman, and a high-profile musician and inventor, Lloyd Loar. Harry Ferris (1923–24) had whipped a dying company back to life in a matter of months.

Hart sits like a huge period at the end of this list of dynamic businessmen. He was not a musician, salesman, craftsman, designer, industry veteran, nor even a longtime employee of the company. He was a 36-year-old accountant who had been hired in 1923 as an in-house auditor. A native of Henshaw, Kentucky, he had worked in a woodturning plant in Chicago before World War I and had moved to Kalamazoo to work for Gibson. When the board of directors appointed him secretary of the corporation, they had to backtrack and vote to sell him a share of Gibson stock so that he would be eligible for the position.

The board saw something—or perhaps a lack of something—in Hart that led them to put their fortunes in his inexperienced hands. Judge Adams, the corporate president who showed up once a year to count the profits, was 65 years old in 1924 and no doubt weary of wild visionaries who lost his money and hot-shot managers who didn't show him enough respect. Hart was no threat in either area. He could be counted on to keep a close eye on the bottom line and to keep the company on a steady course.

Under Hart, Gibson developed and manufactured a line of archtop guitars, topped by the Super 400, that are still considered the best of their kind by a major manufacturer. In the flattop line, which hadn't even existed before Hart arrived, the SJ-200 put Gibson in a class by itself. Gibson's prominent place in the electric guitar market during his tenure was based on the famous "Charlie Christian" electric models (ES-150 and ES-250) and the development of the P-90 pickup. In the banjo arena, the "flathead" tone ring and one-piece flange—the combination of equipment most sought by bluegrass players today—are products of the Hart era.

These accomplishments are as important as any of the Reams and Williams eras or of the Ted McCarty era that followed Hart. Yet Hart was not as respected by those who worked for him as were these other company executives. Kate Harris, who had been working at Gibson for three years before Hart arrived, recalls Williams as "a splendid man" and Buttleman and Loar as "very, very nice people to work with." When asked about Hart, though, she hesitated. "Maybe I'd better not say anything about him." Asked again, she replied, "Mr. Hart was, I thought, a little below the schedule of the others. I never felt that he was as well-taught."

Ted McCarty, who succeeded Hart, found upon his

arrival at Gibson in 1948 that employees' opinions hadn't changed much. "It isn't fair to say it, I guess, but Guy Hart was hated by his employees," McCarty said. "They just despised the man, because he would walk around the factory with a notepad and a pen, make notes about something that he saw, never say anything to anybody. They used to tell the story about one fellow who was wiping the stain off a guitar that was in production. It was one of these flattop round-soundhole jobs. Anyway, I think the quitting bell rang, and he took the rag that he had been using and threw it into the hole. And Guy Hart saw him and fired him. Out! Now! Just like that. That's the way that he operated, and as a result people didn't give a damn about him and they didn't give a damn about the company.

"I got along with Guy all right. Guy was one of these guys, if you didn't work for him, he was a gentleman. He was a real fine person. But for his employees, they were just so many hands to do the dirty work, and he never had any understanding for them whatsoever."

John Huis, who worked under Hart from 1926 until the arrival of McCarty, remembered him as a man whose moods ran hot and cold: "He was the type of guy who'd flash off on a moment. He'd say to me, 'I want you to get rid of so-and-so,' and he wouldn't give me any reason why. Then he'd call me on a Saturday morning. 'Did you fire… whoever, yesterday?' 'No, I didn't see any reason.' I figured he'd be mad as all getout. He'd say, 'I'm glad you didn't.'"

Huis was not so lucky when his own number came up. "On a Thursday he gave me a $200 bonus. Friday night he fired me. Two years later he hired me back as superintendent of the plant."

The company's success under Hart should be credited to the employees, Huis feels,

particularly sales representatives like Wallace (Doc) Caldwell, Clarence Havenga, and Tom Peacock. He singles out Peacock, sales rep for the southern region, as the man responsible for the J-45, the highly successful dreadnought flattop introduced in 1942. Peacock was well known for sending a messenger ahead of him with a cold bottle of Coca-Cola to announce to dealers that the Gibson representative would arrive shortly. At the home office, he was known for sending Georgia pecans to the staff. When he saw a demand for a solidly built, affordable flattop, he delivered the message to Kalamazoo personally and, according to Huis, "He stayed right there 'til we built one."

Hart was not nearly so strong a presence. "He'd go away for weeks at a time," Huis said. "He never did come in before 10 or 11 in the morning. He'd go home at 2. I never did find out what the heck his deal was. He wasn't much of a manager. He wasn't much of an engineer. One of the things he had in the back of his mind, he wanted to make a ruler, a fancy 12-inch ruler. Every few years, he'd pull out that idea about a fancy ruler.

"He was an odd fellow to figure out."

A close examination of Hart's leadership does not put him in a favorable light. Time after time, his company was beaten to the market. He does not seem to have been a man of vision nor of personality. He seems to have acted only when his company—his job—was threatened, which happened often during this period of furious innovation. When Hart found his back to the wall, however, he came out fighting. If he was short on engineering skills, vision, work ethic, or anything else, he at least knew enough to hire people who possessed those qualities.

As an accountant, Hart would no doubt direct historians to look at the bottom line. Regardless of what anyone said about him, he took care of the bottom line. He took over during a period when

Gibson's reputation as a mandolin company was a liability in a booming banjo market, and he pulled the company even with its competitors by the time that market went bust. The wooden toys Gibson made during the Depression, the Kalamazoo-brand instruments, and other budget brands may not have enhanced Gibson's reputation, but they kept the company in business and kept the paychecks coming for the workers. And as the country began its economic recovery in the mid 1930s, he did oversee the buildup of Gibson's reputation and opened new markets overseas. He may not have shown any of the brilliance of those who came before and after, but he had none of their brilliant failures to show either—none of Loar's expensive f-hole mandolin family instruments in the middle of a bull market for banjos, none of McCarty's all-too-modern Korina-wood guitars. Hart seems to have been able to abort his failures before bringing them to market (except for the oddball HG-series Hawaiian guitars). He did not try to recreate a dead market or create a new market out of thin air; he recognized and responded to markets opened up by others—and he responded quite successfully.

Appropriately, some might say, but sadly, nevertheless, Hart's career ended with the same lack of flair and vision that had been his management style. The Chicago Musical Instrument Co. bought a controlling interest in Gibson in 1944, and Hart, after 20 years as secretary and general manager, was finally promoted to president. He was probably elated, but if he had stopped to

compare the mid 1940s to the late 1910s and early '20s, he should have been worried. The earlier chain of events went like this: a world war, promotion from within the company (Williams from sales manager to general manager), severe financial problems, arrival of an outside troubleshooter (Ferris) who takes over leadership.

History repeated itself. Hart converted the factory from wartime production back to instruments, but he could not show a profit. In 1948, CMI head M. H. Berlin dispatched industry veteran Ted McCarty to fix the problems. But unlike the 1920s, when Lew Williams gracefully resigned, Guy Hart hung on. McCarty came in as vice president, but he was in charge. As John Huis remembers, McCarty's authority was immediately and clearly established: "Ted took his [Hart's] office, and they shoved him over in a corner."

Effectively retired, Hart continued as president until 1950, when Berlin ordered McCarty to get his resignation. This time, with his back to the wall, Hart did not come out fighting. He was not in the best of health, and he resigned without comment. He remained on Gibson's board of directors until his death in 1961 of a heart attack.

Hart's aggresive sales force included, from top, Clarence Havenga, Tom Peacock, and Charlie Edwards.

GIBSON BANJOS

BY ROGER H. SIMINOFF

With the Bella Voce and Florentine in 1927, Gibson challenged the frontrunners in the race for ever-more-ornate banjos.

The banjo was king in 1924, but Gibson wasn't its castle. Guy Hart's primary task after taking over the general managership was to make Gibson competitive in the banjo market.

Hart's predecessor, Harry Ferris, had told the board of directors, "The Gibson banjo had the worst reputation of any banjo on the market." Indeed, Gibson had been playing a furious game of catch-up. Lewis A. Williams, the sales manager who took over as general manager when Sylvo Reams died in 1917, did not believe the tenor banjo craze of the postwar period would last. He thought an improved mandolin (the F-5 of 1922) would revive the mandolin orchestra and, along with it, Gibson's prewar glory.

Not surprisingly, Gibson's first banjo, the TB (for Tenor Banjo), was not the head-turner that Gibson employee Jimmie Johnstone described in the first TB brochure (page 58). The craftsmanship was good, as one would expect from Gibson, but the construction was nothing more than basic. The laminated maple rim had a cavity between laminates (1) to act as a "tone chamber," but the head rested directly on the rim. It listed for $141.84 ($80.00 dealer net), a mid-line price.

Similar to many other banjos of the day, the TB was an "open-back" model, with no resonator. Consistent with other instruments in the Gibson line, the banjo quickly became a family: the GB guitar-banjo (introduced with the TB), followed by the MB mandolin-banjo and CB banjo-cello in September 1919. Later additions included the UB, RB, and PB (uke, "regular" five-string, and plectrum, respectively) in 1924.

In the meantime, Gibson's engineering staff went to work improving these instruments. One problem that had plagued fretted instrument makers was neck warpage, and banjo necks, which were thinner than guitar necks and longer than mandolin necks, were particularly troublesome. Gibson's Thaddeus "Ted" McHugh invented an adjustable

Drawings of headstocks and rims, courtesy Roger H. Siminoff, © *Frets* magazine

truss rod in 1921 that made thin, fast-action, straight necks a reality on guitars as well as banjos. Also in 1921, McHugh and Delmont C. Mafit invented a better way to fasten and adjust the angle of the banjo neck to the body.

These two inventions represented giant steps forward for Gibson. The banjo line was expanded to include cheaper and more expensive models, topped by the gold-plated Style 5. A hollow ring **(2)** was added between the skin head and the maple rim to give the instrument a more bell-like sound. Legendary engineer Lloyd Loar made his contributions before resigning at the end of 1924: a tone ring that rested on 20 small ball bearings **(3)**, and a new name for the top models —Mastertone—to be consistent with his Master Model wood-bodied instruments.

Despite the design progress, Gibson was still slipping backwards in the banjo market. The resonator, a device attached to the back of a banjo to project the sound forward, had become a common feature on other makers' banjos. Gibson's answer, however, was a flat piece of wood, hinged so that the player could play with it open or closed. This "trapdoor" resonator debuted in 1922. It was replaced by a Pyralin (plastic) disc-like resonator in 1924, but the Pyralin resonator got such a cold reception that Gibson had to keep the trapdoor available as an option.

Factory workers pose ca. 1920 with instruments-in-progress. A harp guitar rim surrounds a banjo rim, which shows the spacers used on Gibson's earliest banjos.

The Bella Voce was not offered as a banjo-uke, but anything was possible by custom order.

Finally, in Februrary 1925, Gibson gained ground on the pack of frontrunners with the introduction of a Paramount-style flange and resonator. (Longtime banjo maker William Lange, creator of the Paramount banjo line, had introduced a wooden resonator with a rounded back, attached to a "flange" that circled the rim, in 1921.) These instruments also sported a new invention from Gibson engineer George Altermatt. The skin heads of banjos had always troubled players

because of their sensitivity to changes in temperature and humidity, and they could only be adjusted by tightening or loosening several dozen bolts. Altermatt put steel springs **(4)** beneath the ball bearings so that a more consistent head tension could be maintained.

Now Gibson was ready to do battle with the competition. A new model, the Granada, debuted along with a modern resonator in 1925. Three super-fancy models were added in 1927 to challenge the ornate creations of such competitors as Epiphone, Paramount, and Bacon. Gibson's Florentine, Bella Voce, and Style 6 brought engraved pearloid (celluloid with a mother-of-pearl appearance), rhinestones, multi-colored binding material, fancy neck and resonator carvings, etc., into the Gibson catalog. The All American of 1930 featured a peghead carved in the shape of an eagle, among other decadent appointments. On the inside of the banjos, Gibson made another improvement, replacing the hollow tone ring (along with the springs and ball bearings) with what became known as the "archtop" tone chamber **(5)**: a U-shaped ring that was open in the area where the head crossed it.

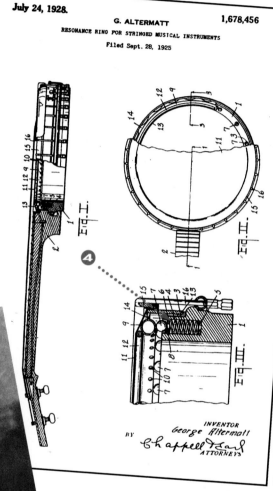

By the late '20s, Gibson was placing Gibson banjos in the hands of popular and influential players.

In the banjo shop, ca. 1930, a worker assembles tension hoops and flanges.

Unfortunately, Guy Hart had no chance to enjoy Gibson's new status as a competitive banjo maker. The Depression killed the market for expensive banjos, and by the end of the Depression, the guitar had replaced the banjo as America's favorite fretted instrument. Nevertheless, while Gibson was fighting for its life in the guitar market of the 1930s, someone at the company kept an eye on banjos, preparing for the banjo's return. The "flathead" tone ring (6), which provided for a larger banjo-head surface, was made available in the early 1930s. It became standard equipment on a new line in 1937 that featured yet another improvement: the "top-tension." (7) With Gibson's top-tension design, head-adjusting bolts were accessible from the top of the banjo, and players no longer had to take off the resonator to adjust head tension. (The problem of maintaining head tension was finally solved in the early 1950s with the development of Mylar plastic heads.)

Ironically, when the banjo finally returned—powered by the advanced playing technique of bluegrass musician Earl Scruggs—Gibson, an also-ran during the golden age of jazz banjos, would become the most revered name in the industry. To further the irony, the style of banjo that became popular was the five-string RB (rather than the tenor), with a flathead tone ring—a 1930s afterthought—as the preferred hardware.

John Hedgecoth

Dan Loftin, courtesy Gruhn Guitars

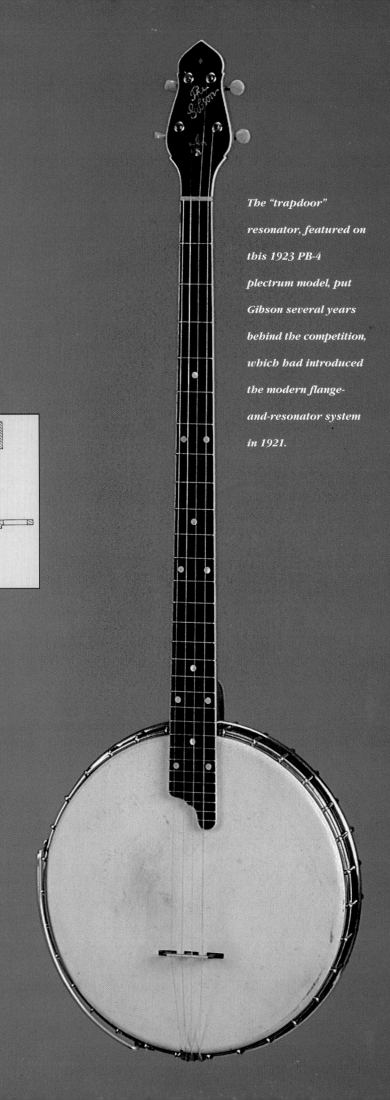

The "trapdoor"
resonator, featured on
this 1923 PB-4
plectrum model, put
Gibson several years
behind the competition,
which had introduced
the modern flange-
and-resonator system
in 1921.

EARL SCRUGGS

B Y   R O G E R   H .   S I M I N O F F

Earl Scruggs, 1980. Earl and the Gibson five-string banjo were both born in January 1924.

Gibson's first banjo, announced in October 1918, and those that immediately followed reflected musicians' familiarity with mandolin-family instruments: The TB (tenor), MB (mandolin banjo), and CB (cello banjo) were tuned in fifths and corresponded in tuning to the mandola, mandolin, and mandocello, respectively; the GB (guitar banjo), tuned like a guitar, augmented the family.

Five years later, in January 1924, Gibson announced a new banjo: the five-string or "regular banjo," designated "RB." It was not even offered in all the current styles, only RB-Jr, RB-3, and RB-4 (the TB was also available in Styles 1, 2, and 5). The RBs featured a 25 5/16" string scale with a suggested tuning of "G major tuning—C, G, B, D, with the 5th string tuned to high G" (old-time or classic tuning, with a low C rather than the low D used by bluegrass players).

RB models were only moderately successful, with no major endorsers popular enough to find their way to Gibson's promotional doorstep. Players in dance bands favored the tenor, and banjo bands were modeled after the earlier mandolin orchestras, with mandolin-related banjos. The future homes of the five-string—bluegrass and folk music—were just beginning to develop. The RB needed a champion.

Coincidentally, another event happened in January 1924 that would have a profound effect on the history of the five-string banjo. On January 6, Earl Eugene Scruggs was born near Shelby, North Carolina, in an area known as the Flint Hill community. His father played banjo and fiddle, and although he died when Earl was only four, the influence was solidified. By the time Scruggs was in his teens, he was performing at local square dances, and he soon envisioned playing music as a way to make a living and support his family. At 15,

he got a job picking banjo with Wiley and Zeke Morris (the Morris Brothers). His three-fingered style and a whole new music genre were beginning to take shape.

In December 1945, Scruggs met Bill Monroe at *The Grand Ole Opry* in Nashville. Monroe and his brother Charlie had been stars in the Carolinas in the mid '30s, and Bill had debuted his own band and his own brand of supercharged hillbilly music on the *Opry* in 1939. After a brief backstage demonstration of Scruggs's magical technique, Monroe immediately invited Scruggs to join his Blue Grass Boys. Scruggs's style, now fully matured, soon became the driving cadence which sparked this newly formed music called "bluegrass."

In February 1948, after three years with Monroe, Scruggs moved back to North Carolina "to get off the road for a while." Two weeks later, singer/guitarist Lester Flatt, who also worked for Monroe, came knocking at Scruggs's door. By month's end, a partnership was cast that was to last more than two decades, and "Flatt and Scruggs" was on its way to becoming a household term.

Their music became a regular highlight on WSM, the 50,000-watt Nashville radio station that broadcast *The Grand Ole Opry,* and dozens of albums followed which showcased their artistry. Stylistically, they were in the bluegrass niche, but they exploded into mass popularity when they recorded the theme song for the hit TV show *The Beverly Hillbillies* and when "Foggy Mountain Breakdown" was used for the chase scenes in the movie *Bonnie and Clyde.* "Foggy Mountain Breakdown" eventually won the prestigious Million-air award from BMI (the performance licensing agency) for one million radio plays.

Scruggs mail-ordered his first banjo from Montgomery Ward. He remembers that it looked like a Kay banjo, "That banjo didn't have any name

©1993 Jon Sievert

lots of pearloid and stenciled ornamentation, it looked more expensive than what it was. Scruggs made that discovery a few years later, when he performed at an outdoor concert and got caught in the rain with his RB-11—a situation in which he remembers "how strange it was that the rain and sun completely ruined the finish on that banjo." Fortunately, he had purchased an RB-3 from a man in Roanoke, Virginia, and used it as his backup. "That banjo was so nice that Don Reno couldn't resist trading me his Granada banjo and a D-18 Martin guitar for it. The gold plating was bad [on Reno's banjo] and the stretcher band was broken, but I loved the tone of that banjo and we made the swap. And, I'm still playing that banjo today."

Standing on the porch of his mother's house in 1947, Earl Scruggs picks a tune on his first Gibson, a model RB-11. ©1993 Roger Siminoff

on it," he recalls. "It was just an inexpensive banjo with geared machines, a wood rim, and a deep resonator. I remember that I paid $10.95 for it." Although he didn't own a Gibson until several years later, it is possible that the "no-name" banjo he bought from Montgomery Ward was actually a Gibson, for the company produced large quantities of inexpensive private label instruments for many mail-order and chain stores over the years. "The Gibson-brand banjos of that period [especially the model he desired] were very expensive," Scruggs remembers. Finally, luck brought him to his first Gibson banjo, a blue RB-11, propped up in a pawn shop window.

The RB-11 was the Gibson-brand equivalent of Gibson's budget-priced Kel Kroydon model. With

In 1947, Scruggs was performing in Kalamazoo. "Someone from Gibson came to the show and invited us on a tour of the Gibson factory," he remembers. "They had two banjo pot assemblies [bodies] on the wall—that was the total amount of banjos in process at that time. They would become whatever anyone wanted—tenor, plectrum, or whatever. There was just no demand for resonator-type banjos, then."

Scruggs was intrigued by the mill room, the stacks of lumber, and he recalls how large the bandsaw was. The final inspection area also caught his attention. "I remember how they had this large canvas bin where they inspected the guitars. If they found a flaw they couldn't repair, they'd throw the guitar in that bin and saw it into pieces. Nothing went by them. I've always thought about that and how much they cared about making good instruments."

As Scruggs's style became popular, sales of RB models soared and sales of tenor and plectrum models declined. Gibson designers continued to proliferate the marketplace with a wide variety of five-string banjo models including the RB-250 "bow-tie" banjo, the RB-100s, RB-250s and RB-800s—all of which came in a wide variety of platings, decorations, and finishes.

By the early 1980s, Scruggs had pushed the five-string banjo into a wider musical arena fronting the Earl Scruggs Revue, and he and Gibson embarked on a project to reproduce his banjo for the Gibson line. This instrument, the Earl Scruggs Model, is a Granada featuring nickel-plated hardware (Earl's banjo was originally gold-plated but the plating has long since worn off), curly maple neck and resonator, hearts-and-flowers inlays, ebony fretboard, and a "flattop" tone chamber. Two models were later added: the Earl Scruggs '49 Classic with bowtie inlays (styled after one of Earl's banjos that was sent back to the factory in 1949 to have a fretboard replacement and received its then-current inlay pattern), and the Earl Scruggs Golden Deluxe with hand-engraved gold-plated hardware.

Bill Monroe and the Blue Grass Boys, 1939. Monroe's first banjo player, Dave "Stringbean" Ackeman, played a Gibson RB-11. Courtesy Country Music Foundation

THE RISE OF RADIO

B Y   M I C H A E L   M c C A L L

Ted Fio Rito's band backed up the Debutantes in the 1934 Vitaphone film 20 Million Sweethearts. His guitarist, Muzzy Marcellino, played a Gibson L-5 and sang "I'll String Along With You," which became a Number One record.
Frank Driggs Collection

As the 1930s began, America struggled to find light while an oppressively dark cloud seemed to grow larger and larger. The Depression was devastation—between 1929 and '31, 10 million people lost jobs, 30,000 businesses folded, and 2,500 banks failed—and events unfolding in Europe added to the impending gloom. In Germany, the Nazi party gained, and by 1933, Adolf Hitler was appointed chancellor and given dictatorial control of government affairs. The Nazi reign of terror erupted, and the Holocaust began.

In America, one of the few glimmers of positive escape came from a little tube-powered box called the radio. The explosion of record sales that occurred in the mid '20s fell even faster than it had risen: In 1928, more than 100 million records had been sold; in 1932, that number dropped to 6 million, even after record companies cut prices from 75 cents to 35 cents.

Musical theater suffered a similarly downcast lot. Broadway productions diminished as ticket sales bottomed out and attendance fell by more than 40 percent. In 1930, 32 new productions were mounted; in 1934, only 10, and nearly all of them

failed. A few successes materialized, most notably the grand *42nd Street,* which premiered in 1933, and Cole Porter's *Anything Goes,* which opened in the bleak year of 1934 and nonetheless went on to become the decade's most acclaimed musical.

Vaudeville all but vanished, and burlesque barely stood on its spindly, shaky last legs. It seemed people just weren't in the mood for entertainment —at least not for the flashy kind that involved hitting the town, living it up, and dancing up a storm. Instead, the early part of the decade was reflected in "Brother Can You Spare a Dime?" The tune from the Broadway show *Americana* was a Number One recording in 1932 for both of the era's biggest new stars: Bing Crosby and Rudy Vallee.

While the public might not have been able to afford to buy music, they still loved to listen to it. In the 1930s, radio became America's fastest-growing business and its fourth largest industry. At the start of the 1920s, hardly anyone owned one of the contraptions. By the mid '30s, estimates suggested that 30 million people huddled around the illuminated dials every evening.

The boxes broadcast more than music. "Soap operas" slipped into the American consciousness.

Eddie Lang, the first great jazz guitar player, accompanied Bing Crosby, the first great crooner, in the 1932 Paramount film The Big Broadcast.
Frank Driggs Collection

The audience for such maudlin melodramas as *Stella Dallas, One Man's Family, Life Can Be Beautiful, Pepper Young's Family,* and *The Romance of Helen Trent* was largely female, and the sponsors typically pushed soap products—thus the nickname.

The serials weren't all soaps, however. Popular comedies included *Amos 'n' Andy, The Goldbergs,* and *Fibber McGee and Molly.* Mysteries and adventures, too, including *The Shadow, The Green Hornet, Inner Sanctum, The Lone Ranger,* and *Buck Rogers in the 25th Century,* kept families glued to the stations. By 1938, some 78 serials were on the air, and they brought in more than $25 million annually to the two national radio networks, NBC and CBS.

Music was also an integral part of the daily broadcast, and it created its own cast of new stars. Bing Crosby, who left Paul Whiteman in 1931 because of what he later termed "youthful indiscretions," emerged as the biggest singing sensation of the decade. Crosby's relaxed, warm baritone proved perfect to take full advantage of the radio microphone, and he made "crooning" the new popular style.

Rudy Vallee, a more strident crooner, hosted his own popular show with a pseudo-collegiate air on the NBC network. His program introduced and even expanded the popularity of many other variety-show entertainers, including Bob Hope, Red Skelton, Fanny Brice,

Milton Berle, Dorothy Lamour, Alice Fay, and the Mills Brothers.

Meanwhile, Kate Smith became known as "The Songbird of the South" through her popular CBS show, which premiered in 1931. Her theme song, "When the Moon Comes Over the Mountain," was a Number One record in 1932, and she went on to record her most famous song, Irving Berlin's "God Bless America," in 1939.

Your Hit Parade, another program featuring well-known vocalists singing the era's most popular songs, debuted in 1935 and would eventually rank as one of radio's longest-running shows, staying on the air for 28 years. It helped establish such singers as Frank Sinatra, Doris Day, Dinah Shore, Snooky Lanson, Margaret Whiting, Martha Tilton, Georgia Gibbs, and Dorothy Collins. Radio also

Before there was "country" music, "billbilly" string bands like Crockett's Kentucky Mountaineers were among radio's most successful products.

The Monroe Brothers, with Bill on the Gibson F-7 mandolin and Charlie on the Gibson Jumbo, were one of the hottest radio acts in the Carolinas in the mid '30s. Frank Driggs Collection

The growing popularity of Hawaiian music prompted the Masqueria Sisters to replace their Spanish Students outfits with grass skirts.

By the late '30s, cowboy music, as played by Louise Massey and the Westerners, reached across the nation, thanks to the NBC radio network. Frank Driggs Collection

showcased the era's great dance bands led by such illustrious maestros as Paul Whiteman, Ted Lewis, Guy Lombardo, Eddie Duchin, and Kay Kyser. A more forceful kind of big band music known as swing also began to emerge from New York ballrooms. Duke Ellington and Cab Calloway's bands, which both gained fame at Harlem's renowned Cotton Club, certainly had that thing called swing. Tommy and Jimmy Dorsey's bands had it, too, in the couple of years the brothers played together as well as in separate bands after their acrimonious split.

Benny Goodman introduced swing to the West Coast during his extended stay at the Palomar ballroom. Bennie Moten, a black bandleader, headed the most famous swing band in the Midwest, thanks in part to the sublime touch of his pianist, Count Basie. By the latter part of the decade, Woody Herman, Jimmie Lunceford, Artie Shaw, and Glenn Miller were adding their distinctive styles to the swing repertoire. By then, it seemed, everyone was doing it, and they were doing it right.

The various barn dances staged by radio stations through the South and Midwest also created stars. At *The Grand Ole Opry,* banjo player Uncle Dave Macon was joined by the singing Delmore Brothers and the Vagabonds. Gene Autry had his

first national hit, "That Silver Haired Daddy of Mine." Autry was a star of *The National Barn Dance* on Chicago's WLS, which also featured the Coon Creek Girls, who, like many country bands at the time, brandished a couple of guitars and a mandolin as well as a fiddle. In Texas, Bob Wills introduced Western swing as a featured artist on three different Fort Worth radio stations before moving on to Tulsa. In North Carolina, Bill and Charlie Monroe played a revved-up style of mountain music that Bill would later augment and call bluegrass.

As the music grew more exotic, there was no telling what odd influence might arise. About the same time Gene Autry nestled his acoustic guitar near a campfire on the silver screen to croon the Hollywood version of a cowboy ballad, the Hawaiian rage that had begun in 1915 reached new heights, shimmying into the American musical sphere with easy rhythms and the distinctive new sound of the electric Hawaiian "lap steel" guitar. Even Bing Crosby got into the act: He starred in the movie *Waikiki Wedding,* which spawned his million-selling "Sweet Leilani" in 1937.

That's right, a million-selling record. By the late '30s, thanks partly to the emergence of jukeboxes, record sales once again became a potent force in the music industry.

EVOLUTION OF THE GUITAR

BY R. E. BRUNÉ

School of Stauffer, ca. 1830. This unsigned German or Austrian guitar has the typical six-on-a-side enclosed tuners. The string length of 60.5 cm permitted tuning the first string to either e or g depending on the gauge of strings. Bruné Collection

Few instruments in history have had such a mercurial and long existence as the guitar and its antecedents. The world's earliest surviving guitar was made by Belchior Dias of Lisbon, Portugal, in 1581, and has five courses (groups of strings), which were probably tuned with a *re-entrant* tuning. In this tuning system, the lowest-pitched note is the fourth-course D-string, which was probably paired with an octave string (like the modern 12-string guitar). The fifth-course A-string was tuned an octave above the modern pitch, producing an effect similar to the ukulele. This 400-year-old instrument is still playable and was made using Brazilian rosewood for the sides and back, a wood still in demand today, though nearly extinct.

The five-course guitar remained popular throughout Europe and enjoyed royal patronage, especially in France where the production of highly ornamented guitars reached a zenith that has never been surpassed. The lavish use of rare and expensive materials became almost a fetish, and some guitars were made using tortoiseshell, ebony, ivory, and other rare exotics. Surprisingly, most of these instruments were meant to be played and were as sophisticated musically as they were visually.

In southern Italy, the wire-strung version of the guitar, called the *chitarra battente,* appeared alongside the five-course gut-strung instrument, and it closely resembles the modern 12-string guitar in concept. Like the 12-string, it was used mostly for popular rather than art music.

With the addition of the sixth course, the guitar was closing in on modern stringing. The change from courses to single strings occurred in southern Europe, where the earliest six-string guitar was made by Francois Lupot in Orleans, France, and is dated 1773. Among its notable features is the pin bridge, an innovation borrowed from the harp makers who used pins to attach strings to the harp's soundboard. In Europe, the pin bridge quickly spread among German, French, and Italian makers; only the Spanish makers retained the lute-style tied bridge.

Early six-string guitars were notable for fingerboards flush with the soundboard rather than glued on top. This limited the amount of tension the guitar could withstand. (It is common for surviving guitars from this period to exhibit a considerable amount of collapsing at the neck/body joint.) As virtuoso composer/players began conquering the public fancy, their demands inspired makers to address this problem around 1820. The invention of the raised fingerboard not only strengthened the instrument but also improved access to the upper frets. Virtuosos were now able to dazzle audiences like never before.

The invention of fixed metal frets provided a fundamental sound change, permitting greater sustain and clarity due to the more solid interface with the fingerboard. The most serious drawback to metal frets was the expense of wearing out costly gut strings too soon, but by 1800, the Industrial Revolution was bringing down the price of many labor-intensive products such as gut strings, and guitarists quickly accepted the metal frets.

In Europe, the guitars of Johann Georg Stauffer of Vienna gained favor among players and spread to other countries. Known for his many innovations, Stauffer patented a neck design in which the fingerboard floated above the top, like the violin. This new model, made with the design input of

THE ÆOLIAN MANDOLIN AND GUITAR CLUB, MEADVILLE, PENN.

Use exclusively Washburn instruments.

Italian virtuoso Luigi Legnani, also featured another innovation: the detachable neck, which attached to the body with a single bolt. By adjusting the tightness of the bolt with a clock-key, the player could easily adjust his own action.

In Spain, the guitar lagged behind European developments. It was not until around 1850 that the appearance of flamenco as an art form created a demand for an instrument to accompany singers and dancers. Foremost among makers was Antonio de Torres, who synthesized all of the great design features in circulation at the time and created a new type of guitar perfectly suited to this new art form. The instrument that originally evolved in southern Spain to be heard above the din of the corner tavern has proven in the hands of artists such as Andrés Segovia to be suitable for the most expressive of music in the modern concert hall.

In America, the status of the guitar evolved from the art music circles of Europe to the more popular instrument of the masses. Waves of European immigrants, quick to shed their accents if not their heritage, created a unique blend of popular musics. With the advances in industrial technology, guitars became more affordable to a wide range of players.

C. F. Martin, who had been a foreman in Stauffer's shop in Vienna, arrived in New York in 1833 and opened shop. He moved to Nazareth, Pennsylvania, in 1839, and his guitars quickly evolved from the Austro-German style of Stauffer into a uniquely American guitar, characterized by a lower bout wider than the upper bout, X-pattern bracing under the top, and a symmetrical, slotted peghead.

Martin's innovations carried the American guitar into the 20th century with no major changes. These small "parlor" guitars began to grow larger and louder around the turn of the century, no doubt in response to the rising popularity of mandolin orchestras and the introduction of a new style of guitar employing Orville Gibson's carved-top concepts. Still, the guitar remained in the shadows of the mandolin and banjo until the 1930s, when its rise to dominance over other fretted instruments spurred a flurry of popular new designs.

After 1850, most American guitars, including these 1890s Washburns, followed the designs established by C. F. Martin.

Johann Gottfried Scherzer, 1861. Not content with six strings, virtuoso Nicolai Makaroff commissioned Scherzer, a pupil of Johann Stauffer, to make a 10-string guitar, of which this is a typical example. Private collection

NICK LUCAS

BY WALTER CARTER

Nick Lucas and his

custom-made Gibson on

Broadway, 1929.

The Crooning

Troubador, still

crooning in 1980.

Courtesy Jas Obrecht

In the 1990s, an era when the guitar rules popular music, a half-dozen or so artists have Gibson guitar models named after them, and over a hundred more endorse Gibsons. In the late 1920s, however, when the guitar was just beginning to raise its voice, there was one and only one artist with his name on a Gibson instrument. He was not only an international singing star, he was, appropriately, the first guitar star—Nick Lucas.

Thanks to campy '60s pop singer Tiny Tim, Lucas is probably best-known today for his original hit recording of "Tip Toe Through the Tulips." But he had started his recording career seven years earlier as a guitarist— as the first to play a hot guitar solo on record.

He was born Dominic Nicholas Anthony Lucanese in 1897, the son of Italian parents who had immigrated to Newark, New Jersey. Coached by his older brother, he learned to play guitar, mandolin, and banjeaurine (a small banjo). Around 1920, playing in a band led by Sam Lanin, he started putting down the banjo and picking up the guitar when the band played a waltz. "The guitar came in handy," he told Jas Obrecht in a 1980 interview for *Guitar Player*. "It blended better." It would be almost ten years before the rest of the music world agreed with him.

Lucas also substituted the smoother guitar tone on recording sessions when his tenor banjo made the cutting stylus jump out of the groove. In 1922, he cut the first guitar solos on a pair of instrumentals he had written: "Pickin' the Guitar" and "Teasin' the Frets."

Lucas moved to Chicago, where his radio performances were so popular that Gibson offered to custom-build a guitar for him in 1924. He had started singing along with his guitar, and audiences liked it. A hit recording, "My Best Girl," in early 1925 elevated him from sideman status to "The Crooning Troubadour."

In the meantime, Gibson was struggling. The mandolin orchestra was dead, and Gibson banjos weren't doing so well against the longer-established competition.

Endorsers—from "Gibson-ites" in the catalogs to performing employees like Jimmie Johnstone and Lloyd Loar—had always played a big part in Gibson's success. An endorser might just ensure the success of the Gibson guitar. The first choice—and practically the only choice in 1928—was Nick Lucas.

The Nick Lucas model, also called the Gibson Special, was a prize, with tastefully ornate fingerboard inlays and a rich, dark sunburst finish. At 13 1/2 inches wide, it looked small, but its extra-deep body (over four inches at the endpin) gave it a big sound.

The timing was perfect. Lucas returned to New York in 1929 to star in the Broadway show *Gold Diggers of Broadway,* and he played his Gibson onstage. He recorded a song from the show, "Tip Toe Through the Tulips," and it stayed at Number One for 10 weeks in 1929.

Nick Lucas went on to enjoy a long and stellar career, and his endorsement model helped Gibson enter the guitar era of the 1930s with a reputation for high-quality flattop guitars.

ROY SMECK

BY WALTER CARTER

In the early 1930s, in an effort to repeat the success Nick Lucas had brought in the late 1920s, Gibson looked for an endorser for a new Hawaiian guitar. Once again, Gibson landed the hottest instrumentalist of the day—Roy Smeck.

Although Smeck had not made any recordings that would qualify as pop hits, he had already secured his place in music history as a film performer and instrument endorser. As a virtuoso on guitar, banjo, ukulele, and Hawaiian guitar—and as a "dummy" act, a non-singer, whose every second of performance was focused on his instrument—he probably had more potential for success with a Gibson "name" model than a musician-turned-crooner like Nick Lucas.

Smeck was born in 1900 in Reading, Pennsylvania, and raised in Binghamton, New York. He dropped out of school in the fifth grade to work in a shoe factory. "Roy would find time to practice and dream of making phonograph records some day," Gibson literature said, and it seems that he found too much time to practice. He was fired from the shoe factory, but he found a music store job that allowed him to practice and work at the same time.

Smeck made up for his lack of vocal ability with dazzling displays of musicianship. He hit the vaudeville circuit in the 1920s billed as "The Wizard of the Strings." In 1926, Vitaphone films featured him in a short, called *Wizard of the Strings*, which may well qualify him as the first music video artist. An instrument maker then signed him up to endorse the Vita-uke, a pear-shaped ukulele with soundholes shaped like trained seals.

The Hawaiian guitar craze, which had started in 1915, was gaining power in the late 1920s. The guitars, too, became more powerful with the introduction of National's metalbody resonator models in 1927. Gibson countered in 1929 with a short-lived flattop that was larger and louder but had a bizarre, double-walled design.

The Depression hit, and Gibson's next round of big acoustic Hawaiians didn't come until 1934. This time, Gibson sought to ensure success with a big name endorser. Two models debuted in 1934—one with mahogany back and sides and one with rosewood—and Smeck got his name on both of them: the Roy Smeck Stage Deluxe and the more expensive Roy Smeck Radio Grande.

Unfortunately for Gibson and Smeck, the *electric* Hawaiian guitar was just beginning its rise, and acoustic Hawaiians were no match for it. The Wizard was no fool. He, too, switched to an electric—a guitar custom-made for him by Gibson—but the electric model did not go into production. He looked for an endorsement model and found the next-best thing: a Gibson-made Recording King model, sold through the Montgomery Ward mail-order catalog.

After World War II, Smeck moved his endorsement to Harmony, where he went on to become the most prolific endorser in instrument history. A 1983 documentary found him still active as a teacher and still, as the documentary's title proclaimed, *Wizard of the Strings*.

The Wizard of the Strings with his Radio Grande, from a 1935 Mastertone magazine.

The one and only Roy Smeck Special lap steel, made for the Wizard of the Strings in 1936. Frank Driggs Collection

The Vita-uke, the first endorsement from the king of the endorsers.

ENTER THE GUITAR

BY WALTER CARTER

Champions of Gibson guitars in the 1932 catalog include a young Alvino Rey, Otto Gray's Oklahoma Cowboys (featured in Grinnell's window display), and the Carter Family.

Gibson's in-house mandolin virtuoso, Jimmie Johnstone, lent his endorsement to the Nick Lucas guitar.

On October 12, 1929, as the stock market came tumbling down, a keen ear might have detected among the wails of American businesses the twang of strings breaking and the clang of metal parts hitting the floor—the sound of the banjo market crashing.

The Depression that followed the Crash of '29 was the death blow for the tenor banjo, but there had been an earlier sign that the banjo's reign over the fretted instrument world was weakening. That sign was the tenor guitar—a four-stringed guitar tuned just like the tenor banjo. Veterans of the instrument business only had to remember back about 10 years, when a four-stringed banjo tuned in fifths (just like a mandolin) pushed the mandolin aside, to know that the banjo was doomed. By the late '20s, the smoother texture of the guitar was replacing the harsh banjo sound, and the tenor banjo provided a bridge for banjoists on their way to the fuller sound of the six-string guitar.

Gibson guitars dated back to the days of Orville, but Catalog U of 1932 gushed with praise as if the guitar were a newly discovered treasure: "The Guitar has been called a Miniature Orchestra in itself, and for centuries an instrument of romance and endless beauty."

"Miniature orchestra" was an exaggeration, of course, but the guitar would soon be accepted as the best all-purpose accompaniment

instrument, the one with the best combination of musical versatility and physical portability. Despite the claim, Gibson shamelessly—on the facing page of the catalog—took the opposite tack and tried to promote the guitar as it had the banjo and mandolin in earlier years, as an instrument suitable for ensembles. Catalog U suggested that a guitar orchestra (with each guitar being its own orchestra, this would be an orchestra of orchestras) could be started with just two guitars—one Spanish and one Hawaiian—and even offered a free booklet called *How to Organize An Orchestra.*

Guitar orchestras didn't catch on, but guitars did sell in orchestral quantities. They became pervasive in all types of music: as a rhythm instrument in the big jazz bands, as accompaniment for country and blues music, and as a lead instrument (like a saxophone or trumpet) in a group setting.

The rise of the guitar should have made established makers like Gibson very

happy, but with the popularity came fierce competition and a flurry of innovation that by mid-decade gave birth to a new unknown factor: the electric guitar. Experience in changing markets turned out to be a valuable trait for makers of fretted instruments. With the exception of National and Rickenbacker—companies with radically new products—no upstart companies were able to jump on the guitar bandwagon of the '30s.

VEGA

Most of the great banjo makers of the '20s failed to make the switch to guitars. Vega was an exception—sort of. The Boston company had a momentary flash of the future in 1928 with the introduction of an electric banjo. It turned out to be a false start that relegated Vega to the back of the field for the next 10 years. Vega catalogs from the late '30s indicate that the company bounced back into the market with a full line of guitars: steels, acoustic archtops, and electric archtops (one of them sporting the first double-coil "humbucking" pickup). But the scarcity of surviving Vega instruments from this era suggests that Vega's switch to guitars was not very successful after all. The company did survive, however, and eventually regained some of its early-1900s prominence when

Tiny Grimes, 1945. The four-stringed tenor guitar helped banjoists switch to guitar, but few were still playing tenor when jazzman Grimes picked it up in the late '30s. Frank Driggs Collection

The window of Grinnell Bros. in 1929 shows banjos still dominating guitars, a situation that would soon be reversed.

its best-known product, the five-string banjo, was revived in the '50s and '60s.

EPIPHONE

From his factory in Long Island City, New York, Epi Stathopoulo was somehow able to see the future of the fretted instrument business. Although the Epiphone brand didn't appear on banjos until 1924, Epi foresaw that boom, as shown by his banjo patents dating back to 1917. And even though he was fully committed to banjos when the boom went bust in 1929, he had seen an archtop guitar on the horizon. Of all the banjo makers, Epi was the

Any Gibson was available with a tenor guitar neck, including the prestigious L-5.

Courtesy Gruhn Guitars

leader in switching over to guitars and was Gibson's strongest competition up until World War II.

GRETSCH

In a technical sense, Gretsch qualifies as a '20s banjo maker that made a successful switch to guitars, but as a distributor of wind instruments and drums as well as stringed instruments, Gretsch was established on a broad enough base so as not to be dragged down along with the banjo. Gretsch jumped heavily into guitars in 1933 and by the end of the decade was challenging Gibson and Epi with big flashy acoustic archtops.

KAY

In 1929, Chicago-based Stromberg-Voisinet showed some foresight by introducing an electric flattop guitar. The Depression and the lack of a modern pickup thwarted the attempt, but the company emerged from the experience with a new, easy-to-remember name—Kay—and a new identity as a leading maker of low-end guitars.

HARMONY

The Harmony name was new but the Chicago company was old. Harmony had built instruments for other makers since 1892 but had just gained its own name-recognition in the 1920s, thanks in part to its 1928 line of Roy Smeck Vita guitars (Smeck, a vaudeville star, had made a short

The Pine State Playboys' guitarist had his own name inlaid into the fingerboard of a Nick Lucas model. Frank Driggs Collection

Fancy ornamentation of the bygone banjo era resurfaced briefly on Gibson's Century guitar, played by Olan and Kenneth Smith, the Plantation Boys, in 1936. Frank Driggs Collection

Gibson

GUITARS
BANJOS
MANDOLINS
UKULELES

The Music Pals
of A Nation

GUITARS
BANJOS
MANDOLINS
UKULELES
MONA-STEEL
STRINGS
and
COMPLETE
ACCESSORIES

Gibson envisioned a

Hawaiian guitar in

every parlor.

Gibson

performance film for Vitaphone). During the Depression, Harmony showed its experience by offering the only kind of instruments the market could stand: inexpensive. By the late '30s, Harmony would be Kay's biggest competitor for the low-end market.

REGAL

By the '30s, the musical instrument business in Chicago had become inbred, with makers supplying instruments and parts for each other. At the center of this family was Regal. The Regal brand name dates back to 1884 in Indianapolis; it passed through several hands, including Lyon & Healy, before a Chicago-based Regal company was incorporated in 1908. Regal became a major maker of low- and middle-grade instruments. Regal made instruments for sale under its own brand; Regal supplied instruments or parts to other makers for sale under various brands; Regal bought instruments from others to sell under its own brands; Regal even had an exclusive license (beginning in 1933) to make Dobros under the Regal brand. Collectors and dealers of vintage guitars today use a blanket term, "probably Regal-made," to cover thousands of instruments of questionable origin.

LARSON BROS.

Carl and August Larson of Chicago are probably best-known for the "WLS" guitars they made for cast members of *The National Barndance,* but this '30s notoriety was their last hurrah. The Swedish-born brothers had been making guitars since the 1880s and had had their own business since 1900. They were the first important makers to build guitars for steel strings, and they made an estimated 12,000 instruments over 40-plus years, but they are obscure because they made few if any under their own name. Their brands included Maurer, Prairie State, and Euphonon, and they also made instruments under dealer-brands for Wm. C. Stahl of Milwaukee and W. J. Dyer & Bros. of St. Paul. Their Dyer harp guitars are the style preferred by most of today's harp guitarists. Carl and August were essentially a two-man business, and their business died when they did, in the mid '40s.

MARTIN

Traditional, conservative, venerable Martin was hit hard by the Depression (Gibson would make wooden toys to get by; Martin toyed with the idea of rosewood jewelry). But Martin hit a surge of innovation just at the right time, just as the guitar was emerging. Martin hadn't had a really great innovation for 80 years—not since C. F. Martin's X-braced flattops of about 1850—but it was worth the wait. The 1930s may not have been Martin's most prosperous years, but they were glory years nevertheless. In the opinion of many of today's players and collectors, Martin flattops from the '30s are the best guitars the company ever made. Martin tried archtops, too, in the '30s but with no success.

NATIONAL/DOBRO

National pushed acoustic guitars to their limit of volume in 1927 with the introduction of the resonator guitar, featuring three aluminum cones (and later a single-cone configuration). These loud metalbody guitars were an immediate success with Hawaiian players and, within a few years, bluesmen. One of National's founders, John Dopyera, left in 1928 to start Dobro, and the two rival resophonic companies merged by 1933. National was an early convert to the electric guitar and a major electric force in the late '30s.

RICKENBACKER

The company whose guitars started a revolution—not just in the guitar business but in all of popular music—came to life as the by-product of a boardroom dispute at National that sent George Beauchamp packing. In 1932, he joined forces with Adolph Rickenbacker, a tool and die man who supplied metal parts to National, and they brought the first modern electric guitar to market. Electro String, as Rickenbacker was called in the '30s, was a major maker of Hawaiian electrics but, surprisingly, was not a significant force in the market for Spanish-neck electrics.

Jazz and big band players embraced archtop guitars, like the Gibson L-5.

The emerging guitar market inspired much innovation and some failures, including this Gibson made for musician Andy Sannella.

Raymond Robert Myers of the Cowboy Loye band played Hawaiian-style with his feet on a '34 L-75. Center for Popular Music, Middle Tennessee State University

THE KALAMAZOO PLAYTHINGS COMPANY

BY WALTER CARTER

Ah, those classic Gibson models. The L-5, the Super 400, the Granada, the J-200…

And who can forget the Enterprise, the Yankee, the Kroydon Rocket, the Boston Bag, the Running Rabbit Wagon, the Fish Sand Pail…

The Gibson name has always stood for high quality, but for a short time—1931 through '33—the Gibson factory was the home of quality toys, from toddlers' items, such as wood blocks in a wagon, to working replicas of racing yachts.

And even though Kalamazoo Playthings and Kel Kroydon Toys didn't sound as prestigious as Gibson Inc., employees didn't mind working for a toy company. The alternative in the middle of the Depression was no work at all.

To Gibson secretary and general manager Guy Hart, the dawn of the 1930s looked like the darkest night. It was undoubtedly the scariest period of his career, the only period when Gibson's survival as a musical instrument company was severely threatened.

The threat is clear from a Gibson serial number list, which shows about 1400 instruments per year from 1925 to '29 (not including banjos), then only 250 per year for 1930 and '31. Guitars were obviously far down the list of necessities for the average worker in the early 1930s, and it was unlikely that sales would pick up until the economy did.

Ironically, for Gibson to have any chance of a future in the musical instrument business, the company had to practically stop making instruments. Hart's top priority was to keep Gibson in business and to keep his workforce (and himself, of course) employed. He made what was probably the boldest move of his career and shifted most of production to wooden toys. It was also a logical move for a company whose workforce included many woodworkers.

Except for the step down in prestige, the move to wooden toys was quite successful. *The Kalamazoo Gazette* of August 16, 1931, told the story under these headlines:

Kalamazoo Plant Making Thousands of Gay Toys

Division of Gibson, Inc., Providing Young America With Model Yachts, Blocks in Boxcars, and Other Novel Playthings

One of the most popular items was a pull toy that contained a set of wood blocks. Hart explained the concept to the newspaper: "We have adopted the plan of boxing our blocks, not in common boxes, but instead in box cars and wagons. That gives the child an extra toy to play with."

Pull toys came with all sorts of decorations, including barnyard animals and Mother Goose characters. The top-of-the line wagons were the "running" models, available with a horse, rabbit, or bear that had wheels instead of feet. (Boston Bags, for the record, were small leatherette carrying bags.)

The *pièces-de-résistance* were the boats. There were five Kel Kroydon sailboats, the largest of which sported a 26-inch hollow hull with a 30-inch sail. The speedboats—the 12-inch Kroydon Rocket and 15-inch Miss Kroydon IV—had a hull of cedar and mahogany and were powered by a rubber band with a five-minute running time. The Kalamazoo line featured scale reproductions of the *Enterprise* yacht, which had recently won the Americas Cup, and the *Yankee,* a frequent race winner on

Kalamazoo's Gull Lake. In April 1932, the yachts were displayed by Marshall Field and Company, the large Chicago retailer, and later entered in a toy yacht race. (Racing results are not available.)

The toy business was brisk enough that Hart moved his sales manager Archie E. Abrams from guitars to the toy division and bought two houses on Parsons St. next to the factory for new toy-making machinery. As business grew, Gibson announced an ambitious new model: a motor-powered merry-go-round, described by the Gazette as "quite a pretentious toy."

The toy venture was shortlived—the plant went back to full-time instrument production by February 1934—but the lesson learned from the experience has become part of the Gibson legacy. "Gibson Inc. Develops New Lines to Speed Recovery," the *Gazette* headlined on June 24, 1934. The toys had been dropped, but the name of the toy line, Kalamazoo, had been introduced as a new budget brand for musical instruments.

BUDGET BRANDS

BY WALTER CARTER

If Guy Hart didn't already know that budget-priced instruments sell faster than high-priced instruments, he learned it during the Depression. The toy division's Kel Kroydon brand spilled over to cheap banjos, mandolins, and guitars, and the Kel Kroydon banjo of 1930 was so successful that Hart added it to the Gibson line in 1931, calling it a Style 11. (In Gibson's scheme of style numbers, 11 did not represent the number after 10. It was more like a double Style 1, which would be the bottom of the line, and doubly so.)

With the nation on its way to economic recovery and Gibson returning to full-time instrument production, Hart didn't forget his budget-priced successes of the Depression. Nor did he forget the catchy name of one of his toy lines—*not* the tongue-twisting Kel Kroydon, but the euphonious Kalamazoo. He launched a complete line of low-priced instruments under the Kalamazoo brand in 1934.

Like a gentleman protecting the reputation of a lady, Gibson had to guard its good name. Instruments made by Gibson had to be of high quality, no matter what name was on the headstock. But it wouldn't make sense to offer a guitar that was every bit as good as a Gibson except for its lower price. The Gibson name had to mean something. And when it came to budget brands, "Gibson" meant an adjustable truss rod. Only the true Gibsons—the ones with the Gibson name—had Gibson's patented adjustable truss rod.

Despite the lack of a truss rod, the budget-brand Gibsons were sturdy, well-made instruments. Thanks to these low-priced models, many players who could not afford to buy a Gibson-brand guitar

or mandolin in the late '30s and early '40s could still afford a Gibson-made instrument.

Kalamazoo is the best-known of Gibson's budget brands, but Gibson-made brands were so pervasive in the late '30s that a guitar buyer might have had a hard time avoiding a Gibson product.

AFFORDABLE PATRIOTISM: ARMY & NAVY MODELS

When Gibson broke tradition, it was for a good cause: America's fighting soldiers. In 1918, toward the end of World War I, a mandolin and guitar with a low-budget design—flat top and flat back (the same mandolin style that was revived in 1977 by the Flatiron company)—were produced for sale at military post exchanges. Because of the special situation, the models were named Army & Navy Special. They carried a different label from other Gibson instruments, but it still credited the Gibson company.

THE DISINHERITED: JUNIORS

What's good for the military is good for the nation. In 1919, a year after the Army & Navy models debuted, Gibson introduced Junior models—trimmed-down versions of low-end models like the L-1 (a small, roundhole archtop) and A-model mandolin. A brochure cautioned the customer to make no mistake—a Junior model was "not a Gibson"—and the Juniors were all without a peghead logo. Like the Army & Navy models, they did have a special label that credited Gibson. They were made until 1926.

NAME YOUR OWN: ORIOLE, PART I

In the late 1920s, the banjo was the most popular fretted instrument, the economy was booming, and banjo makers were dreaming up fancier and fancier ornamentation. It was the plainer and plainer models that were selling, however, and Gibson came up with a plan to let everybody in on the boom. A budget line of banjos with the Oriole brand was introduced, but that's not all. Dealers ordering these banjos in quantities of 25 or 50 could have any brand they wanted on the headstock.

IF IT WORKS FOR TOYS: KEL KROYDON

The Kel Kroydon brand began appearing on instruments in 1930 or '31 as an offshoot of Gibson's toy line. The Kel Kroydon Company was advertised as "one of Kalamazoo's oldest manufacturers." In reality, Gibson wasn't all that old by Kalamazoo industry standards, and Kel Kroydon was brand new.

MAIL-ORDER ROYALTY: RECORDING KING

By 1936, Montgomery Ward, one of the biggest mail-order houses in the country, took Gibson up on the offer made a decade earlier with the Oriole. Ward contracted with Gibson and other makers to build instruments with the Recording King brand, and Gibson made some of the high-end Recording King models, including the small-bodied Carson Robison flattop (endorsed by the country

singer/songwriter) and the rosewood dreadnought Ray Whitley (endorsed by the singing cowboy movie star). Still, they had no adjustable truss rod.

THE BUDGET BANDWAGON

Many distributors figured out that the easiest way to "make" a low-priced guitar of decent quality was to buy it from Gibson and put their own brand on it. In the late 1930s and early '40s, Gibson-made instruments wore such distributors' brands as Cromwell, Fascinator, Martelle, Capital, and Washburn. ●●●●●●●●●●●●●●●●●●●●●●●●●●●

KALAMAZOO ANEW, AND ANEW

The Kalamazoo brand was revived after World War II, but only for a few breaths, as a lap steel and amp set in the late 1940s. Twenty years later, it was exhumed for a small line of solidbody electrics. In 1970, it was finally laid to rest for good.

SOUND RULERS: MASTERTONE

As the Oriole took wing and ascended in the Gibson scheme of things, the Mastertone designation took a dive. Inaugurated in the 1920s (and still in use) on high-end banjos, Mastertone appeared in the late 1930s on an acoustic Hawaiian model and then, in an oxymoronic use of the name, achieved full-fledged brand name status in 1941 on a budget line of electric guitars, whose tone was anything but masterful.

THE BIRD IS BACK: ORIOLE, PART II

Even a budget brand has its pecking order. The Oriole was revived in 1940 to distinguish the high-end of the Kalamazoo line from the regular models—sort of an upper-lower class. These Orioles had a natural finish, tortoiseshell plastic binding, and a bird on the headstock.

Dan Loftin, courtesy Gruhn Guitars

GIBSON STRINGS

BY ROGER H. SIMINOFF

The hard economic times and fierce competition in the emerging guitar market of the early 1930s brought out the best from Gibson. The company's accomplishments in guitar design are near legendary, but just as important—yet not nearly so well known—are the innovations Gibson made in string manufacturing.

From the very beginning, strings have been the heart of every instrument Gibson made. Simple as they may seem, the design and manufacture of musical strings had as much critical attention as every other Gibson product.

At the turn of the century, the development of a high-quality drawn wire of consistent thickness was still in its infancy, and materials were prone to failure. The wire used for musical strings had to be capable of stretching, had to have anti-corrosion and anti-tarnishing properties, and had to be elastic enough to survive hours of being stressed from side to side.

The earliest strings were silver-plated copper wire for the high strings and silver-plated copper wire wound on a silk core for the lower strings. Although strings were always available from Gibson, "Gibson Brand" strings were first promoted as an accessory product in 1909 in Catalog H. These copper strings were soft, prone to breakage, and lacked the power of the steel strings in use today.

In 1927, a gold alloy wrap-wire was introduced, but it stayed in production only a few years because of its softness, high cost, and high tarnish rate. Gold Medal brand strings followed, featuring gold-plated steel wrap-wire, which was more durable and provided somewhat better tarnish properties.

In the early 1930s, Gibson introduced a line of strings made from Monel, the trade name for a very strong metal similar to stainless steel. It was capable of withstanding the rigors of playing and provided low tarnish and oxidation properties. These strings were initially promoted under the name Mastertone DeLuxe Mona-Steel strings and later just as Mona-Steel.

With the advance in wire-drawing technology, the thin Monel wire allowed a winding of a smaller outer wire over a heavier center core wire. By adding mass in this manner, the string could be brought to a playable tension while still providing the lower note.

Initially, Gibson strings were only available with straight ends. Musicians had the responsibility of twisting a loop in the end of each string to secure them to the tailpiece hooks. Gibson's first step to keep the hand-twisted loops from slipping came in the form of a patented double-locking tailpiece in which the loops of the plain strings were secondarily locked by an extra tailpiece hook. (Wound strings did not need the second lock because of the holding qualities of their coarse surface.)

A major advance in string making occurred in the early '30s with the introduction of the "double-lock loop": a tight twist close to the loop or ball, followed by a few long twists and then another series of tight twists about a half-inch from the loop.

By 1934, Gibson had introduced a wide variety of strings to satisfy the tastes of all players: acoustic, classical, and electric. In addition to a broad spectrum of gauges, there were several compositions to choose from, including Mona-Steel, gut and compound, hand-polished silvered steel, aluminum or copper wound on gut (for violin only), silver wound on silk, and bronze wound on steel. Each string provided a uniquely different property for the instrument on which it would be used.

As wire-drawing techniques improved, hexagonal wire became available, which provided a more secure non-slipping core for wound strings. This major development of the '60s provided better string life and more reliable manufacturing techniques.

In 1973, in response to the continuing growth of the stringed instrument market and in an effort to help meet the need for more instrument-making space in Kalamazoo, Gibson moved the string manufacturing to a separate larger facility in Elgin, Illinois. During this period, the popularity of phosphor-bronze strings inspired Gibson's development of several anti-tarnishing and on-line polishing techniques to provide smoother, brighter strings.

The mid '80s was a period of intensified string manufacturing techniques in Elgin. The company developed better winding machines and applied advanced methods in string winding technology. Automated systems were employed to assure the precise tensioning of core strings during winding, to straighten the wrap-wire as it was removed from the spool, and to provide precise control of wrap-wire tension during the winding process.

"Grabbers," featuring a unique pin affixed to one end and pre-cut lengths to fit a wide variety of guitars, were introduced in 1984. The pin provided self-locking string installation that prevented slippage, eliminated the need to cut off the excess, and generally sped up the string installation process.

Today, Gibson's technology of gauging, winding, and loop- or ball-ending strings has advanced to a science with elaborate equipment monitoring each step of production—advances in the art of string making that provide musicians with reliability and tonal properties never achieved before.

Gibson string production in the '50s.

Maybelle Carter's 1928 L-5 gave a distinctive sound to the Carter Family's recordings. Courtesy Gruhn Guitars

The first great jazz guitarist, Eddie Lang, set the standard for all jazzers of the '30s with his Gibson L-5. Frank Driggs Collection

AN ARCHTOP BLITZ

BY WALTER CARTER

By rights, Gibson should have owned the market for archtop guitars in the 1930s. After all, the company had been founded on Orville Gibson's invention of carved-top mandolins and guitars, and Gibson guitars had been the overwhelming favorite of players in mandolin orchestras. Lloyd Loar, in perfecting the mandolin in the early '20s, perfected the guitar along with it, and his creation, the L-5, was the best f-hole archtop guitar available in the late 1920s. In the jazz world, Eddie Lang used an L-5 to create the very concept of a jazz guitarist. In country music, another emerging musical style, Maybelle Carter of the Carter Family picked out her distinctive bass-string melody style on an L-5.

Gibson was certainly aware of its superior product. An early '30s catalog gushed in its description of the L-5: "The King of all guitars—a thousand dollars couldn't build a guitar with a finer tone. A tone that satisfies—listen for quality—it's there; listen for power—it's there; listen for clearness and balance, and you'll find it in this guitar."

The L-5 stood above its competition—that much was true. But there was virtually no competition for the L-5 because there was so little demand for a fine guitar in the age of the tenor banjo. Like all Gibson guitars, the L-5 was conceived as a member of the mandolin family, and since the mandolin orchestra was passé,

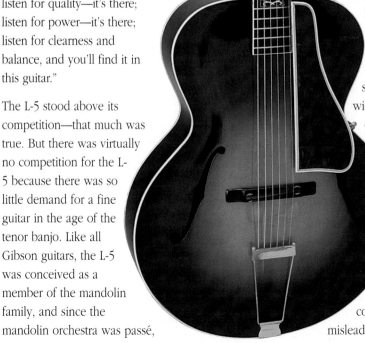

Billy Mitchell, courtesy Gruhn Guitars

the L-5 would seem to have been on a course for oblivion. Indeed, the L-5 would not gain glory in mandolin ensembles, nor would it replace the tenor banjo in the early jazz bands of the '20s. But it was just the opposite of passé; it was ahead of its time. The music for which it was perfectly suited—big band jazz—did not emerge until the '30s.

While the L-5 waited for popular music to swing its way, banjos boomed. As banjo buyers looked for fancier and fancier models, Gibson tried to attract some of them to the L-5 by dressing up the guitar a bit, replacing the dots on the fingerboard in 1929 with large pearl blocks.

The closest thing the L-5 had to competition in the '20s was the Epiphone Recording Series: small, odd-shaped guitars (the upper treble bout looked as if someone had lopped it off) with a round soundhole. Next to the 16-inch-wide L-5, they looked more ornamental than functional, as if they were the archtop equivalents of the small flattop "parlor" guitars of the 19th century. In 1928, Epiphone became officially the Epiphone Banjo Corporation, seemingly a sign that the company didn't take guitars seriously. The sign couldn't have been more misleading.

Epiphone's small ornamental guitars of the '20s gave Gibson little competition, but Epi's f-hole archtops of the '30s, such as the Emperor, ran neck-and-neck with Gibson's.

Gibson L-12, 1933.

Carl Kress's 1934 L-10 brings a smile. Frank Driggs Collection

Ed "Snoozer" Quinn, the premier jazz guitarist from the New Orleans area, plays a 1920s L-5. Frank Driggs Collection

As 1931 began, Gibson general manager Guy Hart focused his attention on selling enough toys to get Gibson through the Depression. In Long Island City, New York, however, Epi Stathopoulo had his sights set on the fast-developing market for the guitar in general and a loud, percussive guitar in particular. In June 1931, while Hart was busy with toys, Epi attacked with all the force he could muster: nine new archtop models, plus five companion tenors and an f-hole flattop. To add a touch of insult to injury, Epi made his top models 16 3/8 inches wide—a fraction of an inch wider than the L-5.

Unlike the typical man who has just been hit from behind, Hart kept his head about him. Rather than gambling the future of the company on an emotional, reactionary counter-blitz, he mounted a methodical campaign to overtake Epiphone.

In response to the Depression, Gibson had already introduced a model in 1931 that was more affordable than the L-5. The L-10 was the same size but plainer, with a black finish, and $100 cheaper than than the $250 L-5. Two more models were added in 1932: the L-12, which was fancier than the L-10, and the L-50, which was smaller and cheaper

Alvino Rey's custom-ordered archtop has the dot inlay of a 1920s L-5 but the large headstock inlay of a Super 400. Frank Driggs Collection

Even in the post-World War II electric era, an acoustic L-7 holds its own against the brass instruments of the Old Heidelberg Band. Center for Popular Music, Middle Tennessee State University

The Spirits of Rhythm, 1940, at Kelly's Stables in New York. The jazz/blues sounds of guitarist Teddy Bunn made this band one of the most popular of the club bands on New York's 52nd St. Frank Driggs Collection

L-5P, 1941. Gibson kept a competitive edge by introducing cutaway bodies in 1939.

(list price $50) than the other models. A year later, in 1933, a fourth 16-inch model, the L-7, appeared, along with a fancy small model, the L-75.

By 1934, Gibson was back on solid ground financially as well as in the archtop arena. Hart discontinued the toy lines and returned full force to instrument production. Toward the end of the year, he revealed his own surprise for Epi. In a move intended to teach a lesson to any maker who dared to challenge Gibson on Gibson's turf, all four of Gibson's large, 16-inch models were "advanced" in width by an inch (the smaller models would also be bumped up to 16 inches in 1935).

The new 17-inch guitars were powerful instruments, and they no doubt inflicted a damaging blow to Epiphone, but just in case Epi had thoughts of one-upping Gibson by advancing its line to 17 inches plus a fraction (which is exactly what Epi eventually did), Gibson delivered the *coup de grace:* a new 18-inch archtop. The huge guitar had a huge sound, a huge price—$400 with a leather-bound case—and, most important, a huge influence on every archtop maker that followed.

Two of country music's greatest guitarists—Merle Travis (with Western band) and Chet Atkins—started out on Gibson L-10s. ....➤

THE SUPER 400

B Y   T H O M A S   A .   V A N   H O O S E ,   P H . D .

Cowboy star Roy Rogers looks at home on the Super 400 range. Center for Popular Music, Middle Tennessee State University

In the electric guitar era, the Super 400– electrified–was the choice of many jazzmen, including Kenny Burrell. Frank Driggs Collection

Don Gibson wrote and sang hit country songs like "Oh, Lonesome Me" and "I Can't Stop Loving You" to the accompaniment of a Super 400. Frank Driggs Collection

A special brochure announced the birth of the Super 400 in 1934.

T he Super 400 guitar of late 1934 was designed to be the centerpiece of Guy Hart's strategy to dominate the archtop guitar market. Gibson, a company that had been focused on building toys for the past three years, could not have made a bolder, more assertive return to guitar production than the Super 400—the biggest, fanciest, and most expensive guitar available during economic times that were perilous at best.

whose handmade guitars are among the most highly sought by players and collectors, had been making 16-inch models, but they both followed the lead of the Super 400. D'Angelico began making his 18-inch New Yorker model by 1936, and Stromberg began making his 18-inch and 19-inch Master 400 models by 1940. The Super 400 was the first guitar of its kind, the first of the 18-inch archtops, and its prominence rests in part on that distinction.

The Super 400 would ultimately achieve many more things than Gibson may have perhaps originally intended. It was so far "over the top" in terms of size and ornamentation that it caught the immediate attention of musicians, instrument makers, and the general public.

The Super 400 certainly caught Gibson's competitors by surprise. Epiphone would follow in 1936 with its own 18-inch-wide Emperor model, and Gretsch would also attempt to play catch-up with the Synchromatic 400 model later in the 1930s. Individual makers John D'Angelico and Elmer Stromberg,

The Super 400 also set a new standard of excellence in guitar making, both for manufacturers and for individual makers. By deliberately picking the choicest materials, utilizing the finest crafts-manship, and sparing almost no expense in construction, Gibson continued to claim the highest standards in the fretted instrument world. The prestige attached to the Super 400 was considerable, because Gibson attached so much significance to materials, design, craftsmanship, and expense. The Super 400 quickly became the symbol of all things Gibson, evoking immediate reactions of awe and desire from all those who viewed and played the instrument. It also made synonymous the notions of almost excessive period decor, quality, and value. And finally, it brought a new acoustic voice to the jazz or popular orchestras of the day, as well as to the emerging field of country & Western music and various areas of radio and recording music.

From its introduction in 1934, the Super 400 went through several evolutionary changes, including

enlarged upper bouts in the later 1930s, cutaway body (designated with a P for Premier) and natural finish (Super 400N) options in 1939, and other less significant changes, until 1941, when production ceased because of the conversion of the Gibson plant to war work.

When production resumed in 1947, the Super 400 would soon lead the way to the next emerging trend: electric guitars. Gibson had become very adept at "catching the waves" of the latest music/musical instrument trends. The company had built its success on correctly identifying and riding out the musical trends involving the use of the

Bandleader Ted Fio Rito directs while Muzzy Marcellino strums a lullaby on his Super 400. Frank Driggs Collection

Muzzy Marcellino's Super 400, one of the first made. Billy Mitchell, courtesy Gruhn Guitars

The Super 400 helped change Lucille Overstake's persona from a Little Maid to Jennie Lou Carson. Country Music Foundation

mandolin, followed by the banjo, followed by the archtop guitar. The Super 400 played a very important role in catching the wave of the archtop guitar's popularity and foreshadowing the eventual popularity of the electric guitar through the introduction of the electric Super 400CES (CES for Cutaway Electric Spanish) in late 1951.

The Super 400 proved to be a versatile instrument, well-suited for musical styles that hadn't even

caught my attention when I was a college student and gave real direction to my early guitar-playing skills. More importantly, Burrell's guitar—a Super 400C pictured on an album cover—was the genesis of my fascination with the Super 400, which led me to begin collecting all the variations of the Super 400, which in turn led me to write a book on the model. Eventually my research and instruments were used as a basis for Gibson's reissues of the 1939 Super 400 and Super 400P.

In the 1990s, the Super 400 still has a home in the hip music of Lyle Lovett, who plays an acoustic model with a floating pickup.

©1990 John Bellissimo

existed when the model was conceived. Singer/guitarist Muzzy Marcellino of the Ted Fio Rito Orchestra was one of the first, if not the first, to introduce the Super 400 to the big bands. The country & Western music that emerged after World War II featured the Super 400CES in the hands of such stars as Hank Thompson, Merle Travis, and Joe Maphis. Bill Haley rocked around the clock on a Super 400CN. In the postwar jazz scene, Kenny Burrell played acoustic as well as electric Super 400s. It was Burrell's blues-tinged jazz improvisation and accompaniment styles that

Although sales of the Super 400 would decline with the changing musical taste of the American public and the rising popularity of rock & roll music (which was better-played on solidbody guitars), the Super 400 would continue to remain a symbol of Gibson's craftsmanship and an enduring sign of the legacy of the past. Its limited production continues to the present day, and the reissue of the 1939 Super 400 Premier is one of the newer high points in the long and illustrious history of this unique carved-top instrument.

BIG BAD FLATTOPS

BY WALTER CARTER

The first SJ-200, made for cowboy movie star Ray Whitley. Courtesy Gruhn Guitars

Ray Whitley wrote a note of thanks to Gibson's John Huis.

In 1931, the last place Gibson's Guy Hart would have expected a new idea in instrument design to come from was the small town of Nazareth in eastern Pennsylvania, home of C. F. Martin & Co.

From Gibson's point of view, Martin operated a full generation behind the times. The venerable, family-owned company had been in business for almost a century, specializing in small flattop "parlor" guitars, but Martin's last guitar innovation had been the X-pattern top bracing perfected by the company's founder by 1850. When guitarists began moving from gut strings to steel strings around the turn of the century, it took Martin 20 years to respond. Martin had recognized a growing mandolin market, introducing bowlback models in 1895, but did not make its first carved-top mandolin until 1929—more than a decade after the mandolin era and Orville Gibson himself had been laid to rest. Martin had given the banjo only a token nod in the '20s, making less than 100 instruments.

Furthermore, Martin was just as preoccupied as Gibson was with surviving the Depression. Gibson inaugurated a wooden toy line; Martin cut up pieces of rosewood to make jewelry, although the jewelry never made it to market. What did make it out of Nazareth in 1931 were two new guitars—with the biggest pieces of rosewood and mahogany Martin had ever made.

If Guy Hart even noticed Martin's 15 5/8-inch-wide "dreadnoughts" (they were named after the

largest battleship of the early 1900s), he had no cause for alarm. After all, big guitars were nothing new. Orville Gibson had made some 18-inchers. And big flattop guitars had been a proven failure in the market. If any company would know that, it ought to be Martin. Martin had made dreadnought flattops for the Oliver Ditson company in Boston as early as 1916. If dreadnoughts had been marketable, they would have had the Martin brand on them long before 1931.

Of course, what somebody at Martin saw, and what no one at Gibson apparently did, was that players were forsaking banjos for guitars and demanding louder instruments. The quickest route to a louder guitar was a bigger guitar. Martin's dreadnoughts got off to a slow start, but within two years, Hart's sales reps in the field no doubt began to ask for a Gibson that could run with the big dogs.

The large-bodied flattop market was a tougher challenge for Gibson than the archtop market had been. Gibson had invented the archtop guitar but had only been making flattops since 1925. By the 1930s, there were only four models available: the plain L-0 and L-1, and the fancier Nick Lucas (with ornate fingerboard inlays) and L-2 (with gold-sparkle binding). Gibson flattops had grown since the '20s—from 13 1/2 inches to 14 3/4 inches—but they were still smaller than even Martin's second-largest size, the 000. Unless, of course, you count an obscure Gibson guitar from 1929, the HG-24. It was a true oddball, with a double-walled body and four f-holes in addition to the standard round hole. The oddity didn't stop there: Though designated HG for Hawaiian Guitar, it was fitted with a 14-fret round neck and a slant-mounted saddle that would have made it impossible to play in tune Hawaiian-style. But the body was the perfect size and shape. It had the thick waist lines of the Martin dreadnought and was 16 inches wide—bigger than the Martin by 3/8 of an inch. (Coincidentally, that

To John

Thanks for

fine music. —

Roy Whitley

was the exact fraction of an inch by
which Epiphone always tried to top Gibson's
archtop guitars.)

Gibson brought out the new flattop in 1934. The
model name—Jumbo—was hardly as imaginative
or as imposing as Martin's battleship guitar, but it
made its point about being a big guitar. The Jumbo

only lasted two years before it was replaced by the more expensive Advanced Jumbo and the less expensive Jumbo 35.

Martin immediately one-upped Gibson—not with a bigger guitar but a bigger guitar *player*. A Chicago country radio singer named Gene Autry had special-ordered one of the new Martins in 1933 with the fanciest ornamentation available; now he was a famous cowboy movie star who was fast becoming identified with his big fancy Martin.

Gibson needed something more than a bigger guitar to top Gene Autry. The answer came walking in the door of 225 Parsons St. in the person of Ray Whitley, another of Hollywood's

Pioneering jazz/blues guitarist Lonnie Johnson (opposite) in Toronto in the early '60s, with his prewar Super Jumbo 100.

Bluesman Mance Lipscomb (opposite cameo) in Monterey, California, 1973, with his '60s J-200.

Blues legend Robert Johnson (above) was photographed by Hooks Bros. in Memphis ca. 1935 with a Gibson L-1. Courtesy Carrie Thompson, ©1989 Mimosa Records Productions, Inc.

Little Jimmy Dickens with a big Super Jumbo 100. Country Music Foundation

Emmylou Harris's custom "Rose J-200" graced the cover of her Blue Kentucky Girl album. ©1989 Beth Gwinn

Country songwriter Cindy Walker plays Gene Autry's custom SJ-200. Frank Driggs Collection

singing cowboys. Whitley wanted a big fancy guitar of his own, and Gibson built him a huge 17-inch body, with a circular lower bout (like the archtops) that made it look even larger. The neck of Whitley's guitar had L-5 features, including the flowerpot on the headstock and large pearl-block fingerboard inlays (engraved with Western scenes).

With a few changes—a new "crest" fingerboard inlay, a new pickguard, and the newly introduced "crest" headstock ornament—Whitley's guitar was put into production. The new model debuted in late 1937. In the spirit of Gibson's super-sized Super 400 archtop of 1934, this super-sized flattop with a $200 price tag was named the Super Jumbo 200.

Whitley showed off his new guitar to his fellow movie stars, and by the time the next Gibson catalog appeared, Gibson had scored a veritable coup in artist relations. Embellishing the picture of the production-version SJ-200 were photographs of Tex Ritter, Ray Whitley, and, yes, even Gene Autry, playing their very own custom-ordered SJ-200s.

The SJ-200 served notice that Gibson was playing for keeps in the flattop guitar game. A less-fancy super jumbo, the SJ-100, and a fancier dreadnought, the J-55, filled in the middle of the large-bodied flattop line, but they weren't especially popular. Gibson's southeastern sales representative, Tom Peacock, demanded that the company give him a dreadnought to compete with Martin's mahogany-body

D-18. Guy Hart took Peacock seriously—so seriously that in 1942, even as he was retooling the factory to begin making war products, he launched two new dreadnoughts: the J-45 and fancier Southerner Jumbo (SJ).

With the J-200 (the S was dropped after World War II) as the symbolic leader—especially in country music—and the J-45 as the workhorse, Gibson could rest secure in the flattop market for decades to come.

The Rolling Stones' Ron Wood shows off a J-200 with double pickguards. Chuck Pulin, Star File

The Johnson County Ramblers made their music on a pair of mid-'30s Gibson flattops, the L-00 (white pickguard) and Jumbo. Frank Driggs Collection

THE ADVANCED JUMBO

BY GARY BURNETTE

In March 1987 at the Dallas guitar show, Gibson CEO Henry Juszkiewicz stopped by my booth and asked what I thought of the new Gibson flattops. I was honest with him. I told him I thought they were pretty bad acoustically. I just reached behind me, got out an Advanced Jumbo, and handed it to him. I said, "If you build a guitar just like this, you'll get back into the acoustic guitar business."

It blew him away. He said, "You'll probably be hearing from me."

I first ran across one in an old Gibson catalog. I said, "Whoa, a Gibson with rosewood back and sides? This would be something to hold up to a Martin." Then a friend told me about a guitar that Wiley Morris had. Wiley and Zeke Morris were early guys; they gave Earl Scruggs his first picking job. Wiley let me in, showed me the guitar, and sure enough, that bugger was a buttkicker. It was a 1936 AJ.

So I started advertising to buy Advanced Jumbos in all the magazines. I bought every single one I could lay my hands on, regardless of price. If it was for sale, I got it. It amazed me when I went out and played at festivals. No one could overpower that Advanced Jumbo. Some of the Martin pickers were quite surprised that Gibson ever built a guitar that would project like that, and by playing this thing in the festivals for several years, word started getting out that these were killers. My guitar got nicknamed "The 'Bone Crusher," referring of course to the herringbone trim of a prewar Martin D-28.

The first Advanced Jumbo, 1935.

As a teenager in the late '30s, country legend-to-be Hank Williams strummed a J-35. Country Music Foundation

The Advanced Jumbo had blown me away the first time I ever touched one. As a bluegrass player, I saw nothing but Martins, but I was more of an outlaw type of guy. If everybody else drives a Chevy I want to drive a Ford, and I was always looking for something different, something that would be just me. The AJ turned out to be that guitar.

A Gibson guitar in the 1930s was every bit as good in tone and power as the guitars Martin was making. Martin and Gibson's construction were very similar. They both tucked the braces under the kerfing and had similar bracing patterns. They scalloped the braces very similarly and used small bridgeplates. Comparing a '37 AJ to a '37 D-28, the tonal qualities are very similar.

Gibson historian Julius Bellson told me many years ago that he loved the Advanced Jumbo. He said he thought the guitar should have been produced on through the years because he figured it was their best flattop. And it was. But he said Gibson would rather produce guitars in bigger numbers and sell them at a cheaper price than compete with high-end guitars. They were not into five, ten, or fifty of one kind; they wanted to sell hundreds. They figured they could probably take some of the lesser-grade guitars and build them quicker and make more money and capture a bigger market share. And they did. It worked; they sold a lot of J-35s. And the AJ was not selling that kind of numbers. So when they got into the war they quit making AJs altogether.

In the 1960s and '70s, when younger kids started getting into country and bluegrass, they were comparing Gibsons from the '60s and '70s with Martins from the same period. They weren't comparing these '30s and '40s instruments, when Gibson was making some great guitars. The

oldtimers, you couldn't convince them a Gibson was bad, because they had good guitars. The newcomers, you couldn't convince them that Gibson was good, because they were comparing the bad guitars from the '60s and '70s.

I did hear back from Henry when he decided Gibson should reissue the Advanced Jumbo. I loaned them my prototype 1935 AJ. Gibson had been going downhill for so long that master luthier Ren Ferguson knew he would have to build a better guitar than anything else that was being built, and he and John Walker came up with what I feel are some of the finest flattops ever built by Gibson. The Advanced Jumbos are Custom Shop guitars now, but the principles are being applied on production line models, too. They are proof that you can build a new guitar as good as Gibson did in the '30s.

At a 1993 guitar show, Gary Burnette illustrated the early history of Gibson dreadnoughts with, from left, a Jumbo, J-35, Advanced Jumbo, Southerner Jumbo, and J-45.

Bill Monroe might have felt like hitting the guitar player but not the guitar, a natural top J-35. Country Music Foundation

AN ELECTRIFYING DEVELOPMENT

BY WALTER CARTER AND A. R. DUCHOSSOIR

Gibson's first electric

Spanish guitar, the ES-150.

Gibson enlisted former

Rickenbacker player

Alvino Rey to help with

the first Gibson

electrics. Courtesy Lynn

A. Wheelwright

By 1942, every band—

including the one on the

Gibson letters—had to

have an electric guitar.

By the end of 1934, Guy Hart could have reasonably looked forward to a moment's rest from the fray, time to take a deep breath and relax while Gibson's new models beat back the competition. As general manager of Gibson, he had weathered the economic threat of the Depression, an archtop assault from Epiphone, and a dreadnought flattop attack from Martin. What else could possibly threaten Gibson?

The answer came from the West Coast in the form of a sustained, piercing sound, unlike anything the instrument business had heard before. It was the sound of an electric guitar—at least it was called a guitar by the obscure little company that made it. It had a small circular body with a long neck attached, and it was made of a solid piece of aluminum. It looked more like a frying pan or a battle axe than a guitar. This was a threat to Gibson?

Electric guitars were a folly. Hart knew that. He owed his position as general manager of Gibson in part to the folly of the electric guitar. Back in 1923, he had seen the oddball prototypes that Lloyd Loar and L. A. Williams wanted Gibson to make. In 1929, he had

seen the amplified guitar that Stromberg-Voisinet (soon to become Kay) brought to market—and brought right back home again. Moreover, he had heard the pitiful sound these instruments generated, whispering and crackling through the small amplifiers of the day. A sharp strum across the strings turned that sound into an irritating mush. Any of Gibson's powerful new acoustic models of 1934—the Super 400 and the advanced-body archtops—could blow these "amplified" guitars off a stage.

Furthermore, Hart had to look no farther than West Kalamazoo Ave., a dozen blocks from the Parsons St. factory, to find solid proof that no market existed for electric guitars. Loar and Williams had opened up their electric guitar business right under his nose in 1933. For all their inventive genius in engineering and marketing, their guitars flopped, and by the end of 1933 they were forsaking guitars for electric keyboard instruments. If those two geniuses couldn't make a viable electric guitar, who could?

Ro-Pat-In could. Ro-Pat-In (soon to be the Electro String Instrument Company) was a

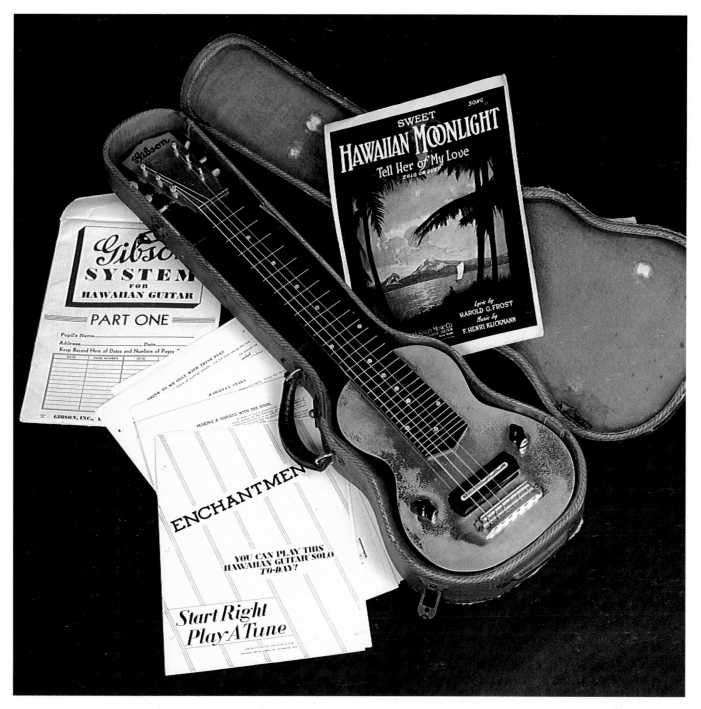

Los Angeles company cofounded by George Beauchamp, a former vaudeville Hawaiian guitarist who had been one of the creative forces behind National's metalbody resonator guitars of the late '20s. By 1932, Beauchamp had been pushed out of National and joined forces with the tool and die maker who did National's metalwork: Adolph Rickenbacker. Their "Frying Pan" got off to a slow start—only a dozen or so sold in 1932—but with its powerful modern magnetic pickup, it made a lot of noise and soon caught on with Hawaiian players.

By 1935, Hart could ignore the electric guitar no longer. Dismissing all previous in-house experiments, he sought outside expertise to devise a lap steel and amp combo as quickly as possible. The initial groundwork was carried out in cooperation with Lyon & Healy, which would design and build the first Gibson amps. A small lab was set up in a Lyon & Healy warehouse in Chicago, and an engineer named John Kutalek was charged with developing a lap steel guitar fitted with an electromagnetic pickup. To help Kutalek, Hart wisely secured the collaboration of musician

Gibson's first electric instrument, 1935. The metal body was quickly replaced by a wood body.

Before the ES-150 guitar, Gibson sold pickup units like the one on this L-7 (above). The electric line included the EM-150 mandolin and the EH-150 guitar.

Electrics filtered down to the budget-priced Kalamazoo brand by 1938.

Alvino Rey, who recalls how he got in touch with Gibson: "I was in Chicago playing in an orchestra, the Horace Heidt Orchestra, and using an Electro Rickenbacker. We were on the networks every night, and so we became quite popular on the air. That's how they knew about me, and they approached me."

Despite the valuable insights offered by Rey, Kutalek failed to deliver, possibly because he was mesmerized by the patent-applied-for design of the Rickenbacker. Within less than a year, the lab at Lyon & Healy was shut down and the experiments repatriated to Kalamazoo. At this stage, Hart asked one of his newer employees, Walter Fuller, an amateur radio operator, whether he could take on the project. The young Fuller accepted the challenge and proceeded to design Gibson's earliest electromagnetic pickup, commonly known today as the "bar" pickup.

NEVER BEFORE
A KALAMAZOO ELECTRIC HAWAIIAN GUITAR
Price $75.00

MODEL KEH

The Gibson Electric Hawaiian Guitar, the first production electric from Kalamazoo, debuted in mid 1935. Like the Rickenbacker, it was built with a cast aluminum body, but all of Rickenbacker's influence was dispelled in early 1936 when a wood body was substituted for aluminum. The guitar and amplifier sold as a set for a list price of $150, and following the example of the $400 Super 400, the new Electric Hawaiian set was named E-150 (soon to be EH-150).

While Electro/Rickenbacker concentrated on Hawaiian guitars, their Los Angeles rival, National, hit the market with a good-looking electric Spanish-

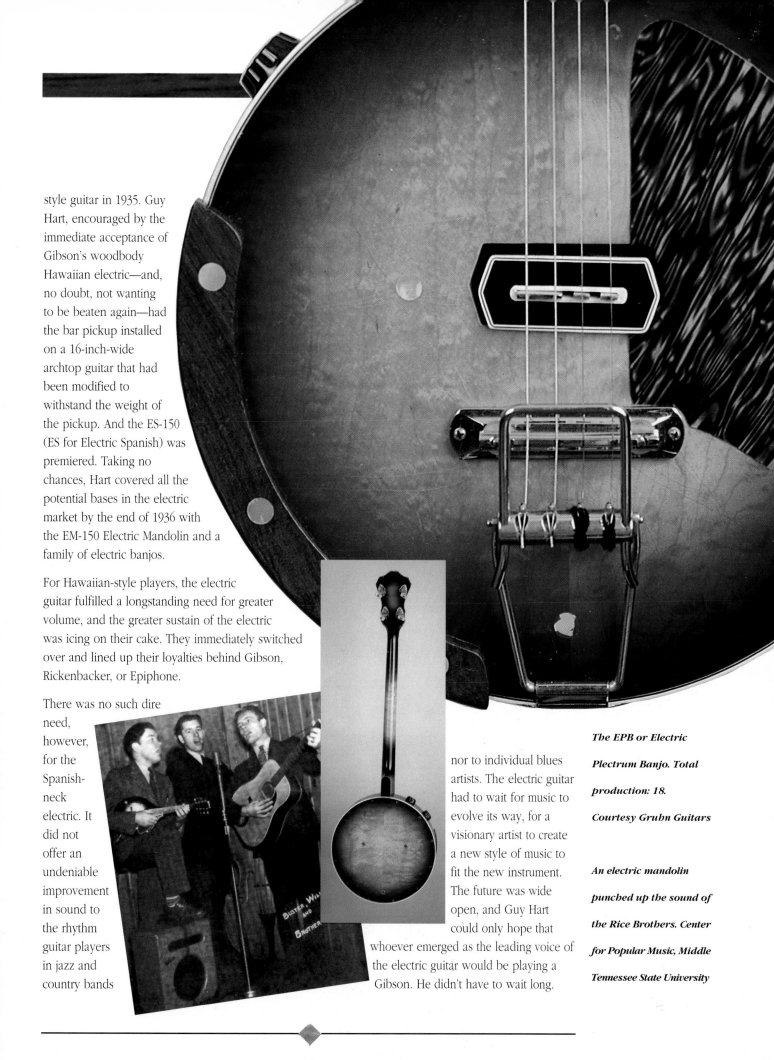

style guitar in 1935. Guy Hart, encouraged by the immediate acceptance of Gibson's woodbody Hawaiian electric—and, no doubt, not wanting to be beaten again—had the bar pickup installed on a 16-inch-wide archtop guitar that had been modified to withstand the weight of the pickup. And the ES-150 (ES for Electric Spanish) was premiered. Taking no chances, Hart covered all the potential bases in the electric market by the end of 1936 with the EM-150 Electric Mandolin and a family of electric banjos.

For Hawaiian-style players, the electric guitar fulfilled a longstanding need for greater volume, and the greater sustain of the electric was icing on their cake. They immediately switched over and lined up their loyalties behind Gibson, Rickenbacker, or Epiphone.

There was no such dire need, however, for the Spanish-neck electric. It did not offer an undeniable improvement in sound to the rhythm guitar players in jazz and country bands nor to individual blues artists. The electric guitar had to wait for music to evolve its way, for a visionary artist to create a new style of music to fit the new instrument. The future was wide open, and Guy Hart could only hope that whoever emerged as the leading voice of the electric guitar would be playing a Gibson. He didn't have to wait long.

The EPB or Electric Plectrum Banjo. Total production: 18. Courtesy Gruhn Guitars

An electric mandolin punched up the sound of the Rice Brothers. Center for Popular Music, Middle Tennessee State University

CHARLIE CHRISTIAN AND THE ELECTRIC GIBSON

BY A. R. DUCHOSSOIR

At a gig in Denver in 1939, Charlie Christian plays Gibson's new top-of-the-line electric, a natural-finish ES-250. Bandmates include Dick Wilson on tenor sax, right, and Sam Hughs on alto. Frank Driggs Collection

The electric line expanded downward in late 1937 with the ES-100. Courtesy Gruhn Guitars

Gibson's ES-150 electric guitar was immediately successful, with a total of 504 units shipped in 1937, its first full year of production. Accordingly, general manager Guy Hart implemented Gibson's usual stepped-up sales approach. The smaller-bodied ES-100 was hatched at the end of 1937, and the fancier 17-inch-wide ES-250 appeared in 1938.

The increase in the number of cataloged electric guitars, however, did not bring in a commensurate increase in sales. It looked for a time as though electrics might not be the next big thing after all, despite the successful debut of the ES-150. The introduction of rival electrics by other companies was probably a contributing factor. The sound of the early Gibson instruments may also be

questioned. Following the input from the sales force, Walt Fuller designed new pickups with adjustable polepieces, which replaced the original bar pickup in 1940.

In retrospect, however, the main problem with the electric guitar was perhaps the guitarists themselves. Some held the electric instrument in awe, partly because it called for changes in their playing. Others were just mentally constrained by the "comping" rhythm role assigned hitherto to the guitar, particularly in orchestras. Only a handful realized then that the electric guitar was not just an

acoustic guitar made louder by amplification. It was a different instrument. Eddie Durham, Les Paul, Floyd Smith, George Barnes, Alvino Rey, and Bus Etri are among the early exponents of the amplified guitar. But the central figure—the one who put it on the map and enacted a resounding musical watershed—was Charlie Christian.

Just as Gibson was not the first manufacturer to market an electric guitar, the young black guitarist from Oklahoma City was not the first to use an electric guitar. But he quickly grasped the essential fact about it, that it was capable of producing single-line solos like a saxophone or a trumpet, at the same volume and with the same fluidity. His style was introduced fully developed on his debut with the Benny Goodman quintet (which immediately became a sextet) in Los Angeles in August 1939.

In a fervent manifesto published by *Down Beat* magazine in December 1939, Christian praised the electric muse by declaring "electrical amplification has given guitarists a new lease on life." He advised fellow guitarists "to save a few dimes to amplify your instrument." His recordings over the next two years, particularly his 1941 masterpiece "Solo Flight," charted new directions and shaped the future of the guitar, musically and commerically. And it was playing a Gibson ES-150 (and subsequently an ES-250) that Charlie Christian established the electric guitar as a recognized solo voice.

Gibson brought out its best new instruments and the best musicians for a demonstration at the New York Band Instrument Co. in 1939: Charlie Christian (top) with Slam Stewart, bass; Teddy Bunn with Stewart. Photos by Michael A. Gould, ©1993 Mimosa Records Productions, Inc.

On March 2, 1942, just two days short of the first anniversary of the recording of "Solo Flight," Charlie Christian died of tuberculosis. He was only 26, but his influence and legacy were critically important. He was pivotal in gaining a wider acceptance for the electric guitar among other musicians and the listening public as well. His inspired work became the textbook of a whole new generation of guitarists, including such Gibson-connected names as Barney Kessel, Herb Ellis, Tal Farlow, Billy Byrd, and Hank Garland. As one of the founders of the bop movement, he also contributed to the emergence of new directions in jazz music. Yet no picture of Charlie can be found in any of the abundantly illustrated Gibson brochures of the prewar era. Despite the awards he won between 1939 and 1941, it never occurred— consciously or unconsciously—to the patricians of the Gibson boardroom to sign him up as a formal endorser.

Be that as it may, Charlie Christian turned out to be a significant, albeit unpredicted, marketing asset for Gibson. He helped raise the profile of the company above its competition at a time when the electric medium was still in its infancy. Gibson's failure to recognize the promotional opportunity—or was it racial prejudice?—was more than adequately made up for by the creative electric flurry spurred by Christian on the threshold of the '40s.

The outbreak of war slowed down the inescapable rise of the electric guitar, but the seeds of a new age had been sown. Other guitarists, like Barney

Kessel, Oscar Moore, and Tony Mottola, to name a few, came to the forefront and confirmed Gibson's leadership in the field of electrics. As for Charlie Christian, time has seen to it that his name would forever remain linked to the ES-150 and the original bar pickup. And more than 50 years later, despite the pickup's technical shortcomings, some jazz players continue to favor the old "Charlie Christian" above all others.

*More from Gibson's
1939 demonstration: Les
Paul (top, with glasses);
Ken Harvey on the EPB
(electric plectrum
banjo) accompanied by
Joe Petroni of the Les
Brown Orchestra.*

*A new pickup with
adjustable polepieces
debuted on the ES-300 in
1940. Courtesy Gruhn
Guitars*

*The "Charlie Christian"
pickup.*

SWINGING OFF TO WAR

BY MICHAEL McCALL

In the late 1930s, as the U.S. economy finally began to improve, more people found work and the Depression started to dissolve. The music industry displayed the signs of better times: In 1938, record sales increased and, for the first time in nearly a decade, several singles topped the 300,000 mark in sales. Those records included Ella Fitzgerald's "A-Tisket, A-Tasket," Will Glahe's "Beer Barrel Polka," and Artie Shaw's "Begin the Beguine."

Two of those top-sellers indicated some of the major trends emerging within the music industry: The big bands now dominated the national music scene and were beginning to develop more distinctive styles as shaped by leaders like Shaw, and vocalists like Fitzgerald were taking more prominent roles within big bands, sometimes drawing as much public notice as the bandleaders themselves.

Along with the sustaining popularity of radio, the jukebox became an overwhelmingly popular addition to American culture in the late 1930s. By the end of the decade, 225,000 Wurlitzers and Rock-Olas bubbled, buzzed, and emitted the latest hit platters, and the colorful coin-operated record players blinked at the heart of the record business' recovery.

Along with big-band swing came the jitterbug, as people reacted to the lively sound of hits by Benny Goodman, Glenn Miller, Woody Herman, and the Dorseys. Goodman was swing's elegant conscience, and his historic concerts at Carnegie Hall in 1938 proved that jazz could be taken seriously as high culture as well as a deep reservoir for popular sounds.

Swing's popularity crested in 1940, when Glenn Miller's "In the Mood" topped the record charts for 12 consecutive weeks. A year later, his "Chattanooga Choo Choo" became the first single certified as a "gold record" by the Record Industry Association of America for selling more than a million copies.

However, the optimistic attitude brought on by better economic conditions was dampened by alarming news coming from overseas. The seeds for a war of a magnitude never previously seen were being planted in the late 1930s. The Nazi Party of Germany, led by Adolf Hitler, occupied Rhineland. Italy appropriated Ethiopia. The Spanish Civil War started. China and Japan squared off in violent clashes. Japan sunk a U.S. gunboat shortly after signing a pact with Germany and Italy. When Japan launched a surprise attack on an American military base in Hawaii's Pearl Harbor, President Franklin Delano Roosevelt joined with the Allied Powers and went to war against Japan, Germany, and Italy.

World War II inspired even more popular songs than America's involvement in the great war of a quarter-century earlier. Songwriters and entertainers mobilized quickly. Two days after Pearl Harbor, Eddie Cantor put a new song, "We Did It Before,"

World War II left a shortage of single men, but it didn't stop people from dancing.

167

into *Banjo Eyes,* a successful musical already running on Broadway. The song, written the day of the bombing, drew a stunning ovation on its first night.

Other popular war songs included "Remember Pearl Harbor" (a hit by its co-writer, bandleader Sammy Kay), "Goodby, Mama (I'm Off to Yokohama)," "There's a Star-Spangled Banner Waving Somewhere," and "Praise the Lord and Pass the Ammunition," the latter so popular that the U.S. Office of War Information asked radio stations to limit the song's airing to no more than once every four hours.

Irving Berlin, meanwhile, composed and produced an all-soldier musical, *This Is the Army.* It featured a cast of 300 soldiers, most of them amateurs. The highly successful show included the national hit, "Oh, How I Hate to Get Up in the Morning."

Novelty songs provided an amusing diversion from wartime concerns and pressures. Comic bandleader Spike Jones was introduced to America with "Der Fuehrer's Face," which first appeared in an animated movie, *Donald Duck in Nutzy Land.* "They're Either Too Young or Too Old," which humorously dealt with the lack of eligible bachelors, was introduced by Bette Davis in a rare singing role in the movie *Thank Your Lucky Stars.* Other witty hits included "Gertie from Bizerte," "The Flat Foot Floogee," "Three Little Fishes," "Hut-Hut Song," and the nonsensical "Mairzy Doats," which was a hit by five different artists in 1944.

Ballads with a strain of loneliness also proved popular for obvious reasons. They included "I'll Be Seeing You," "You'll Never Know," "Sentimental Journey," "Don't Sit Under the Apple Tree," "When the Lights Go On Again," and "I'll Walk Alone."

But the war's most popular song, written by Berlin, was not directly connected to the war effort. "White Christmas," as sung by Bing Crosby in the 1942 movie *Holiday Inn,* became the longest-running hit in the history of the radio program *Your Hit Parade* and one of the most successful songs of all time. By the mid '70s, it had sold more than 108 million copies in North America and another 25 million overseas, where it was translated into 30 languages. According to *Variety,* it is the most valuable music copyright in the world.

The Broadway musical continued to thrive, with the biggest hit being 1943's *Oklahoma!,* the first collaboration between Richard Rodgers and Oscar Hammerstein II. After writing the score for a movie musical, *State Fair,* the two returned to Broadway with another enduring smash, *Carousel.*

Record industry politics and legal wranglings disrupted the booming business. Breakdowns in contract talks between the American Society of Composers, Authors and Publishers (ASCAP) and radio broadcasters in 1940 resulted in a nine-month blackout of ASCAP-licensed songs and the founding of a rival licensing agency, Broadcast Music Inc. Two years later, the American Federation of Musicians initiated a ban on recordings by bands because of a dispute concerning musicians' royalties.

Meanwhile, folk singers like Leadbelly, Woody Guthrie, Burl Ives, and Josh White brought a new style of socially and politically conscious lyrics to American music. And rhythm & blues began to surface into the mainstream, thanks to popular acts like Louis Jordan.

Country music also enjoyed widening popularity, thanks to live radio barn dances and the jukebox, which made stars of Roy Acuff, Ernest Tubb, Jimmie Davis, Bill Monroe, Bob Wills, and Ted Daffan. During the battle of Okinawa, soldiers

reported that the Japanese troops had learned to yell "To hell with Roosevelt! To hell with Babe Ruth! To hell with Roy Acuff!" in hopes of riling the American troops by attacking their heroes.

The musicians' recording ban, as well as the war, had a deadening effect on big bands. By the end of the war, tastes focused more on individual singers like Frank Sinatra, who became the first American music star to create riots among swooning fans at his concerts. Another musical force also was emerging, as jazz instrumentalists like Dizzy Gillespie, Charlie Parker, and Thelonius Monk unveiled an exciting, more improvisation-based musical style built around smaller combos. In addition, blues bands in Chicago, Memphis, St. Louis, and Houston enjoyed growing appeal.

The melting pot finally reached radio and popular music in the late 1940s. It was a time of great creativity and great change, and music began to reflect the increasing pace of the American lifestyle.

WORLD WAR II AND CMI

BY TOM MULHERN

By mid 1942, American manufacturers as well as individuals had dropped what they were doing to help with the war effort. But the prewar and postwar eras were delineated at Gibson by more than a hiatus of guitar manufacturing. Gibson entered the war owned by a group of stockholders, led for over 40 years by one of the company's founders, a contemporary of Orville Gibson. Gibson emerged owned by CMI, the Chicago Musical Instrument Company, a modern, diversified business headed by M. H. Berlin, a man who hadn't even been born when Orville Gibson opened shop.

The war was a test of everyone's mettle, changing every business as no previous war had, as no depression had. Long-idled factories had to be rebuilt or refitted, and workers had to be hired and trained to build the multitude of new equipment that the war effort demanded. World War I—just more than two decades earlier—was mostly a ground war with few tanks, few planes, and mostly footsoldiers supplied by horsedrawn wagons; communication had been largely by telegraph or courier. World War II was totally different, a conflict in the modern age of radio, plastics, and huge numbers of sophisticated aircraft, tanks, and rockets. In order to defeat the Axis forces—who had used the previous several years to gear up their warmaking technologies—a massive effort on the part of American industry was coordinated by the government.

Gibson, like most other companies, had to put almost all of its peacetime activities aside and work in concert with other companies—many of which were peacetime competitors. The workforce made electrical and mechanical radar assemblies for Western Electric, Crosley, RCA, Zenith, and others, plus small screw-machine products, glider skids for airplanes, and precision rods for use in submachine guns.

Metal was carefully regulated—*over*-regulated in some cases—by the War Department. In a case of one hand not knowing what the other was doing, one office of the War Department would order products from Gibson, and another office would then challenge Gibson's need for the metal required to make those products. Only about 10 percent of Gibson's activities were related to musical instrument manufacture, and the shortages of

During World War II the ranks of female workers increased dramatically at 225 Parsons St.

materials forced heavy rethinking of even the most fundamental design features. Guitars were made without truss rods in order to meet metal restrictions, tailpieces on archtop models had a wooden crosspiece to save an ounce of metal, and production of metal-heavy electric guitars and amplifiers was out of the question.

As if general manager Guy Hart didn't have enough problems, the temporary switch to metalworking opened the gate for the United Steelworkers of America to unionize Gibson's workforce, which under normal circumstances was made up primarily of woodworkers.

In the spring of 1944, M. H. Berlin, the founder of the Chicago Musical Instrument Co., was traveling to New York and casually mentioned to a business broker that he was interested in owning Gibson. John W. Adams, the last of Gibson's five founding partners, was 85 years old and ready to sell. In only two months, CMI acquired Gibson. On May 18, 1944, Adams resigned, Guy Hart was elevated to president, and Berlin became treasurer. Gibson, Inc. was now

Gibson's Guy Hart accepts a banner for the first of three E Awards given to Gibson for contributions to the war effort.

Gibson celebrated the first Army-Navy E Awards in March 1944 by throwing a dance.

CMI founder M. H. Berlin.

concerned only with developing and making instruments; marketing would be handled by CMI.

Gibson might not have been able to make the transition from wartime to peacetime operations had it not been for M. H. Berlin, a man who was almost universally known and respected throughout the music industry. And even if it had successfully made the changeover, Gibson certainly wouldn't have grown in the way it did without Berlin's vision and leadership.

Maurice Henry Berlin (known almost universally as "M. H.") was born April 15, 1895, in Bessarabia, an area of Moldavia, east of Romania on the Black Sea. The youngest of nine children, he emigrated with his family to the United States in 1900. Raised in Chicago by an older sister after his parents died, he quit school following eighth grade and became an errand boy for Wurlitzer's music store on Wabash Avenue, in the heart of Chicago's music industry. He worked his way up to salesman, becoming one of the store's best. After a stint in the Navy band during World War I, Berlin briefly

worked in New York for a jewelry wholesaler and then took a job in September 1920 as sales manager for Martin Band Instruments in Elkhart, Indiana (not related to Martin guitars).

Both M. H. and his wife, Elsa, were used to big-city life and were unhappy with tiny Elkhart (then with only about 25,000 inhabitants), so he persuaded his boss, Orville P. Bassett, to help him launch a sales organization for the company. He opened the Martin Band Instrument Co. on Wabash Ave. in Chicago in 1919 and six months later renamed it Chicago Musical Instrument Co. It became a full-line wholesaler for musical equipment, and although extremely small (M. H. and one other employee), it grew quickly.

M. H. Berlin was smart enough to know that a  company could only grow so much as a distributor or wholesaler, so he sought opportunities to manufacture instruments. His first big success came from a plastic recorder called the Tonette. Introduced at the height of the Depression in the mid 1930s, the simple wind instrument was a hit, and by 1941, sales surpassed $1 million a year. (Among the first consumer goods made of plastic, a Tonette is part of a permanent exhibition at the Smithsonian Institution in Washington, D.C.)

In addition to distributing Martin Band Instruments, CMI handled Scandalli and Dallape accordions (big sellers), Penzel Mueller clarinets, Olds trombones, and Symmetricut reeds. In August 1941, CMI became the exclusive U.S. distributor for National guitars. According to Jim Cruickshank, CMI's advertising manager from 1954 to 1968, "CMI was *the* music company of the era. At trade show time, all the salesmen would come and line up to interview with M. H. Berlin to try getting a job with the company. CMI was that sought-after and respected by the industry. There was CMI and there was everybody else.

"One of the great things about M. H. Berlin was that he was a believer that you should compete with yourself. CMI had Olds band instruments and Reynolds band instruments. Some dealers would have a deal worked out with a school district supplying, say, Olds band instruments, but if the demand was too great and they couldn't supply all that were needed, the dealer would take on another line to fill the need. M. H. felt that they shouldn't take on an outside competitor's line, like Conn or Selmer; they'd take on one of our other lines. It was friendly competition and enjoyable."

In a lengthy article following M. H. Berlin's death on August 23, 1984, *The Music Trades* referred to Berlin as "a man whose rare abilities made a lasting impact on the American music industry and a wide range of executives and musicians throughout the world." Indeed, after the war ended, Berlin would lead CMI to the preeminent role as the largest distributor of musical instruments.

Johnny New, left, and Curly Kinsey, better known as original members of the Oak Ridge Quartet, with a wartime Gibson J-45. Center for Popular Music, Middle Tennessee State University

Bluegrass singer Mac Wiseman with one of the new wartime models, the Southerner Jumbo. Country Music Foundation

KEYNOTE RECORDINGS

K-646 A
Recorded in Chicago,
Sept. 23, 1946

QUIET - 2 GIBSONS AT WORK
(Geo. Barnes)

GEORGE BARNES and his

1948–1966

THE TED McCARTY ERA

AN ENTERTAINMENT EXPLOSION

BY MICHAEL McCALL

World War II ended on August 14, 1945, with the Japanese surrender five days after the second atomic bomb destroyed Nagasaki. Nonetheless, the world continued to change at a dizzying pace.

British prime minister Winston Churchill aired the first major warnings of Soviet communist expansion in his famous "Iron Curtain" speech. Despite the formation of the United Nations and the Yalta Conference, the Soviet Union rejected a U.S. proposal for controlling the proliferation of atomic energy and weapons.

President Harry S. Truman proposed the Truman Doctrine as a means for the free world to contain communist expansion. In a similar plan for foreign relations, the U.S. government put forth the Marshall Plan, which provided economic and social aid to war-torn countries.

The rest of the world also underwent historic shifts of power. The British Empire further dissipated: India and Pakistan gained their independence in 1947, and a year later, Burma and Ceylon were freed from British sovereignty. The nation of Israel was proclaimed, as was the independent Republic of Korea. Soviet-backed communists seized control of Czechoslovakia, and Mao Zedong formally set up the Communist Peoples Republic of China.

Peace seemed shaky at best as Truman ordered development of the H-bomb, and public concern about the threat of communist world expansion created a situation bordering on panic. Several Congressmen, led by Joseph McCarthy, began a campaign to expose American communists as "the enemy within," and Julius and Ethel Rosenberg were sentenced to death for allegedly passing atomic secrets to the Soviets.

In 1949, war returned. North Korea invaded South Korea, and the United Nations called for a cease fire and asked leading U.N. nations to assist in bringing order to the divided country. On the same day of the U.N. request, Truman ordered U.S. troops to Korea.

In the music industry, major changes were also at hand. The fastest metamorphosis took place in the profit column: twice as many records sold in 1946 as in the previous years. Sales continued to soar high into the next decade. Through all of the 1930s, only 26 records were million-sellers. From 1945 to 1950, an unprecedented 82 records reached that impressive plateau. As an indication of the industry growth, RCA became the first company to issue its one billionth recording—a commemorative version of John Philip Sousa's "Stars and Stripes Forever."

The return of the soldiers, the reuniting of families, and the stabilization of the postwar economy all played a role in the growing popularity of recorded music. But another factor was the increase in audio quality. With the advent of "high fidelity" recordings and players, music simply sounded better.

French jazz legend Django Reinhardt tried an electrified L-5 in 1949. Max Jones Files

Country meets pop, 1947 style, with Eddy Arnold and Al Jolson. Arnold picks a J-200. Frank Driggs Collection

Country star Hank Williams, early '50s, with a Southerner Jumbo, backed by Chet Atkins. (Chet has traded in his old L-10 for a D'Angelico with an added pickup.) Country Music Foundation

Columbia Records introduced the 33 1/3-rpm recording on 10- and 12-inch disks. Now whole musicals and symphonies fit on one record, instead of a cumbersome "album" (in the true sense of the word) of 78s, and popular recording acts could release collections featuring eight or ten songs. Shortly afterward, Victor initiated the 45-rpm single, which also increased song quality and fit a song onto a smaller vinyl platter.

The record industry expanded in other ways. Until the 1940s, Columbia, Victor, and Decca dominated the music industry. By the mid '40s, Capitol, Mercury, and MGM had emerged as worthy competitors.

Singers were now the stars, and the few big bands that remained struggled. By the early 1950s, most big bandleaders threw in the baton and organized small combos, but a few continued to advance artistically through the postwar years, most notably Count Basie, Duke Ellington, Woody Herman, and Stan Kenton, all of whom incorporated some bebop musical progressions into their arrangements.

But the swing era was over, replaced primarily by singers who earned their stripes fronting big bands. Sinatra, Crosby, and Ella Fitzgerald continued to lead the charge, but plenty of others joined the pack, including Perry Como, Dinah Shore, Peggy Lee, Tony Bennett, Nat King Cole, Rosemary Clooney, Doris Day, Vic Damone, Frankie Laine, Sarah Vaughan, Billie Holiday, and Vaughn Monroe.

The demise of the big bands was greeted by great artistic strides in small-combo jazz. The hard-charging, freewheeling sound of bebop stormed forward in a flurry of unpredictable and exhilarating notes, led by Dizzy Gillespie, Charlie Parker, Thelonius Monk, and Bud Powell. By the end of the '40s, a few developing jazz masters

responded with a more relaxed, more pensive, prettier sound; cool jazz was born from the souls of Miles Davis, Lester Young, Lennie Tristano, and Lee Konitz.

Country music continued to attract a larger audience, helped greatly by the emergence of Hank Williams, who remains one of American music's most enduring figures. Country also started to diversify: singers as different as Williams, Eddy Arnold, Tennessee Ernie Ford, Roy Rogers, Ernest Tubb, Cowboy Copas, and Red Foley topped the hillbilly charts.

As the war ended, radio served as the nation's nerve center, and it probably seemed as

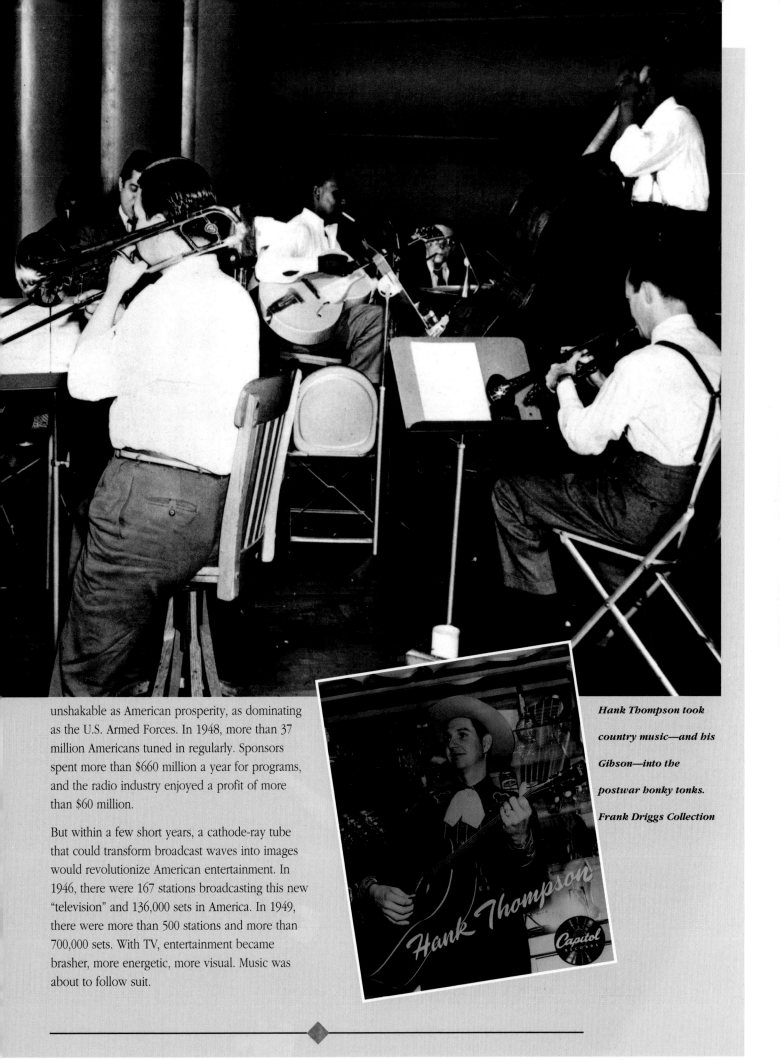

unshakable as American prosperity, as dominating as the U.S. Armed Forces. In 1948, more than 37 million Americans tuned in regularly. Sponsors spent more than $660 million a year for programs, and the radio industry enjoyed a profit of more than $60 million.

But within a few short years, a cathode-ray tube that could transform broadcast waves into images would revolutionize American entertainment. In 1946, there were 167 stations broadcasting this new "television" and 136,000 sets in America. In 1949, there were more than 500 stations and more than 700,000 sets. With TV, entertainment became brasher, more energetic, more visual. Music was about to follow suit.

Hank Thompson took country music—and his Gibson—into the postwar honky tonks.
Frank Driggs Collection

ELECTRICS, YES!
HAWAIIANS, NO!

B Y   W A L T E R   C A R T E R

By the early '50s, Hawaiian guitars were out, but electric guitars were definitely in.

As World War II came to an end and guitar makers switched from war work back to guitars, they might have taken a look back at World War I for guidance. They would have seen a relatively new instrument, the tenor banjo, nudging the mandolin aside after World War I, and they could have drawn a parallel to the electric Hawaiian guitar. Electrics were new, having been introduced just before the war, and the majority were Hawaiian. It seemed historically safe to assume that the Hawaiian electric market would be booming as soon as manufacturers could get the guitars made.

Gibson's first postwar catalog for Hawaiian and Spanish (in that order) models featured a fancy new lap steel on the cover.

Gibson's cover girl for the 1949 catalog was the new, ultramodern Ultratone Hawaiian guitar.

The lead guitars in Epiphone's catalog were also Hawaiians.

Gretsch, a major competitor in the prewar acoustic market, apparently believed the electric market was limited to Hawaiian instruments; Gretsch's 1949 catalog featured highly ornamented 17- and 18-inch acoustic archtops, and only one plain electric, plus a couple of Hawaiians made by Valco.

Valco, the parent company of National and Supro had envisioned the electric future earlier than any major company (the Supro brand was introduced in 1935 strictly for budget electrics). After World War II, National essentially abandoned acoustic instruments, dropping its Dobro-brand resonator guitars entirely and buying the bodies of its few acoustic models from Kay or Gibson. National put "Hawaiian" above "Spanish" on the cover of its first postwar catalog, and the first guitar pictured was a doubleneck lap steel.

Rickenbacker, which had made the first modern electric in 1932, continued with faith unshaken in

180

Hawaiians. From the company's founding up until its sale in 1953, Rickenbacker never offered more than one Spanish-neck guitar at any particular time, and Rickenbacker bought the bodies of those models from other makers.

These companies were half right. Electric guitars would be the guitars of the future. But not the Hawaiian guitars. Whether it was a case of old age—Hawaiian music had been the rage for over 30 years—or the destruction of Hawaii's exotic, romantic image by the bombing of Pearl Harbor and the war in the Pacific, Hawaiian guitars had no future after World War II.

That lesson was there in World War I, too, but one had to look a bit beyond the banjo-mandolin scenario to find it. In the aftermath of the war had come louder, more raucous music, and the tenor banjo was an effect more than a cause. The same phenomenon would occur after World War II. Urban Chicago bluesmen with raw electric bands replaced the solo acoustic Delta blues players. In

country, a rough-edged, Western-influenced honky tonk style replaced the rural string bands. The transition would be complete and total when rock & roll muscled its way into the pop mainstream.

The guitar, which had only recently become the dominant fretted instrument, would soon become the dominant instrument, period, in popular culture. The powers at Gibson, National, Gretsch, Epiphone, and Rickenbacker failed to see the quantum changes in store for them, but they were not alone. The man whose solidbody electric Spanish guitar would revolutionize the guitar world had no better vision of the future. Out in the Los Angeles suburb of Fullerton, Leo Fender had started making electric guitars—electric Hawaiian guitars exclusively.

Fortunately for Gibson, fresh leadership had just arrived, and Gibson would lead rather than follow the pack as the electric guitar era began to take shape.

Everyone thought electric Hawaiian guitars would be the wave of the '50s. Even Fender's 1950 catalog, which introduced a revolutionary solidbody Spanish model, featured Hawaiians on the cover.

Bluesmen were quick to adopt the electric guitar. In the early '50s, B. B. King, flanked by horn players Evelyn Young and Bill Harvey, played the top-line triple-pickup model, the ES-5.

After World War II, Merle Travis graduated from the Drifting Pioneers and an L-10 guitar to solo star status and a personalized Super 400 electric. Country Music Foundation

Ernest C. Withers, ©1990 Mimosa Records Productions, Inc.

At a fair in Berlin, Germany, in 1958, Ted McCarty hosts a "tour" of Gibson. Kalamazoo was chosen to represent a cross-section of American life.

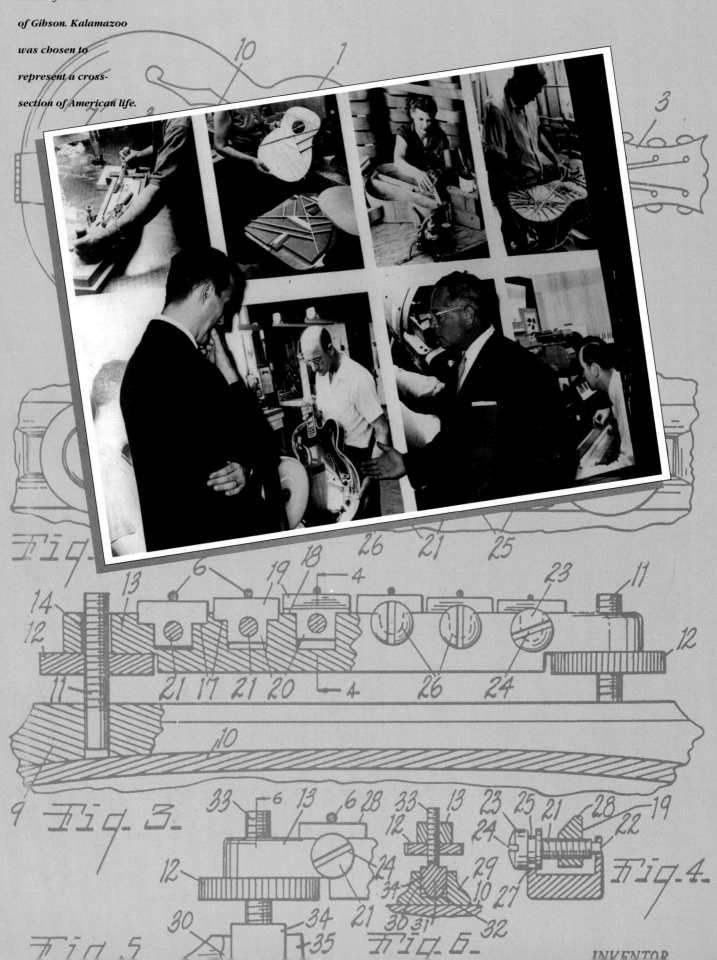

TED McCARTY

BY WALTER CARTER

In 1948, Ted McCarty was offered a job running Gibson. This job would link his name forever with such monumental instruments and inventions as the Les Paul, the Flying V, the ES-335, the Firebird, the tune-o-matic bridge, the pickguard-mounted "McCarty" pickup, the "McCarty" single-piece bridge/tailpiece, the humbucking pickup, an all-new Epiphone line, the Johnny Smith, Barney Kessel, and a half-dozen other artist models. This job would make him a legendary figure in guitar history as president of Gibson during the most exciting, innovative, and successful era since the company's founding.

Ted McCarty's response to the job offer: "Not interested."

McCarty had had his fill of the instrument business and was determined to get out. He had been with Wurlitzer for 12 years, having been an accountant, head of the real estate and insurance division, and merchandise manager for the entire chain of retail stores. He had a job lined up with the Brach candy company, had interviewed with every Brach vice president, and was waiting for Mr. Brach to return from a vacation in Bermuda to approve his hiring. If Mr. Brach had not taken such a long vacation in early 1948, no one in the guitar business would have ever heard of Ted McCarty.

Through McCarty's Wurlitzer years, he had moved his family to eight different cities; his son, 11, and daughter, 8, had been in five different school systems. They had finally settled down in the north-Chicago suburb of Winnetka in a beautiful center-hall colonial home, within walking distance of the schools and the beach at Lake Michigan. He would be joining Brach in the secure position of assistant to the treasurer, who was near retirement. If anyone had suggested that within three months he would be living in a hotel in Kalamazoo, Michigan, he would have laughed. Wild horses couldn't drag him to Kalamazoo.

The ES-175, the workhorse guitar of the jazz world. Billy Mitchell, courtesy Gruhn Guitars

In the mid '50s, B. B. King's band—and his Gibson Byrdland—await his arrival.

The "McCarty" fingerrest pickup offered an easy conversion from acoustic to electric. Courtesy Gruhn Guitars

Gibson's thinbody guitars were inaugurated with the Byrdland, played here by its co-designer, Nashville session star Hank Garland.

Bill Gretsch, head of the Gretsch guitar company, and M. H. Berlin of CMI proved to be stronger than wild horses. While waiting for Brach to return, McCarty came into Chicago to have lunch with Gretsch. Gretsch offered his unsolicited and unwanted help, McCarty recalls. "He picks up the phone and calls Berlin and says, 'Hey, a friend of yours is sitting right here by my desk. He wants to come over and see you.' You'd have to know Bill to understand this. There was no such thing as telling Bill no on anything."

into a trip to Kalamazoo to see if he could figure out what was wrong. McCarty reported back: "They were top heavy. They had more people in the office, deadheads, than they had working out in the factory." Another problem was the attrition of skilled guitar builders during the war.

Berlin offered McCarty the general managership of Gibson. Again, the answer was "Not interested." More lunches, more drives

Joe Rudis, courtesy *The Tennessean*

McCarty had lunch with Berlin, who told him Gibson was losing $100,000 a month and asked for his help. McCarty declined. Berlin lived in Glencoe and offered McCarty a ride home. More lunches and more talks on the drive home followed, while Mr. Brach lingered in Bermuda. Finally, Berlin talked McCarty

home, and Berlin upped the offer: Go in as the boss, chief executive officer (despite Guy Hart's title of president) with the title of vice president and general manager, turn the company around, and you'll be president within a year. The salary offer was more than McCarty had made at Wurlitzer.

McCarty talked it over with his wife. He would have a chance to use not only all the business and

The triple-pickup ES-5, Gibson's top electric of 1949. Billy Mitchell, courtesy Gruhn Guitars

managerial experience he had acquired in 12 years at Wurlitzer, but also the knowledge acquired in earning an engineering degree from the University of Cincinnati. The kicker, he told his wife: "I'll be the sole boss."

McCarty started at Gibson on March 15, 1948. He renovated a center-hall colonial home and his family moved into the house in August, but it would be years before they felt at home in Kalamazoo. "Any time in the first two years," McCarty recalled, "if I'd said we're going back to Chicago, she'd say, 'I'll be packed in the morning.' This was a very cliquish city. You had to be born here or you were not accepted."

Long before his family moved into their new home, Ted McCarty had turned Gibson around. The company lost money in March and April but was in the black for May and forever after as long as he was in charge.

Unlike his predecessor, McCarty did not rest contentedly once the company was profitable. He forged ahead—not always in the right direction, but always ahead. He secured Gibson's position as the premier maker of archtop electrics with the three-pickup ES-5, the jazz workhorse ES-175, and a "fingerrest" pickup that would convert any acoustic archtop to electric, all in 1949. He followed with the CES (Cutaway Electric Spanish) versions of the Super 400 and L-5 in 1951. He missed the beginning of the solidbody market (Fender's Esquire of 1950) but then charged into it with the Les Paul in 1952. His improved bridge of 1954—the tune-o-matic—is still an industry standard. His modernistic Korina-wood guitars of 1958 failed, but his ES-335 semi-hollowbody of the same year established a new genre of electric guitar. In the 1960s, his artist endorsement models and his second attempt at modernistic solidbodies, the Firebirds, were only moderately successful, but his expanded flattop line pushed Gibson sales to record figures.

By 1965, McCarty had had his fill again of the instrument business. He had started with 150 employees; he now had 1200. The plant was four times its 1948 size, now covering an entire city block. In his first year there, Gibson shipped out a little over 5,000 instruments; in his last year, 1965, shipments topped 100,000—a company record that stands today. He had nothing left to prove.

conflict of interest, and when they said it was, he and Huis resigned. Huis got Bigsby Accessories going while McCarty remained at Gibson until a successor was found. McCarty still makes and sells Bigsby vibratos to various guitar makers, including Gibson.

McCarty solicited ideas from industrial designers but in this case did not put them into production.

Before the Tal Farlow model was introduced in the '60s, Tal played an ES-350. Frank Driggs Collection

Jazz guitarist George Barnes liked the humbucking pickup, a McCarty-era innovation, so he put one on his pre-McCarty (ca. 1946) ES-300. Frank Driggs Collection

Out of the blue, Paul Bigsby, the man who made Bigsby vibratos, called McCarty offering to sell his business. McCarty and John Huis, his longtime factory superintendent, bought Bigsby and moved it from California to Kalamazoo. McCarty asked CMI's lawyers to decide if it was a

THE BIRTH OF THE LES PAUL

BY TOM WHEELER

Les and his wife Mary Ford didn't need the Les Paul Model as a vehicle to fame. They were already one of America's most popular acts.

The Les Paul Model, 1956 version, with Ted McCarty's tune-o-matic bridge.

We've taken the Les Paul for granted for so long (most of us grew up with it) that it's easy to forget what a formidable challenge it presented to Gibson's designers in the early 1950s. The company was running at peak performance, boasting a roster of leading jazz, classical, and pop endorsers and basking in worldwide acclaim as a dominant builder of exquisite archtops and popular flattops. Having struck what seemed to be the perfect balance of productivity and quality, it had everything a guitar company could hope for: impressive sales, the envy of its competitors, and a revered status among discriminating artists.

But change was in the air. It was now five or six years since the end of the war, and with the dawn of the new decade everyone looked toward a future of seemingly unlimited promise. On the auto front, Detroit's heavy cruisers were about to sprout tailfins. Scientists were talking about sending satellites into orbit. And in music, irreverent upstarts, both white and black, were mixing styles into a volatile brew that would soon be dubbed rock & roll. Gibson, which wore its heritage the way Cary Grant wore a tuxedo, found itself in a world where people talked less about heritage and more about newness and accelerating change. The response to all this: a Gibson solidbody.

But "Gibson" and "solidbody" seemed to be an inherent mismatch.

Danny Davenport

Compared to an L-5 or a Super 400, Rickenbacker's little lap steels looked like, well, frying pans. The embryonic Fenders were dismissed as "planks." Solidbodies were associated with California assembly lines, not with the image of a craftsman, steeped in old-world traditions, fine-tuning an instrument with hand tools. Gibson was going to put its esteemed name on a solidbody? It was as if Barney Kessel had announced his forming a rockabilly band, a stylistic shift whose risk for failure, even ridicule, was substantial. Gibson had a lot to lose.

And yet with the Les Paul, Gibson not only met the challenge but scored one of the most impressive commercial and aesthetic triumphs in the history of the industry. It was all new, yet every inch a Gibson. Ted McCarty told me, "We didn't like the idea in a way, because it didn't take a great deal of skill to build a plank guitar." But with the solidbody's undeniable potential, Gibson climbed aboard the bandwagon. "We made solid maple bodies," McCarty reported, "but they were too heavy and sustained too long—couldn't keep them quiet. So the original had a mahogany back with a carved maple top laminated to it. That gave us the balance. The reason we carved the top was that Fender didn't have any carving equipment, so I decided, let's do something different. So we built this guitar, but then we didn't know what to do with it."

Ted was of course familiar with Les Paul, who had for years championed the idea of the

One of Les Paul's contributions to the original Les Paul Model was the trapeze-style combination bridge-tailpiece.

When a third Les Paul Model, the Junior debuted in mid '54, guitarist Melvin Lee bought one to accompany the Brewsteraires, a Memphis gospel group. *Hooks Brothers, ©1993 Mimosa Records Productions, Inc.*

Freddie King played his early blues on a Les Paul goldtop, ca. 1954. Courtesy Memphis Music Hall of Fame

Les Paul envisioned a gold guitar and a black one. The Black Beauty, or Les Paul Custom, debuted in 1954.

Courtesy Gruhn Guitars

recalled. "Les played it, and his eyes lit up. We worked all night long on a royalty contract, and when we were finished, it was only a page-and-a-half long. After that we submitted things to Les for his advice."

Ted McCarty explained in the summer of 1993, "No one person designed the Les Paul. I was involved in the shape and the crowned top, and our engineers worked on the pickups. Then we'd get together and discuss sketches. We mainly wanted it to embody the things that Gibson stood for. We didn't believe in a screwed-in neck, for example. So the design just sort of grew. We worked on it for a year or so."

Les Paul told me, "I had two models in mind right from the very beginning. I picked the gold color because no one else had one, and because it's always associated with quality, and black because it's classy, like a tuxedo." Ted McCarty recently added, "We didn't want Leo [Fender] and the rest of them to discover our combination of maple and mahogany, so we figured the solid colors would make it difficult to see the separate pieces.

Officially introduced in 1952, the goldtop Les Paul Guitar, or Les Paul Model, featured P-90 pickups, as well as a cylindrical bridge/tailpiece that Les Paul had specified (it was replaced by the stop tailpiece in late '53). The tune-o-matic bridge was added in 1955, and the coveted patent-applied-for humbucking pickups in '57. In the following year the cherry sunburst flame maple top replaced the gold, and this incarnation (now called the Standard) is likely the most desirable production vintage guitar ever produced. Several have sold in the tens of thousands of dollars. (The goldtop was joined in

solidbody. It seemed that Les's success as a recording and performing star and his reputation as a technological wizard made him the perfect choice for a professional association. Ted met Les's financial adviser, Phil Braunstein, and they journeyed to Les's mountaintop recording studio at Delaware Water Gap, Pennsylvania, carrying the new solidbody, a sunburst with a regular Gibson trapeze tailpiece. "I showed the guitar to Les," McCarty

1954 by the black Les Paul Custom, nicknamed Black Beauty or Fretless Wonder.)

The most impressive thing about that first goldtop is that Gibson got it so right the first time out of the chute. In any field of design there are radical departures and there are classics, but rarely does one creation fall so squarely into both categories. A quick comparison of the '52 Les Paul to other guitars of its day—Gibson's own archtops or other companies' solidbodies—readily establishes its departure from existing designs, and one need only look on any music store wall today to see that its decades-long influence remains potent. One mark of true innovation is a product's adaptability to unforeseen applications, and let's not forget that the Les Paul, an essential rock & roll guitar the world over, was conceived years before the style of music to which it proved so ideally suited. Sure, Gibson has refined it over the years, but while the differences between the 1952 and 1993 models may be noteworthy, the similarities are more remarkable. Most guitars are designed to fit a style of music; it is no exaggeration to say that rock & roll guitar styles were shaped in part by the Les Paul.

No company of such stature had produced solidbody Spanish guitars on a significant scale, so the new instrument was the talk of the industry in 1952. Until that time solidbodies were seen as specialty items, products on the fringe, but manufacturers believed that Gibson's entry into the market would lend legitimacy to the very concept of solidbody instruments. Of course, they were right. As McCarty explained, "Fred Gretsch, a good friend, called after he heard about it and said, 'I am sorry to see that Gibson has decided to go into solidbody guitars,' but I told him that the solidbody was here to stay." More than four decades later, Les Paul, the man, is still a valuable member of Gibson's family, and the guitar, as Ted McCarty predicted, is here to stay indeed.

The fourth member of the original Les Paul family, the Special, sported a "TV" finish. Courtesy Gruhn Guitars

Blues great John Lee Hooker holds one of the original versions of the Les Paul Model. Courtesy Richard James Hite

LES PAUL

BY MARY SHAUGHNESSY

Late one evening in the spring of 1931, 15-year-old Lester Polfuss snuck into a Genesee, Wisconsin ballroom to check out a hot guitarslinger named Sunny Joe Wolverton. Too young to walk in the door, he slipped through a lavatory window and rushed to the front of the ballroom. There he spied Sunny Joe in the midst of Rube Tronson's rollicking cowboy band, alternately playing two of Gibson's most prized instruments: an elegant Florentine banjo and a gleaming L-5 guitar. During intermission, Sunny Joe sized up the eager youngster. "You play guitar, I suppose?"

"Well, I thought I did," Les answered, "but I don't think I do now."

Nevertheless, within a year, the fledgling guitarist joined Sunny Joe's new hillbilly band, the Scalawags, and enjoyed his dual status as Joe's star pupil and professional partner on several Midwestern radio stations.

Les had started playing harmonica, banjo, and guitar when he was still in grade school. He practiced relentlessly, trying his best to sound like the old pros he listened to on live radio broadcasts of Chicago's *National Barn Dance* and Nashville's *Grand Ole Opry*. His favorite was Claud J. Moye, better known as Pie Plant Pete, an itinerant showman who crooned country ditties and simultaneously played guitar and harmonica. Whenever Pete performed within a hundred miles of Lester's Waukesha, Wisconsin, hometown, he'd see the boy in the audience. One day he brought Les backstage after the matinee and taught him a few chords. Pretty soon, Pete later said of his protege, "This fellow sounded as much like me as could be."

Dubbing himself Red Hot Red, Les began working dance halls, stock pavilion shows, festivals—anyplace that called for live entertainment. He had

Pete's hillbilly act down cold by the time Joe plucked him out of Waukesha in 1932. Renamed Rhubarb Red (a clever variation on Pete's moniker, rhubarb being another name for pieplant), he was a lively addition to the Scalawags. But Joe decided the boy's twangy resonator guitar had to go. One day he drove him from St. Louis to Kalamazoo to buy him his first Gibson, an L-50 archtop (Joe later bought Les an L-5). Under Joe's tutelage, Les blossomed into a guitarist to be reckoned with. Within two years, though, the pair went their separate ways.

Barely 19 and on his own for the first time, Les continued to make a splash on Chicago radio as Rhubarb Red. However, he soon began jamming with noted jazz players in clubs all over the city. Trouble was, his guitar couldn't be heard above the din of the brass players and hard-drinking patrons. In the mid '30s, he commissioned the Larson Brothers, who made guitars for many WLS performers, to build him an electric guitar. In order to boost the volume and sustain, Les ordered a half-inch-thick top of solid maple with no sound holes.

He was still peforming his country bumpkin routine in 1937 (often with his new Super 400) when he met singer/guitarist Jimmy Atkins (Chet's older half-brother). United by an ardent desire to escape the hillbilly scene, they recruited bassist Ernie Newton to form a jazz trio. The following year the threesome set out for New York City, where they quickly won a featured spot on Fred

Les Paul in his home studio, 1988. Courtesy Waukesha County Museum Collections

Les Paul has modified practically every guitar he's ever owned. This one probably started out in the late '30s as an ES-100, but he installed a "Christian" pickup from the ES-150. Fred Waring's America, The Pennsylvania State University

Waring's radio show, sponsored by Chesterfield. Now Les's amplified single-string solos were heard nationwide several evenings a week, influencing such guitarists as Charlie Byrd, Tony Mottola, and Johnny Smith. "As far as I'm concerned," said Smith, "Les did more to popularize the electric guitar than any other player." Chet Atkins concurred: "I used to ask my brother how Les Paul managed to play so damn much guitar."

Les, however, was still intent on finding an instrument that would give him the sound he was after. In 1941, he built a 20-pound monstrosity he called "The Log," named after the four-by-four piece of pine he used for the body. He added a Gibson neck with a Larson fingerboard, two pickups he fashioned from the inner coils of an electric clock, and a pair of side wings from an old Epiphone to make it look like a guitar. But he was never quite satisfied with its tone, preferring

Les Paul, left, and Jimmy Atkins play Gibson L-7s with Fred Waring's Pennsylvanians in the late '30s. Fred Waring's America, The Pennsylvania State University

for the most part to stick to his modifed Gibson, or later, one of his hot-rodded Epiphones.

Les moved in 1943 to Hollywood, where he scored chart-topping disks with Bing Crosby and the Andrews Sisters. Four years later, after painstakingly experimenting with a variety of overdubbing techniques in his own garage recording studio, he turned out a solo record that turned the music industry upside down. Released in February 1948, "Lover" was a feverishly fast, multilayered arrangement for eight guitars—all played by Les. This at a time when the major labels were failing to get a good clean sound out of two or three overdubs.

Despite a near-fatal car crash that year that almost cost him his picking arm—he had to be fitted with an artificial elbow—Les soon joined forces with a stunningly talented singer/guitarist named Colleen Summers, whom he married and renamed Mary Ford. "How High the Moon," one of 27 hits they made together, went to Number One in Billboard and stayed there for nine weeks in 1951. It was also Number One on the rhythm & blues charts—a first for a white act—and a consistent frontrunner on BBC radio's *Housewife's Choice*. "'How High the Moon' had terrific verve, proof at last that pop music could provide stylish instrumental inventiveness," Rolling Stone Bill Wyman remembered in his 1991 autobiography.

By the end of 1951, the husband-and-wife team became the first artists to simultaneously hold four spots on *Billboard's* Best Selling Pop Singles Chart and the first big-name performers to allow their names to be used to sell everything from beer to mouthwash. In the November 1953 issue of

Metronome, writer George Simon summed up Les's career to that point: "What Benny Goodman did for the clarinet, Harry James for the trumpet, Tommy Dorsey for the trombone and Coleman Hawkins did for the tenor sax, Les Paul has done for the guitar."

When Gibson completed the prototype of its first solidbody guitar, Les Paul was the logical choice to help market it. Ironically, the electric guitar that Les had worked so hard to popularize eventually became the instrument of his professional doom. Unable to stem the tide of rock & roll, he and Mary precipitously slipped off the charts in the mid '50s and split up in 1963, the same year Les's name was removed from Gibson's SG-style models.

However, by 1968, the old Les Paul Standard had become the guitar of choice for such rock luminaries as Jimmy Page, Keith Richards, and Eric Clapton. The upsurge of interest in the discontinued models prompted Gibson to introduce the first of many new Les Paul models, and it is now the bedrock of Gibson's success in the solidbody guitar market.

Les, too, is basking in renewed fame. His professional renaissance began with the Grammy he won in 1977 for *Chester and Lester,* his downhome LP with Chet Atkins. Since then he has been inducted into the National Academy of Recording Arts and Sciences Hall of Fame as well as the Rock and Roll Hall of Fame. In 1991, Capitol released a critically acclaimed four-CD retrospective, *Les Paul: The Legend and the Legacy.* And today, at 78, he is still drawing full houses every Monday night at Fat Tuesdays, the New York City jazz club he has called home since 1984.

Guests at Les Paul's 72nd birthday party at the Hard Rock Cafe in New York included pop star Tony Bennett.

Rhubarb Red in a 1930s Gibson catalog.

LES PAULS ON PARADE

BY WALTER CARTER

Birth announcement of the 1956 three-quarter-size Les Paul Junior.

The king of the Pauls, a "flametop" cherry sunburst Les Paul Standard from 1960.

Courtesy Gruhn Guitars

The Les Paul Model was an unqualified success: 1,715 instruments were shipped in 1952, the first year of production, and 2,245 the next year. Even so, no one— not even Les Paul or Ted McCarty—would have dared predict that the number of Les Paul models would eventually be greater than the number of all guitar models Gibson offered in 1952.

The expansion began slowly in 1954, with one fancier and one plainer model: the Les Paul Custom and Les Paul Junior, respectively. The Custom outsold all the other high-end electric models put together, with 355 shipped in 1955. And, as is usually the case with Gibson instruments, the cheapest model was the most popular—2,839 Juniors in 1955. The Special, essentially a better-looking ("TV" yellow finish vs. yellow-to-brown sunburst), double-pickup Junior,

also made a successful debut in 1955.

It was a promising start, to be sure, but there was one serious problem. Nobody famous was playing a Les Paul except Les himself, and as Les's star began to fade in the late '50s, so did the models that bore his name. A third pickup on the Custom and a cherry sunburst finish on the Standard failed to stop falling sales.

One change did help, however. A double-cutaway body, instituted on the Junior in mid 1958, caused Junior sales to almost double. In early 1961, the whole Les Paul line was revamped with a new body style— thinner and lighter with bold, sharply pointed double-cutaways. The changes worked. Sales of the Custom, Standard, and Special turned upward. Les, however, didn't care for the new style, and his contract (signed in 1952 for five years, then renewed for another five) was expiring

196

anyway, so in 1963, the Les Pauls were renamed the SGs (for Solid Guitar).

SG sales held steady in the mid '60s, but a new demand arose for the old Les Pauls. A goldtop Standard and a Custom were brought back in 1968, and Les was back in the guitar endorsement business—with a vengeance. By 1970, the Les Paul line warranted its own brochure, with five guitars, a bass, an amp, and a preamp.

Dozens of variations of the original Les Paul models would eventually be born, and a great many of them live on today. As of 1994, Gibson had more than 25 different Les Paul guitars and basses in production, plus handmade Historic Collection reissues of nine early Les Paul models. Here's a sampling of Les Pauls through the years:

PROFESSIONAL, PERSONAL, AND RECORDING (1969–79)

Practically every modern electric guitar has high-impedance output—except for Les's personal guitars. He has always preferred low-impedance. Les admits, "The only difference between high and low, basically, is you can run longer lines and get better frequency response [with low], and you have less noise problems, and it's easier to work with."

Nevertheless CMI head M. H. Berlin thought there was some hidden ingredient in Les's personal guitars, and around 1967, he asked Les what the secret was and if Gibson could use it. Les has always considered that information proprietary. His position was, "As long as I'm active I will not give that to Gibson. That is my sound." But in 1967, he was not active. He thought he was

Billy Mitchell

retired, so he lent his name to Gibson's new low-impedance models.

Even though he had been using low impedance for most of his career, he had no interest in being a crusader. "This is like high-definition television," he explained in 1993. "It's very difficult to get everybody to scrap their TV sets. It would be very hard for me to get everybody to switch to a low-impedance guitar and then get a low-impedance amplifier."

Furthermore, Les felt that most players didn't want his sound anyway. "What the guitarists liked the most was a high amount of output, a tremendous amount of level, and a big round sound. I went for a brilliant sound, but the average guitar player wanted a rounder sound."

The original Personal and Professional required transformers to be played through standard amps. The Les Paul Recording that replaced them alleviated that inconvenience with a built-in transformer and a high-low impedance selector switch. There was still a fatal flaw, according to Les. "[Gibson president] Stan Rendell felt that it should be a little different than the high-impedance Les Paul models, so the body was made a little larger. It was more like The Log and played like a hog. I said, 'I'm going up to

The 1962 catalog pictured Les with Mary Ford and the full line of double-cutaway Les Paul models. Les was not getting along with Mary by this time, and he didn't like the guitars much either.

It looks like an SG Custom, but the official name in 1961 was still Les Paul Custom. Courtesy Gruhn Guitars

197

the Mayo Clinic and I'm going to pick out a room and call it the Les Paul Room for people who come in with back pains.' But they sustain, I'll tell you that."

DELUXE (1969–85)

For reasons unknown to today's players and collectors, Gibson introduced small "mini" humbucking pickups on the Deluxe in 1969. It sold fairly well until 1975, probably because there was no Les Paul Standard available with full-size humbuckers. The Deluxe is virtually ignored by collectors, but not by Les. "In every conversation I have with any Gibson president, I will bring up Deluxe, Deluxe, Deluxe," he says. "It was one of my favorites. It still is one of my favorites. It sustained so good. Evidently they had some problems with it, and/or it wasn't one of the models that just happened to be one that the public wanted. It's very much like running a saloon. The fellow doesn't think about how good the entertainment is, it's how the cash register looks. If the cash register doesn't ring, they're gone. It doesn't matter if you have Sinatra there or the Nosebleeds."

ARTISAN (1976–81)

Banjo-style fingerboard inlay and peghead inlay.

ARTIST (1979–81)

Active electronics, "LP" on the peghead.

STUDIO (1984–CURRENT)

Trimmed-down Standard.

Les Paul Recording.

JUMBO (1969–72)

A big-bodied flattop with a cutaway and a low-impedance pickup. Les: "What I wished to do, and Gibson did do, is place the pickup way up right to the fingerboard and to bury it in there so that no one would ever see it. There was just room enough by moving the hole down a little bit. Thumbs Carlille loved it, John Pizzarelli loved it, I loved it, and many others. The protoype is just excellent, but when they made it they made some changes. I'm not blaming them for it, but they didn't make it exactly like the prototype. It didn't go, but maybe not because it wasn't good but maybe because Les Paul was known for solidbodies."

SIGNATURE (1973–77)

Sort of a low-impedance ES-335 (semi-hollowbody) that stayed in the sun too long, also available as a bass. "There was one thing missing in our repertoire," Les recalls. "I always felt there were people like Wes Montgomery, Barney Kessell, George Benson, they like to wrap their arms around something so that they can love their instrument. They like something that isn't just a little bitty piece of wood, a broomstick sitting in their hands."

Like the production version of the Jumbo, the Signature that came off the line was different from the one Les had in mind. "I was going to run it stem to stern, from the nut all the way down to the bridge, very much like The Log. It was going to be one piece." Instead of neck-through-body, however, there was only a T-shaped piece under the top.

Billy Mitchell

THE LES PAUL (1976–79)

With ultra-fancy ornamentation (wood knobs, wood pickguard, wood bindings, etc.), The Les Paul was expensive—then and now.

THE PAUL DELUXE (1980–85)

With a slab body (no top contour), no binding, not even pickup covers, The Paul Deluxe is not to be confused with The Les Paul or the Les Paul Deluxe.

LITE (1987–CURRENT)

Chromyte (balsa) core for lighter weight.

CLASSIC (1990–CURRENT)

Essentially a 1960 reissue without pickup covers.

PLUS TOP, PREMIUM PLUS, BIRDSEYE, PREMIUM BIRDSEYE, ETC.

The degree of figuration in the wood grain of the Les Paul's maple top cap can make a difference of thousands of dollars to vintage buyers. Tops of new models are carefully graded into separate model designations, with a Premium Plus or a Birdseye top pushing the list price up $500 or more over a "regular" top.

HERITAGE 80 (1980)

The first reissue attempt that came close to the revered cherry sunburst Les Paul Standard of 1959. Les's working guitar is a Heritage 80 Elite (ebony fingerboard instead of rosewood), but with low-impedance pickups, of course. "It's just my favorite guitar," he says. "It's the only one that comes close to the sound I like and the sound that I'm known for."

Les Paul Signature.

Courtesy Gruhn Guitars

Les Paul Jumbo.

Courtesy Gruhn Guitars

THE ELECTRIC GUITAR AS CULTURAL ICON

BY TOM WHEELER

Postwar America was one of the most dynamic peacetime periods in modern world history, characterized by unprecedented commercial expansiveness, personal prosperity, and a sense of newness, a "make way for the future" optimism. Paralleling a virtually unchallenged patriotism and a limitless faith in progress was a rock-the-boat rebelliousness of a new kind of music, born of a union (unholy, said the critics) of rhythm & blues and hillbilly. Deejay Allan Freed called it rock & roll, and the name caught on. Of all the pop-culture icons and images of the era—tailfinned Detroit landrockets, "New and improved!" products of boggling variety, buzz-cut astronaut trainees—perhaps it was the electric guitar that best symbolized the blend of faith in all things American, the excitement of technological horizons, and the kinetic energy of consumer society's sudden superstar, the teenager.

Of course, electric guitars were hardly new; Gibson had been making them since the '30s. They had been invented for one reason: volume. Remember that many pop and jazz guitarists were essentially rhythm players who strummed and comped while vocalists and horn players took the spotlight. As bands got bigger, these supporting guitarists were often drowned out by horn sections and drum kits. But in one of countless examples of technology's unforeseen effects, the electric guitar not only gave rhythm players the punch they needed, it opened up entirely new possibilities. As demonstrated with astonishing clarity by Charlie Christian, the guitar could now function as a solo instrument in a band setting, giving those vocalists and horn players a run for their money as the featured attraction. For guitarists, it was suddenly a whole new game.

The mid-'50s birth of rock as a hybrid of black and white

John Bellissimo

Chuck Pulin, Star File

styles has been endlessly dissected by musicologists, but there was obviously more going on than melodies and harmonies and rhythms. Sex appeal and exhibitionism, for example. Taking a cue from T-Bone Walker and Guitar Slim, early rockers helped change the persona of the onstage guitarist from a technically accomplished journeyman, content to perch on a stool behind a music stand, to a showstopper attraction in his own right—a performer—and they couldn't have done it without the mobility and looks of the electric guitar. Watching Chuck Berry duckwalk across your little black-and-white TV screen with a Gibson ES-350, you could turn off the sound and it would still look too cool for words.

While they were being used in exciting new ways, the guitars themselves were familiar and generally conventional. By the time Scotty Moore went into Sun Records to record with Elvis, he had plenty of gear to choose from—big Gibson archtops whose features had been refined for years by some of the world's best designers and

craftsmen. We'd seen instruments like these in the hands of players with Bob Wills or Nat King Cole. To the general public, anyway, there was nothing new about them.

Enter the solidbody. Pioneered by Les Paul and others, it represented not just a new way to solve old problems. Like its hollow electric forebear, it marked a whole new approach to what the guitar could do, what it could be, what it could mean. For one thing, it provided a low-feedback, relatively buzz-free sound at volume levels far beyond the needs of those tuxedoed jazz compers back there in the rhythm sections or even the new generation of soloists following in Christian's footsteps. The Les Pauls were ahead of their time, suited not only to the music of the day but to styles that wouldn't even be conceived for years. It would be more than a decade before rock stars like Pete Townshend would discover the Joy of Loud—new, artistic uses for volume and feedback. But meanwhile, one attribute of the solidbody was immediately grasped by

Bill Haley, playing a Super 400 acoustic with a DeArmond pickup, started it all with "Rock Around the Clock" in 1955.

The Les Paul guitar has worked its way into architectural designs at the Dallas Hard Rock Cafe.

Chuck Berry with an ES-355, still duckwalking.

British guitarist Jeff Beck takes aim with his Les Paul.

Scotty Moore, described in this 1958 Gibson Gazette as a backup player for "crooner" Elvis Presley, defined rockabilly on Gibsons.

David Bowie takes a bite out of Mick Ronson's axe.

manufacturers: They could saw it into any shape they wanted.

The earliest Les Pauls were innovative, but they still looked like Gibsons; their Kalamazoo heritage was apparent. Soon, though, Ted McCarty and his crew began to have fun. If the primary considerations were now weight and density rather than resonance and vibration, why not get wild? Let's shape this baby like a lightning bolt and call it the Explorer, or a pair of tailfins and call it the Flying V. We can even take an existing guitar silhouette, more or less, reverse it, and call it the Firebird. In the words of Elvis Presley, "Let's get real, real gone for a change."

From the moment designers first experimented with them, it was apparent that solidbodies would have to be small. No longer half-hidden behind their instruments, the new generation of players would be more exposed, out front. The guitar practically encouraged its player to step forward, and hey, while you're at it, take a step or two,

strum with a flourish, shake it up a bit, run across the stage if you feel like it, see how high you can jump. With their compact size, powerful sound, and radical new shapes, solidbodies were tailor-made for players tapping into the heady abandon of rock & roll.

Before we knew it, electric guitars sounded like nothing else and looked like nothing else, and the same could be said for music and its performers. Furthermore, music was now seen as more than mere entertainment, almost a way of life or a vehicle for social change. These simultaneous trends were obviously connected, self-stoking. Whatever players may have required in tone and versatility, they also had an endless array of lifestyle symbols to choose from—the guitar as a piece of craftsmanship, a work of art, a token of individuality, a sidearm of social protest, even an extension of your sexuality. By the mid 1960s, the electric guitar was many things to many people, but in every case it carried with it all the power and magic of music itself.

SCOTTY MOORE

Rock 'n' Roller Scotty Moore plays lead guitar with the group backing well-known Crooner Elvis Presley. The versatile guitarist—here using a Gibson L-5CESN—is also the proud owner of a Super 400CESN. Scotty appeared with Presley on a recent Ed Sullivan TV show, during which Presley used his new J-200N. Both made their purchases from O. K. Houck of Memphis, Tenn.

Record Tips:

"Intimate love songs" is the fetching theme of a new album by one of the best mandolin players in the business, issued recently through Romance Records of Hollywood, California.

Definitely a cut above the usual mandolin release on the market, this record features the well-known Dave Apollon's Romance Recording Orchestra. Backing the artistry of Mandolinist Dave Apollon is a blend of woodwinds and strings playing tunes both rhythmic and dreamy.

The album is entitled "Lot of Love," DA 101, issued by Romance Records, 1750 N. Serrano avenue, Hollywood, California.

◆ ◆ ◆

Classic guitar fans will be interested in the new release by Renato Rossini— the RCA Victor LP M1303 album which came out recently.

Titled "Renato Rossini—My Guitar," the album has an attractive cover that

There Are No "Short Cuts" To QUALITY In
EPIPHONE BASSES

Made expressly for the professional ... with ALL the desirable features ... fine tone ... perfect adjustment ... properly fitted bridge ... correct angle of neck ... etc.

ONLY AN EPIPHONE GIVES YOU
* Natural Woods Throughout
* Genuine Straight Grained Spruce Top
* Genuine Curly Maple Body
* Genuine Carved Scroll
* Superlative Grade of Strings
* Extremely Accurate Fingerboard
* Fine Weight Balance
* Hand Rubbed Finish

TRY AN EPIPHONE AT YOUR DEALER OR WRITE ... Department B-MST

EPIPHONE, INC.
142 WEST 14 STREET, NEW YORK, N. Y.

WORLD'S LARGEST FIRST GRADE FRETTED INSTRUMENT BUILDERS

EPIPHONE ADS (similar to the one above) are appearing regularly. They mean **MORE BUSINESS** for you. There's an EPIPHONE BASS for every popular price. Send for folder.

EPIPHONE FALLS

BY WALTER CARTER

A. STATHOPOULO
FOUNDER

E. A. STATHOPOULO
PRESIDENT

O. A. STATHOPOULO
VICE-PRES. & TREAS.

F. N. STATHOPOULO
SECRETARY

From the early 1930s to World War II, Gibson and Epiphone vied like contenders in a title bout, a rivalry that brought out the best from both companies. Epi landed the first punches in 1931 with nine new archtops. Gibson countered with a bigger and better model. Epi made an even bigger one. Gibson switched to an electric attack; Epi responded with the first pickup with individual polepieces. Gibson won the last round before World War II with the introduction of cutaway bodies.

When World War II ended, they resumed the rivalry. Ted McCarty recalls that when he arrived at Gibson in 1948, "Our biggest competitor was Epiphone. Les Paul was playing an Epiphone. I tried for a couple of years to get that away from him and get him to play a Gibson—without much success, I might add."

Epi had come out of the corner with fists raised, in the form of catalogs featuring new electric models—with cutaways, of course. But before long it was clear that Epi's heart wasn't in the fight anymore.

Epiphone had lost the heart of the company, literally, with the death of Epi himself during World War II. Epaminodas Stathopoulo was a third-generation luthier. His father Anastasios was born in Sparta, Greece, in 1863 and made violins and lutes. Epi was born in 1893 and the family emigrated to New York in 1903. Anastasios died in 1915. Two years later, Epi began labeling instruments "House of Stathopoulo." His name inspired the Epiphone brand on a new banjo line in 1924, and the company was renamed Epiphone

in 1928. In the 1930s, guitar players were caught in a tug of war for their endorsements between Kalamazoo and New York. Like Gibson, Epiphone severely cut back instrument production for World War II. In the middle of the war, on June 6, 1943, Epi died of "pernicious anemia" or leukemia. The company would never be the same again.

Epi's brothers took over, with O. A. (Orphie) Stathopoulo as president and F. N. (Frixo) as vice president, but they didn't have Epi's talent or interest in the guitar business. In 1952, they licensed distribution in some territories (they held on to the lucrative New York area, among others) to Continental, a wholesaler owned by the C. G. Conn band instrument company of Elkhart, Indiana. Conn didn't fare any better with Epiphone, and Orphie regained control after a couple of years, but it didn't matter. Gibson's once-formidable competitor was now making guitars that were, according to McCarty, "so poor you couldn't give them away."

McCarty was in Washington state buying spruce when Orphie called, wanting to sell Epi's bass business. That was the one area where Epi had always had the edge over Gibson. Epiphones were among the most respected American-made upright basses. Gibson's challenge to Epi's basses in 1939 was a typical one-up attempt: an entire violin family of instruments. Gibson's line was moderately successful, but it was not resumed after the war.

CMI head M. H. Berlin recognized an opportunity to get back into the bass business with no expense for design and tooling, and he sent McCarty and John Huis to New York to talk to Orphie. They

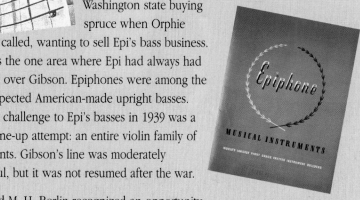

In the late '30s Gibson one-upped Epi's basses with an entire violin family.

Epiphone
MUSICAL INSTRUMENTS

The lure of Epiphone basses hooked Gibson into buying the company.

Epiphone Emperor electric, 1960 edition: thin body and pickups by Gibson, neck from the old New York Epiphone stock. Courtesy Gruhn Guitars

learned the price Orphie wanted: $20,000. They also learned that parts and assembly were spread over three locations: Manhattan, New Berlin (a small town in central New York), and Philadelphia. So off they went to Philadelphia. "When we got there," McCarty said, "we discovered that all of the tools, dies, fixtures, forms, and whatnot to make the Epiphone guitars were there, and they were included in this sale."

McCarty paid the asking price and received everything: 35 completed basses, bass manufacturing equipment, and rights to the name, plus the guitar parts and equipment. The possibility of making Epi guitars sparked an idea for Gibson to continue the Epi heritage, to make the more highly regarded models with the same forms and the same techniques used by Epi craftsmen.

Then a better idea hit. Gibson had a waiting list for dealers, some of whom were

successful dealers of other CMI products but because of Gibson's protective territorial policy were not allowed to deal Gibsons. A second brand—especially one that already had a level of name recognition equal to Gibson—would appease new dealers without directly threatening established Gibson dealers. Gibson would be careful to keep the perception of Epi at a level below—but only slightly below—that of a Gibson, by such means as smaller, "mini" humbucking pickups and slightly thinner solidbody models.

Gibson announced the acquisition on May 10, 1957, along with expectations for basses to be available "within the very near future," some guitars by fall, and a complete line, including solidbodies, by early 1958. McCarty remembers the result: "Within about three years we were doing about three million dollars worth of business. We were going great guns."

But the road to profitability was rocky. For starters, Epi's reputation had fallen as low as its instruments. A statement after the first six months (October 31, 1957) shows that Gibson pumped another $18,000 into the Epi project, most of it on building, machinery, and office expenses. Sales of all items—supplies, strings, and repairs, as well as instruments—totaled a meager $1,621.82.

Those 1957 sales were the last gasps of the old Epiphone—the company that the Stathopoulo family knew. There was even a funeral pyre. In

Billy Mitchell

family knew. There was even a funeral pyre. In April 1958, Paul Gazley of Conn reported a fire in the New Berlin warehouse, where a stash of old Epi parts, now owned by Gibson, were stored. A memo from CMI salesman Howard Kelley to Gibson's Clarence Havenga revealed that the fire was no accident, that Gazley had given employees whatever Epi parts they wanted and then burned the rest in a bonfire. "Some cooperation, eh?" Kelley said in closing.

Bass production hit a snag in February 1958 when temperature variations caused finish checking on the tops and backs. Every single bass had to be refinished. To make matters worse, when they finally hit the market, the B-4, the professional model, listed for $345; Kay, the most successful American bass maker, sold its C-1 model for $275. Upright basses—the reason CMI bought Epiphone in the first place—were clearly not going to carry the company, and they faded out of production by the early 1960s.

Fortunately, Gibson was not counting on any help from bass sales or from Conn. New Epiphone guitar and amp lines had been on the drawing board since the first announcement, and on February 6, 1958, McCarty met with Clarence Havenga, Clyde Rounds of CMI, and M. H. Berlin to finalize the new Epi models. By May 16, McCarty was putting a rush on production for the upcoming summer trade show. By September most of the models were ready for shipment.

Epiphone was back as a competitive brand, but now the competitor was part of the Gibson family.

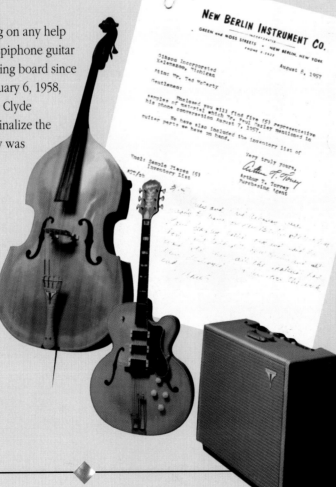

The mysterious Epi warehouse fire turned out to be a farewell bonfire.

A Deluxe acoustic, natural-finish upright bass, and Emperor electric—the pride of the new Epi line— represented American instrument makers at an exhibit in Moscow, Russia, in the summer of 1959.

THE MODERNISTIC KORINA TRIO

BY TOM WHEELER

Ted McCarty was annoyed. That Leo Fender fella was going around saying Gibson was stodgy and hadn't had a new idea in ages. Gibson's softspoken boss responded with a triple-barrel blast of innovation intended to raise the stakes in the hotly contested solidbody market. But the Explorer, Flying V, and Moderne, didn't raise much of anything except a few eyebrows, not at first. The trio of distinguished duds was ahead of its time, but when the rest of the world caught up with them, two of the guitars soared into the rarified air of vintage guitar Valhalla, and the third attained an even mistier status, that of the ultimate six-string phantom, the Lost Guitar of Kalamazoo.

The rivalry got underway in 1950, with the debut of Fender's Esquire/Broadcaster/Telecaster. McCarty countered with the elegant yet forward-looking Les Paul. (Not that Fender and Gibson were the only players, but when it came to the solidbody sweepstakes, it was pretty much a two-team league.) The Stratocaster of '54, all curvy and splashy, was a major score, and the game's next play was once again in the hands of Ted McCarty. He threw long.

"We were pretty close in the industry," he recalled in 1993. "Fred Gretsch, Fred Martin, the fellows at Harmony and Kay—we were all friends. But Leo didn't mix much. He was going around saying Gibson hadn't had any new ideas in a hundred years, and I guess my attitude was, well, we'll show 'em."

Gibson brought three new designs to trade shows, and they made an impression on Fender general manager Forrest White. "He did that on a lark," White said of McCarty's new ideas. "He was making fun of what Leo had done. When I looked over there and I saw those things, I looked at him and he looked at me, and he had a big grin on his face. He thought I would be mad, but I had to laugh. I thought Leo's stuff looked crazy. I thought this guy was off his rocker."

Gibson ultimately produced two of the three models, the Flying V and the Explorer, but they fizzled on the launching pad. McCarty said that some of the dealers who did purchase V's wanted them mainly as display props, not because they were taken seriously as instruments (when it came to Gibson dealers, Leo Fender was right—they were stodgy). But during the first tremors of the vintage guitar boom, the quality, rarity, utility, and zigzag sex appeal of original V's and Explorers made them among the most lusted after chunks of wood on earth, and they started selling for thousands of dollars, then tens of thousands.

It's simple enough to track down the Gibson execs of 1957 and record their recollections of the birth of the V, the Explorer, and the triplets' third sister, the fabled Moderne. But getting them to agree on what happened—that's a different story. Who actually sat down at the drafting table and came up with those shapes is a matter of dispute, or perhaps

Lonnie Mack ordered his guitar after seeing only a drawing of the new model, and his dealer, Glenn Hughes Music in Cincinnati, fashioned a metal support piece so the Bigsby vibrato could be mounted. The '58 V generated the sound for Mack's 1963 hit "Memphis."

Dan Loftin, courtesy Gruhn Guitars

© 1993 Jon Sievert

of dimmed memory. When I was researching *American Guitars,* Ted McCarty did say that he designed the trio "with the help of a local artist." Today, Mr. McCarty does not recall that person's name but reports: "He's dead and gone. In fact, there was more than one—they worked for a company here in town. I drew out the guitars freehand, and all they did was get them acceptable for the patent application, cleaned them up a little. They did no design work." We do know that the sketches—dozens of them, perhaps as many as a hundred—crossed McCarty's desk for approval, and that it's his name on the paper where it counts: a U.S. patent filed in June 1957.

"The public in general was requesting natural finishes," he told me in 1978. "If we had made them out of maple, they would have been too heavy. If we had used mahogany, we would have had to bleach it to get the color we wanted—we called it a limed finish—and bleaching is unsatisfactory because the wood discolors after a few years. Korina [the trade name for a type of African limba] is pale yellow, the grain is similar to mahogany, and it works like mahogany. So Korina was ideal."

Officially introduced in 1958, the Flying V featured three in-line knobs, squared "shoulders," gold-plated hardware, PAFs, all frets clear of the body, a metal wedge through which the strings passed, and a peghead logo of raised plastic letters. McCarty noted: "The idea for the strings extending through the body came about when we discovered the shape did not leave room for a tailpiece and bridge. And the very first models had a tendency to slip if you were sitting down, so we came up with a piece of corrugated rubber on the lower wing that kept it from sliding off." Some original bodies were stored at the factory until 1962–63; they are often considered originals, although they have patent-number pickups and nickel-plated parts.

Still "modernistic" after all these years, a custom-made transparent V inspires the body language of the Scorpions' Rudolph Schenker.

The Explorer was similar to the V except for its lightning-bolt shape, stop tailpiece, rim-mounted jack, and scimitar peghead (a very few of the earliest models, unofficially called Futuras, have a forked peghead). It was promptly discontinued, in 1959, although some of the originals were shipped as late as 1963.

Speaking of the Moderne, Marc Horowitz and Mandolin Bros.' Stan Jay said, "It's generally agreed that it had a shape only its mother could love... a totally nonappealing silhouette." It may have resembled a cross between a '57 Chevy tailfin and Gumby, yet it's among the most storied electrics in Gibson history, perhaps in guitar history, period. But why? Well, what sets Modernes apart from other interesting instruments is the same thing that sets pterodactyls apart from ordinary rare birds: They vanished, every single one of them.

The fog began to shroud all three Korinas right at their birth, since Gibson's "system" of classification was not a model of precision or logic. Various sources cite three batches of 40 original Flying V's, with 81 shipped in '58 and another 17 in '59 (accounting for 98 of the 120; the rest were presumably stored until 1962-63). It seems that a single 40-guitar batch of Explorers was made (there is some speculation that two batches were made, but in an ad for Explorer reissues Gibson itself referred to the original 38), and yet they do not show up on the shipping records. No one knows why. There is a notation for "Korina (Mod. Gtr.)," indicating 19 shipped in 1958 and 3 more the following year. These might have been Modernes as the designation would suggest, but they could have been the Explorers, or some of them, that otherwise are missing from the records.

Courtesy Gruhn Guitars

Employees sometimes adopted different nicknames for works-in-progress while the marketing guys were settling on model names; remember, these records were for internal purposes, not for catalogs or promo materials. The Explorer prototype, for example, was remembered by different Gibson vets as the Futura, the Futurama, and the Futuristic. But wait—it gets worse. Both the V and the Explorer were grouped in the July 1, 1958 price list under the designation (get ready) Modernistic Guitars. Each sold for $247.50, by the way, which today wouldn't even begin to cover the sales tax on the sale of an original Korina Gibson.

So how many Modernes were there, anyway? Ted McCarty once guessed that only a handful were produced, maybe a half-dozen. Other veterans of the late '50s factory put the figure between 40 and 50. But because Gibson never sold or even advertised the model through normal outlets, and because so few Modernes seem to have actually left the factory, we can logically conclude that it never slipped beyond the prototype stage. John Huis, in charge of Gibson production

Steve Earle assaults country music with a camouflaged Explorer III, a 1985 variant with three soapbar pickups.

©1993 Beth Gwinn

213

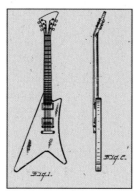

The Flying V and Explorer were revived with a restyled mahogany body in 1966 and 1975 respectively. Bluesman Albert King plays his new lefty V at the Ash Grove in Los Angeles in early '68. Blackfoot's Rick "Rattlesnake" Medlocke bends his body and his strings on an Explorer in a 1981 concert.

at the time, guesses that 30 to 35 Modernes were made but that "most of them just hung around in a rack for a long time." He told me in August 1993: "Some were raw wood, most of them. They sat there dormant. We may have put a finish on only five or six. I'm not sure after that. I don't think most of them ever left the factory. Maybe they finally just sawed them up."

If even a substantial portion of a single 40-guitar batch of Modernes had been finished and distributed, a few would likely have turned up. After all, we've been searching for them hard enough and long enough. But although tantalizing rumors have floated through the ether for some years, turning the Moderne into the guitar equivalent of Anastasia, lost daughter of the Czar, there's not a single authenticated example known to exist. I don't know exactly how many were made, or how many left the factory, or which model is referred to by the "Korina (Mod. Gtr.)" hieroglyphic—maybe it even refers to several models, a mix of "Modernistics." Huis, 84 at the

Stephen C. LaVere, ©1993 Mimosa Records Productions, Inc.

©1993 Beth Gwinn

time of this writing, is admittedly unsure of the details, but he is a credible source; after all, these guitars were built under his direct supervision. His version is at least convenient, because it accounts for the recollection of some eyewitnesses as to the total number produced, it is generally in accord with Gibson's typical production practices, and it explains the scarcity of finished models flying the coop.

There's no reason to believe that the Moderne was any better than the Explorer or Flying V. No, it achieved its status because of its incomparable rarity (it seems extinct as a dodo—now that's rare) and because of family ties to its legendary Korina sisters. Gibson built plenty of other laboratory experiments, perhaps even one-of-a-kind prototypes, but none has generated a level of interest even approaching that of the glamorous Gumby guitar. The Moderne mystique is a matte of juxtaposition: There it is, big as life, right alongside the other two in the famous patent drawing. Today, an authenticated missing triplet would shock the guitar community, almost like the appearance of Elvis's twin, who we all thought had died at birth. "If a genuine late-'50s Gibson Moderne were to surface and be available for sale," says Stan Jay, "it would be worth about half a million dollars." Stan didn't mention whether that figure would include the case, but you get the idea: The Moderne remains Gibson's Holy Grail.

Artist's drawings of the Moderne and "Futura." The Futura grew a scimitar-shaped peghead and survived briefly as the Explorer; the Moderne disappeared without a trace. A note on the Moderne drawing specified poplar rather than Korina wood—the famous modernistic Poplar Trio?

BIRTH OF THE ES-335

BY TOM WHEELER

The best of both worlds? It's a tempting concept. Take the essential features of two great products, mix them together, and come up with something even better. But often these attempts wind up as "neither fish nor foul" combos that seem just plain wrong, like the alien creature described in *Flight of the Navigator* ("sort of like a hippopotamus—but with feathers"). Once in a while, though, a person with exceptional foresight rubs together two familiar sticks and creates some fire.

The most inspired meddling of existing concepts in electric guitar history may well be the ES-335, one of Gibson's longest-running success stories. Conceived by Ted McCarty, the guitar did precisely what it was intended to do: It blended the resonance of a hollowbody with the high end and sustain of a solidbody. "Some players didn't like the acoustic electrics because they had the same problems all acoustic guitars had," Ted explained in July 1993. "They weren't loud enough, or if you did turn them up they were hard to control. And other players thought the sound of the Les Paul was too bright. So we needed something for the player who wanted the body reverberation of an acoustic and more highs than, say, an L-5 but not as much treble as a solidbody. The 335 was an in-between deal."

In between, and right on the money. Introduced in the spring of 1958, the guitar was not only a new model, it inaugurated a whole category of guitars called semi-hollowbodies or semi-solidbodies. While other electrics had combined solidbody and

B.B. King refined the ES-335 style into his own "Lucille" model– without f-holes.

The ES-335 started with a sunburst or natural finish, but cherry red was the family color for the '60s. From the dot-neck 335, the line ascended to the ES-345, with split-parallelograms and Vari-Tone/stereo controls, then on to the ES-355, with large pearl blocks and fancy peghead.

Beth Gwinn

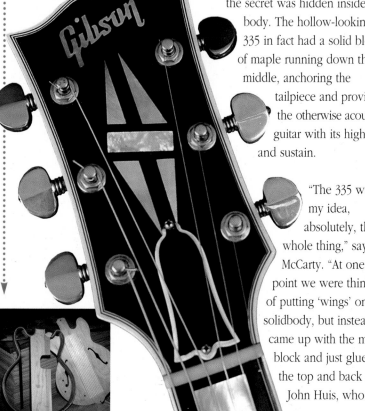

Masaki Rush

hollowbody details (Gretsch's "pseudo-solidbodies" come to mind), the 335's design derived from considerations of tonal versatility rather than production convenience or weight, and it wasn't camouflaged as a conventional instrument. One glance revealed the new Gibson's bold departure from the norm, and yet, as they had done six years before with the Les Paul, McCarty's crew was able to break new ground while maintaining the guitar's palpable Gibson personality, its Essence of Kalamazoo. Three years before, Gibson had introduced its thinbody style and now offered it on various single-cutaway and noncutaway hollowbodies such as the ES-125T, ES-225T, ES-350T, and Byrdland. Still, the 335 was unlike any predecessor. A double cutaway on a hollow guitar (or at least a guitar that looked hollow) was itself innovative—for any manufacturer. A stop tailpiece on a hollow-looking guitar not only was unusual but seemed physically impossible. But of course, the secret was hidden inside the body. The hollow-looking 335 in fact had a solid block of maple running down the middle, anchoring the tailpiece and providing the otherwise acoustic guitar with its high end and sustain.

"The 335 was my idea, absolutely, the whole thing," says McCarty. "At one point we were thinking of putting 'wings' on a solidbody, but instead we came up with the maple block and just glued the top and back to it. John Huis, who was the superintendent and vice president, and I sat down and came up with the idea to take some softer wood that we scored, and it provided a gluing surface for the other pieces."

Available in sunburst or blonde (also called natural), the debut model had rounded cutaways, a single-piece neck of mahogany, dot fingerboard markers, a stop tailpiece (also designed by McCarty), a long pickguard extending below the bridge, an orange oval label, and clear-top knobs. The sonic icing on the cake: patent-applied-for humbuckings. "Walt Fuller was the head of the electric lab," Ted McCarty recalls. "He worked on amplifiers and pickups. I said, fellows, some of our players are complaining about the noise, the squealing of the pickups, so we've got to come up with a way to buck that hum somehow. Seth Lover was on our team, too, and he went to work on a new pickup. That's how the name came about, and Seth designed it."

A cherry finish was offered beginning in late 1959. A shorter pickguard became stock in 1960, and block markers replaced the dots in mid 1962, about the time that patent-number pickups replaced the PAFs (a few stock guitars for the period have one of each type of pickup; some block-marker guitars have PAFs, and some '62s have dots). Another essential feature of the debut 335, the stop (or "stud") tailpiece, was gone by late 1964 or early 1965, replaced with a trapeze; this final change marked the passing of the classic 335, which years later would be dubbed the "dot neck" and would become one of the half-dozen or so most desirable vintage guitars in the world. There were three alterations that occurred in about 1970: the flat neck/headstock joint was reshaped in back to include a protruding volute, the orange label was dropped, and MADE IN U.S.A. was stamped on the back of the headstock. Once again, some stock guitars have an overlap of features: the newer volute and U.S.A. stamp, and the older orange label.

McCarty's other radical designs of 1958, the Flying V and the Explorer, were ahead of their time and drew mainly puzzled looks and raised eyebrows. The 335, though, was immediately accepted by players and dealers alike. "It got a great reception right off the bat," Ted recalls. "It started with a bang."

Its success immediately spawned two upscale versions, the ES-345TD (1959; triple-bound top, stereo wiring, Vari-Tone circuit, gold plating, split-parallelogram markers) and the top-of-the-line ES-355TD (a few in '58, according to shipping records, officially 1959; even more top binding, gold plating, split-diamond peghead inlay, block markers, ebony fingerboard, vibrato tailpiece, mono and stereo versions).

Beth Gwinn

© 1993 Jon Sievert

The hollow/solid appeal attracted players from many styles, including (from left) studio king Larry "Mr. 335" Carlton, bluesman Freddie King, and jazzer Lee Ritenour.

Over the years Gibson has introduced many variations on the semi-hollowbody theme, from reissues of the classic dot neck to a 12-string to the unique B. B. King artist model. The essential rightness of McCarty's vision has been readily demonstrated by the adoption of the 335 and its Gibson successors and offshoots by players ranging from Otis Rush to Lee Ritenour to John McLaughlin. Eric Clapton recorded with one during his fertile Cream period, Alvin Lee wowed 'em at Woodstock with one, and Chuck Berry has duckwalked across countless stages with various examples in recent decades. Because of its renowned versatility, the 335 is practically a staple on sessions (studio king Larry Carlton was so closely associated with the guitar that for years he happily bore the nickname "Mr. 335"). Ted McCarty's durable brainchild has become such a familiar archetype that to this day, 35 years after its appearance, a semi-hollow guitar is often called a "335-type"—even when made by another manufacturer.

SINGING THROUGH THE SIXTIES

BY THOMAS GOLDSMITH

Bob Dylan onstage, 1964, and recording **Bringing It All Back Home,** *1965. If the neck inlay looks familiar, check the label. It's a '29 Nick Lucas Special, reworked with a natural top, new bridge, and new pickguard.*

Gibson's response to the folk boom was a deluge of folk instruments.

The '60s, as they're popularly remembered, didn't really unfold until nearly the middle of the decade. In the 1960–61 television season *Gunsmoke* was king, the Oscar winner for best picture was *The Apartment,* and the most popular song was Marty Robbins's fine Western ballad "El Paso."

Then, along with miniskirts, swinging London, and the Kennedys, came the era-defining stars—the Beatles, Bob Dylan, the Rolling Stones, the Supremes, et al.

There were rumblings early on of the musical and social uproar that was to characterize the decade. By 1960, a clean-cut young folk group, the Kingston Trio, had started a landslide that built on the work of the Weavers and earlier groups. The sound was folk music through a bland blender, musically far from most indigenous sounds. But the folk boom's banjo, guitar, and vocal harmonies struck a deep chord with a nation that had been listening to even blander pop music. Folk *à la* Kingston Trio was well within the playing skills of almost anyone, and a sudden wave of new folk groups appeared not just on record labels, but on virtually every campus. Homemade music was hot.

Pop acts such as Percy Faith and Bryan Hyland, who continued to crank out '50s-style formula hits, were superseded creatively by pop stylists like Phil Spector, Gerry Goffin and Carole King, and Burt Bacharach and Hal David. Together with a vibrant rhythm & blues scene, highlighted by Ray Charles and the Drifters, these new sounds provided underpinnings for the adventuresome hits of the Beatles, Motown, etc.

Folk music hit even greater heights with the arrival of Peter, Paul and Mary, New York City performers flush with musical and show-biz polish. The trio was among several folk acts identified with the rise of the civil rights movement, as music began to accompany and express the decade's turning social tables. Notable among PP&M's hits were tunes by recently arrived New Yorker Bob Dylan, who had rambled in from Minnesota with eyes and ears open and a yen to meet his idol, ailing folk legend Woody Guthrie. Dylan's early appeal was not just in his imaginative songs, but also in his deep contact with the roots of folk music. Next to the rawness and spirit of Dylan's blues and country excursions, the carefully arranged harmonies of earlier folk popularizers sounded like the Mormon Tabernacle Choir.

Just as Dylan was touching the national consciousness for the first time, the climactic pop music event of the decade occurred with the January 1964 arrival of the Beatles in America. Talented, good-looking, and sarcastically funny, the Liverpool boys smashed conceptions of rock & roll, staid Britain, and hair lengths for men. They were, people said, a musical craze of no substance—a "direct hit on a guitar factory" in the Old Wave humor of Bob Hope. Happily ignoring all that, the "Fab Four" settled in as the prime movers of pop for the rest of the decade, bringing together Everly Brothers harmonies, R&B grooves, pop melodicism, and indefinable sparks of genius in captivating, three-minute slices of listening pleasure.

And the race was on. British acts headed by the raucous Rolling Stones and Dave Clark Five

invaded. Other Brits, including the Kinks, Herman's Hermits, Gerry and the Pacemakers, and the Who made it in America. U.S. bands started popping up to match the challenge and fun quotient of the Fabs: the Lovin' Spoonful, the Sir Douglas Quintet, the Young Rascals, the Mamas and the Papas, et al.

Meanwhile, rhythm & blues was going mainstream with the high-quality, danceable work of Motown acts like the Supremes, the Temptations, Marvin Gaye, and Smokey Robinson and the Miracles, as wall as the Memphis sounds of Otis Redding, Booker T. and the MGs, and Wilson Pickett. Country music had survived the threat of rock & roll, in Nashville by taking on some pop gloss and in California by twanging harder than ever in the Bakersfield sound of Buck Owens and Merle Haggard.

It was a great period of musical cross-pollination. The Beatles were copping licks from American soul and country music, while a whole U.S. generation was being reacquainted with American masters like Chuck Berry and Little Richard through the English band's recreation of their hits.

Cocking an ear to the Beatles' success and musical flair, Dylan came up with a new sound that blended his folk roots with the surrealism of French poetry and backbeat of rock & roll. Folk-rock, a term Dylan never liked, became a trend that produced hit acts such as the Byrds, Sonny and Cher, Simon and Garfunkel, and the Turtles, and also sowed seeds for the country-rock sound of the last years of the decade.

It's not possible to look back at the musical and social seismic shifts of the '60s without talking about drugs. By 1966, much of the work of Dylan and the Beatles dripped with trippy or stoned visions, which listeners freely interpreted as they wished. Then came a whole generation of bands built on the fondly remembered—but only briefly groovy—hippy era. The multi-colored sky was the limit for bands such as the Grateful Dead, Jefferson

© Beth Gwinn

Airplane, and Big Brother and the Holding Company in San Francisco, the Doors in Los Angeles, and mind-boggling guitarist Jimi Hendrix in London via New York. Everywhere, guitars were making new and very startling sounds.

The real hippy movement, of course, had already peaked by the time it made the cover of *Time* in the summer of 1967, but that didn't stop it from exploding worldwide following the release of the Beatles' mind-expanding masterpiece, *Sgt. Pepper's Lonely Hearts Club Band* in June of that year. Soon, every rock band worth its stacked amplifiers was releasing its own bid to match Pepper, with the Stones' *Their Satanic Majesties Request* only the most embarrassing.

The tie-dyed and paisley culture collapsed under its own weight following the summer of 1969, when a crowd of 500,000 descended on a farm in Woodstock, New York. Musically, the festival had its moments, but rainstorms turned it into a chilly mudbath, and the promoters took their own financial bath. The era, as well as the decade, was coming to an end. Jimi Hendrix, whose guitar-screaming version of the national anthem highlighted Woodstock, died in 1970. Dylan returned to a sparse country-based sound. The Beatles broke up. As if that weren't enough, the presidency of

Richard Nixon and the escalation of the Vietnam war brought a generation that had been high on music back down to a confused reality.

The Kennedys ruled and died, hemlines rose and fell, pop music grew very complex and then regrouped, people took tons of drugs and then reconsidered: A lot really did happen to *some* people in the '60s. Why, by the end of the decade the Number One television show was the innovative, mildly hip *Rowan and Martin's Laugh-in*. And *Gunsmoke?* It had slipped all the way to Number Two.

Pictorial Press Ltd., Star File

225

THE FLOWERING OF THE GUITAR INDUSTRY

BY TOM MULHERN

In 1960, as 70-year-old Dwight Eisenhower was about to turn over the Presidency to John F. Kennedy, the voice of the new generation and a man 27 years his junior, the youth of America was more than ready to embrace a new beginning. And it was no coincidence that the guitar industry was at the threshold of explosive growth.

In the first years of the '60s, it seemed that the guitar was everywhere. Radio and records, of course, had been the major media for music, but TV was becoming a major force, too. More sophisticated with each passing year (regular broadcasts had only begun in 1948), it helped to spread the six-string message. If Elvis or Ricky Nelson weren't wagging a guitar on the tube, then the Beatles were. Shows with "modern" names like *Shindig* and *Hullabaloo* joined *American Bandstand* to capture the burgeoning youth-oriented marketplace.

Guitars were literally everywhere in the '60s— if this Gibson catalog shot can be believed.

At the decade's beginning, the folk revival began in earnest, with songs of protest and alienation, angst and doom. The Cold War left its mark on the music, too, but if this was indeed the "Eve of Destruction," then—by golly—everyone was going out with an acoustic guitar in hand.

Electricity, anyone? Surf Music, that phenomenon with driving rhythm and reverb-drenched electric guitars, was beginning to catch fire. The obligatory guitar break in almost every song was a major hook; some practitioners like the Ventures and Dick Dale dispensed with the vocals and used the guitar to provide the melody, too. The British Invasion shifted the guitar demand into high gear. More precisely, it was like pouring gasoline on a fire: Every garage and basement in America seemed to sprout a band.

Gibson, with plant expansions in 1960, '62, and '64, was already geared up to produce more guitars for the rapidly expanding market, and the company's sales doubled between 1964 and '66. And Gibson wasn't alone. Fender was making 1,500 instruments a week at the end of 1964, surpassing $10 million in sales. When Leo Fender sold his company to CBS, it was a clear sign that the establishment was taking the guitar seriously as a means to profit. When the deal closed in early 1965, Fender cost CBS $13 million—about $2 million more than CBS had just paid for the New York Yankees. Similarly, other industrial concerns saw dollar signs in the guitar biz, and Avnet purchased Guild in 1966.

Other makers of high-grade guitars—Guild, Gretsch, Rickenbacker, and Martin—saw sales go through the roof. Martin, the conservative acoustic maker, even ventured into several electric guitars and amps and more than tripled guitar production during the decade. Harmony and Kay, supplying the lower end of the spectrum, were typical in that they couldn't keep pace with demand. More workers, more plant floor space, and more guitars: Sales soared.

The huge demand increased the number of imports, but it also provided a perfect opportunity for some upstart U.S. makers. Besides selling affordable, utilitarian instruments under its own name, New Jersey's Danelectro was supplying Silvertone guitars for Sears, then the world's largest retailer. Among the most famous "Dan-Os" is the

guitar that came with its own amp built into the case. Later in the 1960s, Danelectro's Coral line, which included an electric sitar, was launched.

Other small companies sprang up. Micro-Frets, of Frederick, Maryland, lasted from 1965 into the early '70s, building unusually shaped guitars and basses. In Green Bay, Wisconsin, the LaBaye Guitar Company made the 2 By 4, a virtually bodyless electric that came and went virtually unnoticed. Hallmark built the Swept Wing, another radically shaped (and not in a good way) instrument that never found its way into the hearts of millions. Standel marketed guitars made by Harptone of Newark, New Jersey. Inexplicably, despite quirky looks, loads of pickups and knobs, op-art advertising, and endorsements by one-hit (or no-hit) wonders like the Cyrkle and the Robbs, these birds became extinct in short order—the total number made was in the low hundreds.

Perhaps one of the biggest success stories among upstarts was Mosrite, which was actually founded in the 1950s and became a minor hit in the early-to-mid '60s, mostly on account of a tie-in with the Ventures, the guitar-heavy instrumental band. At its peak, the Bakersfield, California, company employed more than 100 workers. Mosrite was in and out and back in business in the ensuing two

decades, never leaving quite the same mark as its larger contemporaries. However, among the small companies, it was a biggie.

Only one company formed in the 1960s grew to sizable proportions later. In 1967, Ovation sprang fully grown from Charles Kaman's empire of aviation equipment. Ovation's round-back acoustic debuted, and a pickup in the bridge—rather than a magnetic pickup—was added. A market for amplified acoustic guitars developed as a result, and Ovation, which was staffed by over 300 people early on, quickly branched out into making semi-solidbody electrics and eventually solidbodies.

But for every new American company to come along in the 1960s, several more reached their zenith and headed for decline. And regardless of who was making the instruments, the guitar boom would last into the early 1970s.

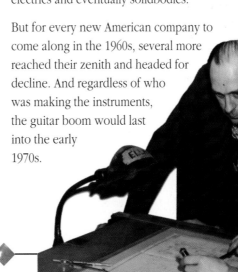

227

GIBSON IN ENGLAND

B Y   T O N Y   B A C O N

*Aladar de Vekey was
the first Gibson
teacher-agent in
England.*

*Aladar de Vekey's wife
also played and
endorsed Gibsons.*

An American guitar, especially a Gibson, was a rare prize for the aspiring British guitarist of the 1940s and '50s. Postwar austerity and restrictions on dealings in U.S. dollars meant that American guitars were not officially available in the U.K. There were really only three ways in which British musicians could get hold of a Gibson guitar back then: 1) if they were successful enough to visit the United States, 2) if they were wealthy enough to order an instrument direct from the maker, or 3) if they were lucky enough to secure one of the small number of secondhand Gibsons that turned up for sale in Britain.

Some of those secondhand guitars were the result of Gibson's original exports to the U.K. before World War II and even before World War I. Aladar de Vekey, a mandolinist, teacher, and "literaturist," according to Gibson catalogs, saw ads for Gibsons in *The Crescendo* around 1908 or '09. He ordered one mandolin, then another and another, becoming in essence Gibson's sole teacher-agent in Britain for the next 22 years. Around 1932, Gibson management began looking for a dealer in a more accessible location—de Vekey lived in the provincial town of Bournemouth—and the import dealership was granted to Francis Day & Hunter of London. Gibson's general manager Guy Hart made at least two business trips to Britain, in 1934 and 1937, to meet and encourage the FD&H people.

By the end of the '30s, FD&H were offering British players a line of some 30 Gibson instruments, including flattop, archtop, and electric guitars, mandolins, banjos, and ukuleles, plus cheaper Cromwell and Kalamazoo branded guitars. Cheapest was a

Gibson Uke-1 at £3/7/6 (pre-decimal prices were expressed in pounds/shillings/pence), most expensive a Super 400 at £90.

British musicians such as Harry Sherman of Carroll-Gibbons Savoy Orpheans and George Dickinson of Henry Hall's BBC Radio Band were typical of the talented guitarists attracted to the fine creations of Kalamazoo. "If you're not playing a Gibson, you're not playing a guitar," said Sherman in an FD&H ad in the musicians' newspaper, *Melody Maker,* in April 1933. But Britain's entry into World War II in 1939 and the cessation of Gibson's production a few years later meant that the FD&H connection had to stop.

It wasn't until 1959 that the British government finally lifted the postwar restrictions on American trade, and musicians in the U.K. once again had easier access to Gibson's guitars. Henri Selmer, a wholesale company in London run by Ben Davis and his brother Lou, began to import Gibsons from about 1960. A Selmer price list from September 1961 itemized a line of 16 Gibson electrics, basses, and flattops, ranging from a J-45 priced at 72 guineas to an L-5CESN at 327 guineas. (Luxury items were often priced then in "guineas," presumably as the word itself sounded extravagant; a guinea equalled £1/1/-.)

London's pop music scene of the 1960s had begun to swing into action, and Selmer's retail shop in the Charing Cross Road was situated in the heart of an area in central London alive with music publishers and instrument retailers, a mecca for both the budding and successful musician. Most of the staff at Selmer's shop were players, some of whom went on to greater fame—at various times John McLaughlin, Paul Kossoff, and Tony Hatch worked

4 POPULAR ENGLISH GUITARISTS WITH THEIR Gibson

BERT THOMAS
London

BILL TRINGHAM
London

HARRY SHERMAN
London

HARRY DAVIS
London

there. Doug Ellis, who in the 1990s runs Gibson's U.K. importer, Rosetti, was a junior salesman at the Selmer shop in the 1960s. He remembers a bustling, exciting place where stars and ordinary customers jostled side by side for the latest musical instruments. "One Saturday a national newspaper came in to take photographs," Ellis remembers, "because they couldn't believe you could get so many people in such a relatively small space at one time. It was horrendous! But Selmer did enormous business then. The boss of the shop at the time was a wonderful guy called Jack Moore, whose main claim to fame was playing the Clavioline on [British comedian] Jimmy Edwards's song 'Little Red Monkey.' I remember it being a very happy time. We were all playing four or five nights a week as well as working in the shop, and it was a delight."

Famous musicians regularly visited the Selmer shop. Ellis remembers Hendrix dropping by and recalls selling his own ES-330 to Andy Summers (then in Zoot Money's Big Roll Band). The Beatles also came in a few times. "I remember them buying a Gibson Fuzztone on one occasion," says Ellis. "Funnily enough, being a weekday morning, the place wasn't swarming with screaming people. Later on, dear old Mal Evans, the Beatles' roadie—a huge, gentle, Liverpudlian giant, one of the nicest guys you could choose to meet—asked if I'd take some left-handed guitars with him up to Paul McCartney, at his home, so that he could have a look at them. They were mostly Gibsons, including a lefty SG Standard.

"We had an enjoyable afternoon, at the end of which I said, 'Well, I really must be going, because my wife's in hospital having our second child.' Paul gave me a fearful telling-off. 'You silly sod,' he said, 'what the hell you doing round here when your wife's in hospital?' So he wrote her a very nice little note, apologizing for keeping me away."

Gibsons were successfully marketed in England before World War II severed the connection.

Guitarists jammed into the small Selmer shop in London, pictured here in the May 1969 issue of Best Instrumental. *Courtesy Tony Bacon.*

Steve Howe bought his favorite guitar, an ES-175, at Selmer's, and he featured it on his 1993 CD cover The Grand Scheme of Things.

Jeff Beck caught the Gibson bug after seeing Eric Clapton play a Les Paul with John Mayall's Bluesbreakers at a club gig in south London. "I already knew Les Pauls sounded good because Jimmy Page had a Custom," Jeff says. "Those models had this deep sound, and I really needed that power in a three-piece, to help fill out the sound. So I went sorting around. There was a guy at Selmer's shop said he'd got a good one, and that's how I got my first Standard... which was subsequently stolen."

Steve Howe was a regular visitor to Selmer's shop in the 1960s. "I'd left school when I was 15 and had nothing to do," he remembers. "So I'd get on the bus to the Charing Cross Road, walk into a guitar shop, and go, 'Can I play that guitar?' They didn't ask if you were going to buy it, they'd say, sure, go ahead and play it. Things were laidback then. And although the other shops were worth a visit, the Selmer shop was Gibson Land. So I'd be sitting in Selmer's playing away, and guys like Doug Ellis would say hello, they'd ask what you were up to, and you'd meet all kinds of people. Albert Lee used to come in and I'd rub shoulders with him; he called me Face. I bought my very first Gibson guitar at Selmer's, my prized Gibson ES-175D, in 1964."

Robert Fripp went to the Charing Cross Road area at the end of 1968. One of the members of his new band King Crimson had managed to persuade a wealthy uncle to loan them a substantial amount of money to kit out the fledgling group. "I thought I was going to get a Fender Strat," Fripp recalls, "but there was this Les Paul Custom staring at me from a shop window. Four hundred quid. The salesman was pretty loathsome. He said, 'All I have to do is phone Eric Clapton and he'll buy it.' And I thought, then why haven't you phoned Eric Clapton and why hasn't he bought it? I had a briefcase with this very large sum of cash in it. So I asked for the manager, opened the briefcase, and showed him the money. I got the Custom for £375, and walked

out with it. It remains to this day the finest Les Paul I've ever played, and I've played a few."

Gibson guitars have continued to attract British players through the years, despite the shifting of background business arrangements and the growth of competition from overseas. Looking back now at one of the first British advertisements for Gibson the 1930s, it is at once depressing and inspiring to note how little has changed. "Your decision to act today without delay may place you years ahead in music," it reads. "Of all the instruments made, Gibsons have helped more musicians to reach their goal—success—than any other." Ad copywriters seem to have been as impudently partial then as they are today, while the attraction of real American instruments to real British musicians also appears timeless.

John McLaughlin was a clerk at Selmer's before becoming an influential jazz artist.

THE PEAK OF PRODUCTION

BY WALTER CARTER

Blueswoman Jessie Mae Hemphill played Gibson's best selling thinbody of the early '60s, the ES-125TC. Trey Harrison, Memphis Blues Museum

"B.B. Mr. Blues Himself" is obviously not B.B. King, nor is his guitar an ES-355 "Lucille." The P-90 pickups are the mark of the cheaper, fully hollow ES-330 model. Center for Popular Music, Middle Tennessee State University

Y ou couldn't play "Tip Toe Through the Tulips," "Satin Doll," or even "Hound Dog" with just two guitar chords. But you could play "Tom Dooley"—the Kingston Trio's folk hit of 1959. Folk music's anyone-can-play attitude spilled over into all kinds of music, and the '60s became the era of greatest growth in the history of Gibson. It was a time of new guitar models, new amplifiers, new facilities, and record sales figures.

SALES LEADERS

In 1965, Gibson shipped over 100,000 instruments (the total includes almost 20,000 Epiphones) for the only time in history. It wasn't as if Gibson president Ted McCarty could do no wrong. It just didn't matter. So many people were buying guitars and amplifiers that slow-selling models never threatened the company's success. As had often been the case throughout Gibson history, the best-seller list from the 1960s was dominated by 1s and 0s and other low-end model numbers. For the record here are the award winners, by category:

Electric archtop, thinbody: ES-125TC and ES-330. The low-end cutaway and double-cutaway models, respectively, vied for top honors in the early 1960s, but both were passed by the ES-335 (the least expensive semi-hollow model) in the later 1960s.

Electric archtop, full-depth: No award given (a model must sell over 500 in at least two years to be eligible).

Acoustic archtop: No award given.

Artist endorsement model: tba on page 236.

Flattop: LG-0 and LG-1. In most years, these small-bodied cheapies easily outpaced the second-place models, the dreadnought J-45 and J-50.

Solidbody: Melody Makers. While the low-end SG Jr. outsold its family members in the SG line, it wasn't in the same league with the even-lower-end MMs.

Classical: C-0 and C-1. Each of these two plain-janes bettered all the other classical models combined. The C-0 took the award for best single year, with 3,979 shipped in 1967.

Bass: EB-0. This single-pickup, SG-style bass set a

Steve LaVere ©1993 Mimosa Records Productions, Inc.

record for bass shipments in 1965 with 2,006, then upped it in 1969 to 3,018.

Model of the Decade: LG-0. With 9,924 instruments in 1964, this small, all-mahogany guitar set a single-model record for the '60s. To put that number in an industry perspective, Gibson sold 50 percent more LG-0s in 1964 than Martin's *total* guitar production (6,299).

ARTIST MODELS

Profits are made from the high-volume, low-end models, but reputations are built on finer stuff. And Gibson had some fine names on guitars of the 1960s. Les Paul's name was still there on the SG line, although it would be gone by 1963, not to return until 1968. Nashville players Billy Byrd and Hank Garland had their names combined on the thinbody, short-scale Byrdland in 1955, but their model lost some name recognition after Byrd left Ernest Tubb's band in 1959. Garland's incapacitating auto accident of September 1961 would effectively orphan the Byrdland. As the 1960s got underway, Ted McCarty looked not just

At a 1969 filming of **A Night at the Barrelhouse,** *T-Bone Walker, left, plays a Barney Kessel, with its unusual full-depth double-cutaway shape. Shuggie Otis plays Gibson's star thinbody of the late '60s, the ES-335.*

In 1972 in Memphis, Jimmy DeBerry plays a B-25, the popular '60s successor to the LG-2, as Walter Horton contemplates his harp.

Stephen C. LaVere, ©1989 Mimosa Records Productions, Inc.

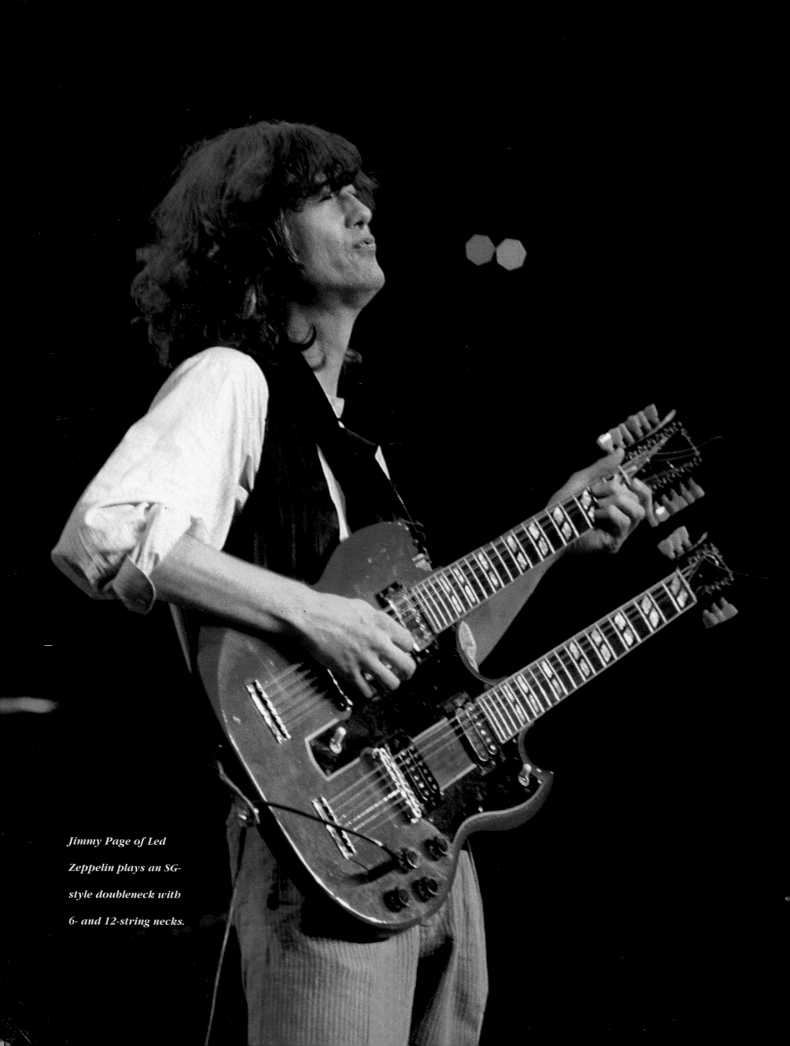

Jimmy Page of Led Zeppelin plays an SG-style doubleneck with 6- and 12-string necks.

The Everly Brothers—

singers and guitars.

Courtesy **The Tennessean**

Tal Farlow's Tal Farlow.

Artists and their models:

Howard Roberts, left,

and Tal Farlow.

Country star Roy Clark

with a '60s Byrdland.

Center for Popular

Music, Middle Tennessee

State University

for one new endorser, but for an entire line of "Artist" models. Several guitarists were making names for themselves in the growing rock & roll crowd—Link Wray ("Rumble"), Scotty Moore (Elvis's early hits), and Duane Eddy ("Rebel Rouser")—but McCarty's list was dominated by jazzers:

Johnny Smith (1961–1988). Smith had had his own top-of-the-line model with Guild (which became the Artist Award after he moved to Gibson). His Gibson was built along the lines of his personal guitar made by John D'Angelico and was essentially an acoustic archtop with a floating pickup. It was slightly different in shape and scale length (25 inches) from any other Gibson.

Barney Kessel (1961–74). Kessel had impeccable jazz credentials, having played with Charlie Parker and Lester Young in the 1940s and in a trio with Oscar Peterson and Ray Brown in the early '50s. In addition to his solo albums, he was a busy Los Angeles session player. Like Smith, he came to Gibson directly from a competitor. He had endorsed a line of Kay electrics, and McCarty gave him his own mini-line of two Gibsons. Both had a full-depth hollow body with a pointed double-cutaway shape.

Tal Farlow (1962–70). Farlow's reputation was built on his trio work with vibist Red Norvo and bassist Charles Mingus in the early '50s and on his solo albums. He was a curious choice for a Gibson artist model, since he had quit the music business in 1958 (he has since returned). His model was just as curious, with binding material inlaid on the cutaway

bout to simulate a scroll and a fingerboard inlay pattern that was an upside-down version of the J-200's.

Everly Brothers (1962–71). By far, the biggest stars of the Gibson roster, Don and Phil Everly had cut their teeth on Gibsons. Their father Ike had been a contemporary of Merle Travis and one of the first to use the thumb-and-finger picking style that came to be known by Travis's name. Don and Phil had played various Gibsons onstage from the beginning of their recording career in 1956. Their endorsement model was a flattop with an oversized bridge (designed by Ike), oversized double-pickguards, and stars on the fingerboard.

Trini Lopez (1963–70). A nightclub act, Lopez had a few Top 40 hits singing folk songs while he strummed

enthusiastically on an electric guitar. He was as incongruous a folk star as he was a choice to endorse a guitar. Make

Johnny Smith with his Gibson Johnny Smith.

The best-selling Trini Lopez, in custom-ordered Pelham blue finish.

that *two* guitars. Two *incongruous* guitars. The Lopez Standard was essentially an ES–335 with diamond-shaped soundholes and a Fender-style headstock (all six tuners on the same side). The Lopez Deluxe was essentially a Barney Kessel with the six-on-a-side headstock and paired-diamonds on the fingerboard.

Howard Roberts (1964–70). Jazz player Howard Roberts was an Epiphone endorsee. Roberts did not see the point of f-holes: The pickguard covered up one and the player's arm covered the other. An oval soundhole gave his electric archtop an acoustic sound that the player could hear. The body was full-depth with a pointed cutaway. A fancier version, the Howard Roberts Custom was added in 1965.

And the winner is… In the category of artist endorsement models, the award for the biggest seller of the 1960s goes to: The Trini Lopez Standard. It may have been the least extraordinary model from the least talented guitarist, but like Trini's recordings, his guitar left the competition standing at the starting gate. In 1967, for example, Gibson shipped 783 Lopez Standards—more than all the Smith, Farlow, Kessel, Lopez Deluxe, Everly, Roberts, Byrdland, Super 400CES, and L-5CES models *combined.*

FIREBIRDS

None of Gibson's '60s endorsers had the kind of pop success—at least not as guitarists—that Les Paul had had in the '50s, nor were the guitars themselves as new and

The Everlys were playing Gibson J-200s long before the Everly Brothers model. From left are Phil, father Ike, mother Margaret, and Don.

innovative as Les's had been. And despite their talents, Smith, Farlow, Kessel, and Roberts were jazz players in a decade of folk and rock music. In 1963, McCarty decided to go after the rockers. Five years had passed since the Explorer and Flying V failures of 1958. Maybe the time was finally right for a bold, new design.

New automobile designs out of Detroit had caught McCarty's eye, and he hired the man responsible, Ray Dietrich, to draw up some guitars. Dietrich sketched a series of models, and one was chosen. The new guitar bucked tradition with a treble-side horn longer than the bass horn—the reverse of conventional style. The headstock, too, was reversed, with all the tuners on the treble side. To avoid an awkward tuning procedure, banjo-style tuners went straight out the back of the headstock. The neck went all the way through the body. The pickups were unique: mini-humbuckers with no visible polepieces. The new creations were dubbed Firebirds, and a flock of four models debuted in 1963. A new set of custom color finishes was introduced just for them.

The Firebirds flew. They didn't soar, but they were no turkeys.

Then Gibson "fixed" them. The first fix was understandable: putting the tuners on the bass side of the headstock for easier access. But then Fender complained that the Firebird infringed on its patented offset-waist body design, so the body was changed to a non-reversed shape and made shorter and fatter-looking. The neck-through was replaced by a glued-in neck. And on the lower two models, single-coil soapbar pickups were substituted for the Firebird-style humbuckers. The only thing that was really fixed was the Firebirds' goose. They were gone by 1969.

©John Bellissimo

Johnny Winter has played his blues on Firebirds since the '60s.

Firebird III, polaris white.

Dan Loftin, courtesy Gruhn Guitars

The Dove flew above the Gibson dreadnought line in the '60s.

Gibson doublenecks were available with any neck. The "Joanie" neck on this one is a five-string banjo.

The Epiphone line blossomed along with the Gibson line in the mid '60s.

FLATTOPS

The flattop line in the 1950s was made up primarily of three styles: the maple-body jumbo with circular lower bout (J-200 and smaller J-185), the mahogany dreadnoughts with squared-off lower bout (J-45, J-50, and fancier SJ) and the LG (for Little Guitar) models.

The line was expanded considerably to cater to the emerging folk crowd. The Hummingbird of 1960 brought a new body shape to Gibson: the "square-shouldered" Martin-style dreadnought with a mahogany body. A 12-string followed in 1961. The next year a fancy, maple-body square-shouldered dreadnought, the Dove, debuted with a mother-of-pearl dove in the pickguard and two abstract dove shapes in the bridge.

ALL GOOD THINGS...

The Epiphone line followed the same upward curve through the early '60s. Thinbody electrics, solidbody electrics, flattops—just about everything sold well.

Gibson amplifiers rose in prestige as well as sales, and they boomed along with the guitars into the mid '60s.

Gibson's growth was tremendous—physically as well as fiscally. A plant addition in 1960 brought the floor space to 120,000 square feet. A new 20,000-square-foot building was acquired for electronics production in 1962. Two years later, a 60,000-square-foot building was bought for amplifier assembly, and the last corner of the city block at Parsons St. was filled by yet another factory addition.

... COME TO AN END

When would it ever end? All too soon.

The guitar market—the American-made guitar market, that is—fell almost as fast as it had risen. By the end of the '60s, Gibson guitar production was half of what it had been in mid-decade. Fifty thousand instruments a year, of course, was still an awful lot—but it was really awful for a company that had just expanded to meet a demand for a hundred thousand. Epiphone fell from about 20 percent of total units shipped to around 7 percent, and plans were made to move Epi production to Japan.

Ted McCarty had left just in time. He and his right-hand man John Huis bought Paul Bigsby's vibrola company in 1965 and moved it from Los Angeles to Kalamazoo. Huis left Gibson immediately while McCarty stayed on until a replacement could be found. After McCarty, Gibson fell quickly from its best years in history to losing a million dollars a year, beginning a fall from grace that would last almost 20 years.

1966–1985

THE
RENDELL/NORLIN
ERA

©John Peden

Gibson provided the power for the power trio Cream. Eric Clapton plays a custom-painted SG Standard; Jack Bruce plays an EB-0 bass.

STAN RENDELL

BY TOM MULHERN

Gibson president Ted McCarty left on June 30, 1966, ending an era of innovation that saw the rise of the electric guitar (the solidbody in particular) and explosive growth in guitar sales. The post-McCarty years would bring the reintroduction of the Les Paul, the end of the Chicago Musical Instrument Co.'s ownership of Gibson, the opening of Gibson's Nashville facility, and a bumpy ride through economic up- and downturns. The man who held the reins through this troubled time, from 1968 to the end of 1976, was Stanley Rendell.

Born on November 11, 1914, in the tiny town of Elkhorn, Wisconsin, Rendell graduated grammar school from a one-room schoolhouse and completed high school before marrying and setting off for a job in Chicago with Belmont Radio, the largest radio maker in the world. He spent 20 years in manufacturing at Belmont, but when the company moved east, he took a job as director of manufacturing at another radio concern, the Hallicrafters Co., which had negotiated a deal with CMI to build Lowrey organs. In 1963, CMI president M. H. Berlin offered Rendell a job as vice president of manufacturing for CMI.

Overseeing factories around the country and around the world entailed constant travel. After five years, Rendell told Berlin he was tired of his itinerant lifestyle and was going to quit if he couldn't settle down and run one plant. He asked to head the Olds horn plant in Fullerton, California, but Berlin told him, "Oh, you could run that plant with one hand tied behind your back," and

©1993 Jon Sievert

convinced him to take on the task of turning around Gibson's manufacturing. After McCarty's departure, Berlin had brought in an accountant, Albert Stanley, to run the show temporarily, but under Stanley, Gibson was losing about a million dollars a year.

Production was Rendell's specialty, and he immediately set about making Gibson's production run smoothly. His first big challenge was, he says, separating the amp, string, and guitar manufacturing, which were all intertwined. "The problem was the steelworkers union," he details (the company had been unionized during World War II, when the plant was making metal-intensive war products). "They were dictating everything. If you needed someone to be a string winder, you had to post the job. Well, maybe someone who was a guitar sander would say, 'I'm tired of sanding; I want to be a string winder.' So, that person became a string winder, and now you're suddenly short a sander. So you had to post the sander's job, and maybe a string winder would say, 'I'm tired of winding strings; I'd like to be a sander.' It was like seven transfers when one job was posted. This was a terrible situation."

Rendell's solution was simple: Move all string manufacturing from Kalamazoo across Lake Michigan to Elgin, Illinois. This reduced the crossover from job to job, and increased efficiency both in guitar production and in string making. It also sent a message to the union that Rendell wasn't going to mess around.

Jim Morrison checks out Robby Krieger's Gibson SG at a Doors concert, ca. 1970. Courtesy Robby Krieger

Sleepy LaBeef plays an ES-150DC, a 1969 addition that put the 335 body shape on a full-depth hollow body.

Stan Rendell, 1971.

David Lindley, playing in 1968 with the Kaleidoscope, found the sound he wanted from a vintage harp guitar (with new fingerboard inlays).

With a company of 1,100 employees and 140 of them salaried management, the levels of bureaucracy were also an obstacle to communication and production. Rendell solved the problem by eliminating 80 salaried positions. The money saved was put into one of Gibson's biggest equipment purchases ever, in an effort to streamline production even further.

Rendell also instituted a purchase order system for a more efficient relationship with CMI. Before

Rendell, the CMI sales force would try to predict what guitars they would need for the year, and the workers at Kalamazoo would build accordingly. Inevitably, lots of guitars weren't sold, and the factory took the blame for "overproducing." No longer: "I said that we wouldn't manufacture anything without a purchase order," Rendell explains.

The Epiphone line felt the cut of Rendell's efficiency axe. New competition from low-priced

"camouflage" finish intended to cover flaws. "They were having problems with the wood checking," he explains. "See, that's a laminated top and back, three pieces. You take the center piece and run it through a gluer that puts glue on front and back. You then set it between two other pieces, cross-banding it—that's with the grain running one way on one side and the other piece going the opposite. You'd set that in a press, and the pressure would form the top. Well, the wood was checking, so they were filling those checks with wood filler and spraying the guitars sparkling burgundy. But some of those guitars went through finishing as much as seven times. We took an inventory, and there were about 2,000 of them as works-in-progress.

"I notified Chicago that we were no longer going to produce Electric Spanish [ES-series] guitars until we learned how to do it. We stripped off the parts we could salvage and then sawed up the guitars and put them in the incinerator. That cost a lot of money, probably a quarter-million dollars. But that's what we did. It took about six months until we could figure out what we were doing wrong. It was a moisture problem in the wood. So we put in a little kiln so that we could control it, and from then on we never had any problem with Electric Spanish guitars."

Other construction moves had mixed results. Neck and body designs were changed to add strength and probably to save money in the process. The one-piece mahogany neck (used on all but the high-end models) was replaced with a laminated three-piece mahogany neck, beginning in the late '60s; by 1975, some models sported a three-piece maple neck. The area where the neck becomes the peghead was strengthened, beginning in late 1969, by the addition of a "volute" or extra lump of wood. The weighty, solid mahogany bodies of

The Les Paul Signature Bass of 1973 did not last long, but the Jefferson Airplane's Jack Casady still cherishes his.

foreign-made guitars squeezed Epiphone out of its market niche as a less-expensive alternative to Gibson. Rendell fought fire with fire and moved Epiphone production to Japan in 1969.

Gibson's problems extended from the corporate level down to basic instrument construction. One day, while walking through the finishing department, Rendell noticed that many ES-335s (semi-hollowbody electrics) were being painted "sparkling burgundy," which he calls a

© 1979 Ebet Roberts

The Deluxe is usually looked down on as the poor man's Les Paul, but the Who's Pete Townshend played several, which he numbered.

With no Les Paul Standard available, Duane Allman got a big sound from the mini-humbucking pickups of a Les Paul Deluxe.

the Les Paul Deluxe and Custom hardly needed strengthening, but they were revamped to include a thin maple laminate between two pieces of mahogany. Players didn't like the volute, and the laminations, while probably not affecting the technical quality of the instruments, certainly made them look cheaper. The "pancake" body went out in 1977, the peghead volute was abandoned in 1981, and the three-piece neck was phased out over the course of the '80s.

Another construction change was not so benign and in fact was an omen of trouble ahead for the Gibson name. Flattops were being returned for warranty work—most of it due to the top being convoluted by the bridge pulling on it—at a rate of 14 percent, compared with a 0.75 percent return rate for solidbody electrics. The solution was to add a second set of "X" braces underneath the top, which did indeed eliminate practically all top movement, including the vibration that provides the fundamental tone and volume of an acoustic guitar. At least the huge number of warranty returns was dramatically reduced.

In Rendell's first year, he reduced the Gibson plant's losses to only $250,000, and afterwards the plant showed a consistent profit. In the meantime, however, Gibson's parent company was having larger problems. For more than a decade, CMI had grown quickly along with the booming market for musical instruments, acquiring Lowrey Organs (1956), Epiphone (1957), F. E. Olds & Son band instruments, Buffet woodwinds, Armstrong flutes, Maestro Electronics, William Lewis & Son Violin Company, Story & Clark pianos, Turner Musical Instruments Limited (Canada's largest musical-equipment distributor), L. D. Heater (a northwestern U.S.

246

distributor), Krauth & Benninghofen (maker of music stands), and Symmetricut Reed Co. Accordion lines included Cordovox, Scandalli, Bell, and Dallape.

Storm clouds first gathered at the piano end of CMI's business. In order to meet the demand of the expanding piano and organ market, CMI built a new Lowrey plant in Asheville, North Carolina. From day one, the Asheville facility was a black hole, draining huge amounts of money from CMI's coffers. M. H. Berlin quickly shut down the plant and sold off all the machinery, but CMI's stock, which was traded on the New York Stock Exchange, eroded.

In the '60s, with the world—and especially the United States—putting so much emphasis on youth and the expanding pop culture, music equipment manufacturers seemed like good investments to larger companies. CBS had purchased Fender in 1965. Baldwin, the organ maker, had purchased Gretsch, and Avnet had bought Guild. With CMI's stock price depressed, it was only a matter of time before the company was taken over.

Ecuadorian Company Limited (ECL for short) began buying up CMI's stock, and on December 19, 1969, became the proud owner of the largest distributor of musical instruments, as well as one of the world's most important guitar makers. A few months later, ECL was renamed Norlin, using the first syllable of ECL chairman Norton Stevens's name and the last syllable from M. H. Berlin's name. Stan Rendell tells how the change hurt Berlin: "We were both at the Mayo Clinic in Minnesota. I was in his room, and the phone rang. And when he hung up, he had tears in his eyes. I said, 'What's going on, boss?' And he said, 'They've just changed the name of the company from Chicago Musical Instruments to Norlin, and they never even consulted me.' That'll give you some idea of how they worked."

Allman Brothers Band Archives, Star File

THE QUIET AFTER THE BOOM

BY TOM MULHERN

t was as if the British Invasion had fattened up the American guitar market, only for it to be devoured by a new invasion of Japanese guitar makers. The boom decade of the '60s saw tremendous growth in the quantity and quality of guitars by Japanese companies, and by the end of the decade, Japanese products were ubiquitous in the U.S. marketplace.

But did Japan have elaborate plans to take over the U.S. guitar market? Or were Japanese makers just learning and growing as the American manufacturers stagnated and stumbled in their attempts to meet the skyrocketing demand? Perhaps it was a bit of both.

Gibson catalogs, 1970.

Following World War II, the U.S. had a lock on most manufacturing. The most productive workers in the world—Americans—made the bulk of the world's TVs, radios, phonographs, autos, and, not surprisingly, musical instruments. The hyperactivity in manufacturing that began during the war actually increased in the U.S. as consumers dived headlong into a virtual feeding frenzy of spending.

In the meantime, Japan was struggling to rebuild every facet of its infrastructure following its crushing defeat and destruction of its manufacturing base. It scrambled to get into the emerging global economy, regardless of the country's lack of natural resources or ability to make many products that rivaled the quality produced by the U.S. It's no secret that most

Americans looked down their noses at products from Japan, viewing them as cheap, cheesy imitations of American goods. Little did they suspect that Japan was learning with each misstep and would eventually become a manufacturing superpower.

By the mid 1950s, Nanyo Boeki in Nagoya began exporting copies of Stella acoustics. By the 1960s, low-quality electrics from Japan reached America's shores and stores, reaching into Sears and Montgomery Ward establishments. At first their effect was negligible on the manufacturers of higher-priced guitars— Gibson among them. However, it was murder on the companies that had been supplying the low end of the market—namely Kay and Harmony. Japan had gained a foothold.

Harmony's downfall was fairly typical. A maker of low- and moderate-priced instruments, Harmony was vulnerable to competition from abroad. At its peak in the mid '60s, Harmony had about 600 employees, producing approximately 350,000 instruments per year. Harmony's president, Charles A. Rubovits, said in Tom Wheeler's *American Guitars*, "At one time Harmony made half of the industry's guitars, three-quarters of the ukuleles, and a major share of the other instruments like banjos and mandolins. We produced more than all the other companies combined." A steep downslide led to Harmony going belly-up by 1974.

Kay's story is similar. They were tripping all over themselves trying to meet production during the

©Roger H. Siminoff

©Beth Gwinn

In 1973, Billy Gibbons led the power blues sound of ZZ Top with a sunburst Les Paul Standard.

Gibson factory, Kalamazoo, 1972.

While Japan conquered the low-end guitar market, performers stuck to their American guns. Duane Allman slides along on a '60s SG Standard.

Duane Allman's guitar case, 1971.

company's rapid growth in the first half of the 1960s, and quality slipped. Acquired by jukebox maker Seeburg in 1965 and then sold to Valco (which made National and Supro guitars) in '67, Kay skidded into the abyss before the sun came up on the 1970s. (The names of many defunct companies outlived the companies themselves, with Kay, Washburn, Epiphone, Harmony, and Vega later applied to imports.)

Japan's Teisco switched in the mid 1950s from hollowbodies to rock & roll electrics, and by the mid '60s, Teisco was the biggest single Japanese guitar exporter, shipping more than 100,000 guitars per year in '66 or '67. Teisco's guitars were licensed for sale under several other names, the most prominent being St. George. (Teisco eventually lost its grip on the low end of the guitar market when it pursued the development of combo organs.)

Most '60s imports came from the Far East, but not all. Baldwin imported Burns electrics from England in the middle and late '60s; Eko guitars came from Italy. Neither made great inroads into the U.S. market. Vox, whose guitars were popularized by the Rolling Stones, and whose amps were tied to the Beatles, specialized in teardrop and irregular geometric-shaped guitars during the '60s, but like their fellow European models (Voxes were built in England and Italy), never made a huge impact. German guitars made a smaller impact, led by the Hofner violin-shaped hollowbody bass popularized by Paul McCartney.

By the 1970s, with a large part of the American market sewn up, Japanese companies such as Yamaha and Ibanez shifted their focus from producing copies of American guitars to designing their own. Part of the reason was confidence in their own abilities to produce better instruments. But a larger part was that Taiwan and Korea, with much lower labor costs than Japanese companies,

were undercutting Japan in the low-end market. No matter. After their advances in the American marketplace, these Asian exporters were now a force to be reckoned with.

Jazzmen Barney Kessel, left, and Herb Ellis, 1974.

©1993 Jon Sievert

Little Joe led the Latinaires with an ES-335. Center for Popular Music, Middle Tennessee State University

Charlie Daniels with the Southern rocker's standard equipment, a Les Paul Standard.

SPLINTERED SOUNDS

BY MICHAEL McCALL

The repercussions of the cultural revolution of the 1960s—including its social upheavals and political pressures—continued to change the world in the following decade. The U.S. invasion of Cambodia in 1970 led to political demonstrations across the country, including one on the campus of Kent State University, where four students were slain by National Guardsmen. Three years later, the end of bombing in Cambodia officially marked the end of U.S. combat in Southeast Asia after 12 years.

In 1971, the Supreme Court unanimously ruled that the busing of students may be ordered to achieve racial desegregation. The same year, the voting age was lowered to 18. In 1972, the Supreme Court deemed the death penalty unconstitutional, only to reverse the decision four years later.

Also in 1971, the United Nations recognized Communist China and unseated Taiwan. In 1972, President Richard Nixon visited China for eight days in an unprecedented trip. The same year, five men were arrested for breaking into the Democratic National Committee headquarters at the Watergate complex in Washington, D.C. Within a year, Nixon accepted the blame but not the responsibility for the scandal that became known as Watergate. In 1973, Vice President Spiro Agnew resigned because of tax evasion charges. In 1974, Nixon resigned, and Vice President Gerald Ford became the 38th President. Two years later, Jimmy Carter defeated Ford in national elections for the Presidential post.

As the 1970s started, music fragmented much as the United States had been separated into several ideological camps. At one time, popular music appealed to all ages and all classes, whether it was big band music, pop vocalists, or Motown. What had started to splinter with the advent of rock & roll now separated in several directions. Perhaps the bitter falling apart of the Beatles served as an omen: The age when America seemed to be swept up wholly into a musical trend ended as radio no longer conformed to one Top 40 chart. Instead, stations preferred to specialize in a particular style, dividing the audience into cultural camps.

"Rumble" man Link Wray still rumbles in 1979 on an SG Standard.

Irish folkie-turned-folk-rocker Donovan turned up in 1979 with an old ES-350.

Jimmy Buffett plays an ES-335, 1978.

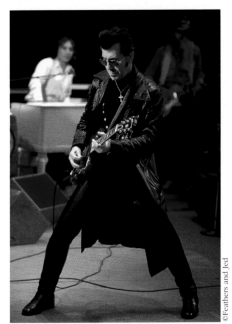

©Feathers and Jed

©Beth Gwinn

©Beth Gwinn

©Clark Thomas

Lynyrd Skynyrd's Gary
Rossington plays a
sunburst Les Paul;
bassist Leon Wilkinson
plays a late-'60s non-
reverse Thunderbird IV.

Jimi Stratton

As the 1970s progressed, fans of a more tranquil style of music were given soft rock by such acts as the Carpenters, Bread, Tony Orlando & Dawn, and Carly Simon. Later in the decade, this contemporary style of adult pop boomed, thanks to the success of Fleetwood Mac, Peter Frampton, Boz Scaggs, and Journey.

Those desiring a more ostentatious and complex style were fed progressive rock by Yes, Pink Floyd, Genesis, Queen, Emerson Lake & Palmer, Jethro Tull, Chicago, the Electric Light Orchestra, and Steely Dan. For those who wanted a sound of regional pride that was musical yet earthy, there was the Southern rock of the Allman Brothers, Lynyrd Skynyrd, the Marshall Tucker Band, the Charlie Daniels Band, and Black Oak Arkansas.

Funk-rock also stepped out to the beat, thanks to the Ohio Players, Earth Wind & Fire, Tower of Power, the Average White Band, Rufus, and Parliament/Funkadelic. Before long, the beat became faster and more uniform, and disco music transformed dance floors everywhere, bringing with it such stars as Gloria Gaynor, Donna Summer, the Bee Gees, Thelma Houston, Chic, and the Village People.

On the other end of the spectrum, hard rock took on a more aggressive sound that also grew more formulaic with time. Bands like Slade, Humble Pie, Foghat, Uriah Heep, Aerosmith, Bad Company, Deep Purple, Blue Oyster Cult, Heart, AC/DC, Foreigner, and Van Halen took their cues from the Who, the Rolling Stones, Cream, Led Zeppelin, and Jimi Hendrix. But the results had more of a streamlined structure than the adventurous rock of the late 1960s.

On the more outrageous side, several rock acts copped a more audacious, theatrical form. Alice Cooper wore thick makeup, carried snakes, and used a guillotine on stage. The members of KISS

wore makeup so thick that it hid their identities, while the Tubes pushed a more sexually outrageous persona through outlandish costumes and arrangements. In an offshoot that became known as "glitter rock," artists flaunted sexual ambiguity and drug use, led by T. Rex, David Bowie, the New York Dolls, and Roxy Music.

By the second half of the 1970s, a brash, stripped-down style of guitar rock emerged as a response to the pomposity of progressive rock and the sterile uniformity of disco. Such acts as the Ramones, Patti Smith, the Sex Pistols, Blondie, the Clash, and the Talking Heads pushed energy and attitude over virtuosity and musicality.

Ignoring these trends was a bunch of distinctively individual singer-songwriters who pursued their own idiosyncratic visions, and many of them became as influential as any particular style or trend. Two of the most significant, Carole King and James Taylor, opened the decade, and they would send many sensitive, poetic types to the acoustic guitar or the grand piano to put their musings to music. Those that followed included quirky individualists like Joni Mitchell, Randy Newman, Leonard Cohen, Neil Young, Cat Stevens, Jerry Jeff Walker, Gordon Lightfoot, and Rickie Lee Jones.

Meanwhile, a similar kind of rock that borrowed from folk and country rose in Los Angeles, no doubt inspired by the Byrds and Buffalo Springfield. The Eagles became the most successful band to come out of this scene, but many others also prospered and proved widely influential, among them Linda Ronstadt, Jackson Browne, Crosby Stills and Nash, Poco, Warren Zevon, America, Karla Bonoff, and Wendy Waldman.

Country music also underwent some fragmentation and expansion. Charley Pride opened the decade by becoming country's first major black superstar. The primary Nashville Sound became slicker, giving the world Barbara Mandrell, the Gatlin Brothers, Tanya Tucker, Lynn Anderson, and Crystal Gayle.

Meanwhile, many singers from the pop world came into the country sphere, some full-time and some adding country to a diversified portfolio. These included Charlie Rich, Mac Davis, B. J. Thomas, Olivia Newton-John, John Denver, Kenny Rogers, and Anne Murray.

However, the most successful country trend of the 1970s was born of frustration. Willie Nelson and Waylon Jennings wrestled creative control from the iron grip of the record companies, and the "Outlaw" movement kicked its spurs into the soft underside of the Nashville studio system. Before long, country stars and stories ascended to the silver screen. Willie Nelson and Dolly Parton became internationally known stars on film as well as on record. Loretta Lynn's colorful life story, *Coal Miner's Daughter,* became a box office draw. And the rumblings of what would turn into a boom at the end of the decade came with the first major exposure of country honky tonks and country line dancing in *Urban Cowboy.*

Saturday Night Live's Dan Ackroyd blows a blues harp with Toy Caldwell, left, and George McCorkle of the Marshall Tucker Band.

Patrick Simmons of the Doobie Brothers plays an ES-335, 1978.

THE LONG DECLINE

BY TOM MULHERN

The company that took over CMI was a virtually unknown concern called Ecuadorian Company Limited, or ECL. According to ECL's official background material, it was incorporated in London in 1913 by E. Hope Norton, an American investment banker. The Panama Canal had just opened a new route for commerce to the Pacific Coast of South America, and Norton foresaw opportunities to participate in the growth of Ecuador. Starting with a cement company and a narrow-gauge railroad—which, according to some stories, Norton won in a poker game—ECL had expanded by the 1960s to include a flower company (which flew carnations to New York City on a regular basis), and a beer company. ECL was the major brewer of high-quality beer in Ecuador, eventually operating breweries in Guayaquil, Quito, and Pascuale. ECL was also contracted to brew Löwenbräu beer in Ecuador. ECL's first venture in American business was Aiken Industries, a company specializing in high-tech electronics and metallurgy.

Norton Stevens, the grandson of ECL's founder, had joined the company in 1958 and served as president and chairman of Aiken. He became president and chief executive officer of ECL in 1962 and chairman in 1966.

The new Norlin regime lost no time in making sweeping changes at CMI. Aside from pitching out the respected name of CMI, they also moved M. H.

Berlin out of the driver's seat and eventually ousted him altogether. Stevens and Berlin's son, Arnold, were firmly in charge.

ECL became Norlin (combining Norton and Berlin) in 1970, a few months after taking over CMI. In the first year under the Norlin banner, the future looked bright, with musical instrument sales accounting for 61 percent of the company's overall activity. However, the 1970s were to be rough on Norlin, and Gibson would undergo a major transformation.

Problems plaguing Gibson included ongoing union disputes, too much management, and too little understanding between layers of management. Stan Rendell, Gibson's president from 1968 to 1976, recalls how Norlin's corporatization of Gibson impacted the company: "We had had a profit-sharing system that was second to none, and Norlin did away with that. Norlin changed Gibson from a profit center to a cost center and destroyed individual incentive. They changed things so that we shipped product and they paid our bills. So, in effect, we had no sales. Prior to that we had a price, and we had to perform under that price structure to make a profit. That's how Gibson's employees got their bonuses, how they got raises, and how we set benefits. Norlin destroyed that."

Rendell also remembers the endless meetings and paper-pushing that created a log-jam in the company's decision-making processes: "They set up an organizational structure in Chicago that made it difficult to get things done. We would come up with a guitar design and ask them what color to make it, and they'd say, 'I don't know; I have to ask my boss.' Then that boss had to report to my boss, and six weeks later we still didn't have a

decision on what color to make these guitars. It was impossible."

With Norlin came an influx of something new to CMI and Gibson: the Harvard MBA—the first of which were none other than Norton Stevens and Arnie Berlin. Rendell describes them as the types who "figured they could solve every problem with a calculator. Any problem—they could put a number to it." Rendell was ordered specifically to hire a Harvard MBA as his second in command. He recalls, "I said, if I have to hire an MBA, what's wrong with hiring one out of the Midwest? I resented the fact that I had to hire someone from Harvard. Norton Stevens said I really didn't, so I subsequently hired a guy who was a graduate of the University of Michigan with a master's degree from the University of North Carolina in wood technology, Tom Fetters. It made sense."

For many years, Gibson had gone along with union demands—mostly, as Rendell explains, because the company could afford it: "We were such an integral part of the corporate profits that they felt even if we acquiesced to the union's demands, we could still generate a profit. So that's what happened." The need for expansion in the early '70s created an opportunity to escape union problems, and to that end, site searches took place in the dozen or so states with "right to work" laws (where unions were allowed, but union membership wasn't mandatory). The field was narrowed to Tennessee, and because Gibson wanted to be located close to a major airport, Nashville was the ideal choice.

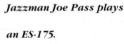

Jazzman Joe Pass plays an ES-175.

The legacy of Django Reinhardt: His first son Lousson (with cigarette), brother Joseph (below), and second son Babik, are all playing the same ES-175.

Joan Jett jumps in the '80s with a modified mid-'60s Melody Maker.

Session star Eric Gale plays a Super 400CES.

In 1974, Jim Deurloo—a Gibson employee from 1958 to 1969, and a manager at Guild for the next five years—was asked by Tom Fetters to come back and work out the tooling, machinery, and processes for the 100,000-square-foot Nashville facility. Although originally planned to produce Les Pauls and the newly introduced L-6S solidbody, Nashville's mission was soon changed to building acoustic guitars—in particular the new Mark Series. A huge crapshoot, the Marks—radical, new high-tech designs—debuted in late 1975 with the expectation that they would cure a multitude of ills in Gibson's acoustic guitar business. Expensive and difficult to make, they only made the patient sicker, and they were gone by 1979. The failure of the Marks caused Norlin to send the Les Pauls—and later, most other production—down to Nashville. As a result of a downturn in the economy and guitar sales, neither plant ran at more

Rock experimenter Frank Zappa, 1978, with what probably started out as a '72 SG Special.

Howard Roberts, a Gibson and Epi endorser since the '60s, introduced a new model in 1979, the Howard Roberts Fusion.

than about half of capacity.

In about 1975, Chuck Schneider—a financial analyst—was elevated by Norlin to the position of Gibson's executive vice president, and Rendell was ordered by his immediate boss, Les Propp, to report to Schneider.

Rendell decided to quit right then. After a meeting in which Propp said that Rendell could have veto power over any of Schneider's decisions regarding the factory itself, Rendell agreed to stay on. However, by 1976, Rendell had reached his limit with Norlin. He announced that he was leaving to start a string company, Sterlingworth, which would produce private-label strings for other companies (it was acquired in the

1980s by Dean Markley). Although he agreed to stay on at Gibson as a consultant, they showed him the door at the end of 1976.

It was a revolving door that Rendell left through. Carl Spinosa, whom Rendell had put in charge of Gibson's string facility in Elgin, Illinois, was summoned to take over temporarily as Kalamazoo plant manager. In 1978, Jim Deurloo was tapped for the job—a natural selection, considering that he had worked his way through almost every aspect of the company since coming to Gibson fresh out of high school in 1958. Except for five years at Guild, he had spent his entire adult life intimately acquainted with Gibson's processes. In 1980, Marty Locke moved over from Lowrey to head Gibson. His job, one insider said, "was to downsize it."

As Norlin's troubles mounted and the recession of the early 1980s wore on, Norlin made the decision

On KISS's Dynasty tour, Ace Frehley cranked it out on a three-pickup Les Paul Custom.

Billy Gibbons of ZZ Top, 1979.

©Beth Gwinn

in July 1983 to close the Kalamazoo plant. "There were feasibility studies going back and forth for years, you know," says Deurloo. "One week, it was decided that Nashville would be closed, and then a couple of weeks later, it was decided that Kalamazoo would close."

Norlin didn't particularly care about Gibson's lifelong identification with Kalamazoo. They weren't even swayed by the fact that it would be virtually impossible to sell off the Parsons St. plant, since there were already 10 or more major factories sitting empty in Kalamazoo's decaying inner city (the Nashville facility was in a prime, easy-to-sell location). "I had said that Kalamazoo is Mecca," Deurloo says. "A lot of people tried to argue that, but it didn't matter. There's an assumption that if you can make widgets in one place, you can make them in another. But I say that only Rembrandt paints Rembrandts."

Deurloo made a run at keeping Kalamazoo in operation. In much the same way as Gibson kept afloat during the darkest depths of the Great Depression by making toys, the factory started turning out non-musical items such as chronometer cases, oak parts for van conversions, and even waterbeds. But the end was inevitable. During the last months at Kalamazoo, semi truck after semi truck carted off equipment for the ride to Nashville. Each week, more people were let go, until only a dozen or so remained.

One longtime employee summarizes the situation in this way: "The spirit of the company was disappearing. There weren't enough people with soul, with sensitivity toward guitars." Another is a bit more blunt: "It was almost impossible for someone to screw up something as badly as Norlin did. You'd really have to work at it."

The doors at 225 Parsons Street—Gibson's home since 1917—closed in the fall of 1984. Jim Deurloo, J. P. Moats, and Marv Lamb, all longtime Gibson employees, decided not to go to Nashville and instead formed the Heritage guitar company and rented part of the Parsons St. factory.

By the time the 1980s rolled around, Norlin was desperate to maximize profits. In a move to recapture the low-end market from Asian companies, models like the Firebrand series, 335-S, and synthetic-body Sonex were introduced. They were flightless birds. Ever-changing information from the corporate headquarters made designing and redesigning an ongoing struggle. "We got Federal Express packages every day," says Tim Shaw, one of the design engineers. "Binding would appear or disappear, colors would change, switches would come and go."

Gibson's reputation was at an all-time low, and Norlin was sinking fast. The only question was whether Norlin would take Gibson down with it when it went under.

BURYING A GOOD NAME

BY WALTER CARTER

The longest-lasting name of the Gibson company has been Gibson, Inc., which endured from late 1923, through the company's purchase by CMI in 1944, through the takeover of CMI by ECL in 1969, all the way to June 1979. The parent company's name, however, was anything but stable in the 1970s.

ECL
ECL Industries, Incorporated (the initials stood for Ecuadorian Company Limited), a Delaware corporation and U.S. subsidiary of ECL Industries, Inc., a Panamanian corporation, took over the Chicago Musical Instrument Co. on December 19, 1969.

NORLIN INDUSTRIES, INC.
In 1970, ECL's U.S. company became Norlin Industries, Inc., and the Panama corporation became Norlin Corporation. CMI was still a subsidiary of ECL.

NORLIN MUSIC, INC.
This small name change in 1972 did away with the CMI name, as it was merged into Norlin.

NORLIN INDUSTRIES, INC.
With the merger of Norlin's technology business into the parent company, the name was changed back to Norlin Industries, Inc.

FRETTED INSTRUMENT DIVISION OF NORLIN INDUSTRIES
Gibson, Inc., became extinct when it was merged into Norlin Industries in June 1979. For the next six years, "Gibson" did not exist as a corporate name; it was just a brand name (along with Epiphone) for products made by Norlin's fretted instrument division.

GIBSON GUITAR CORP.
"Gibson" returned to the corporate name on January 15, 1986, with the purchase of Norlin's fretted instrument division by Henry Juszkiewicz, David Berryman, and Gary Zebrowski. Since then, Gibson Guitar Corp. ("Gibson USA" is a logo and not a corporate name) has become the parent company for a number of brand names.

The L-5S, envisioned as a solidbody equivalent of the L-5, is one of the more respected models from an era that garners little respect.

The sound of Diana Ross playing a B-25 never made it onto record.

Neither a rotary tone control nor Carlos Santana's endorsement could help the L-6S of 1973–79.

THE GREAT SYNTHESIZER SCARE

B Y   T O M   M U L H E R N

By the mid '60s, the electric guitar had practically blown the saxophone out of rock music, and guitarists were exploring effects like fuzz and wah-wah in search of new lead voices. Concurrently, the first generation of all-electronic music machines—synthesizers—were being developed by the likes of Robert Moog, Donald Buchla, and ARP. Big, unwieldy, and temperamental, they were mostly studio dwellers until 1970, when the first performance-oriented portable synths hit the music stores. Moog's Minimoog and ARP's 2500 and 2600 were portable enough to use onstage and novel enough to pique the interest of keyboardists who had long toiled behind cheesy-sounding combo organs or big pieces of furniture intended for living rooms and churches.

Like the blossoming electric guitar of several years earlier, synthesizers were new, sometimes startling,

Little Milton (left) and Robert Cray demonstrate the bluesman's semi-solidbody preference, the ES-345.

and gimmicky enough to perhaps help to sell records. In the "art-rock" movement, players such as Keith Emerson of Emerson Lake & Palmer and Rick Wakeman of Yes were heralded, while in jazz, Chick Corea, Jan Hammer, Herbie Hancock, Josef Zawinul, and George Duke were stretching out with the new sonic vocabulary afforded by these instruments. Even classical music was expanded by bold sounds created by Wendy Carlos and Isao Tomita.

This proliferation of synths had little bearing on the guitar's fortunes, however, since synthesizers were still few in number and virtually all monophonic—they could only play one note at a time. In addition, very few hits featured synthesizer—Edgar Winter's "Frankenstein" and Emerson Lake & Palmer's "Lucky Man" were probably the biggest. Synths were lead instruments or bass instruments, but certainly not substitutes for piano, organ, or guitar.

By 1975, the polyphonic synthesizer appeared. No longer was the keyboardist limited to one or two simultaneous notes. Full chords—and lots of them—were possible. By 1978, the first microprocessor-equipped, fully programmable synths appeared. The pioneering companies, Sequential Circuits, Oberheim, E-mu, Moog, and ARP, all approached polyphony and programmability from different directions, but did so wholeheartedly.

By the time the recession at the dawn of the 1980s got into full swing, sales of all instruments, including synthesizers, sputtered. Gloom and doom swept the music industry, accelerated by the collapse of disco, and with it many record companies. It was easy to point fingers for poor sales: interest rates around 20 percent, high unemployment, double-digit inflation. Synthesizers were a scapegoat for allegedly taking away from sales of traditional instruments. In addition, some musicians were worried about being put out of work by these instruments touted as "keyboards with all the sounds of the orchestra." Some musicians were

indeed eventually replaced, but by synthesists, not synthesizers.

Meanwhile, to some it seemed only natural to adapt the synthesizer so that guitarists could use it. Unfortunately, this involved much more than the simple on/off switches inside a keyboard. It meant extracting the fundamental pitch of each note and converting it into a voltage to control the pitch, duration, and loudness of each note emanating from the synthesizer. The real wet blanket in this conversion process came from simple physics: Every note played on a guitar is rich in harmonics, enough to cause the most sophisticated circuitry to stumble. More money was thrown at the problem, which of course would eventually mean higher prices.

Prices on early guitar synthesizers were astronomical, especially considering that most

U-2's guitarist The Edge plays a Les Paul Custom.

Todd Kaplan, Star File

©Beth Gwinn

©Beth Gwinn

pickers viewed them as a sort of super fuzztone. And most didn't work worth a darn if you played fast, sloppy, or… well, any number of ways that make the guitar fun to play and great to hear. But to make matters worse, you often had no choice other than to buy the guitar that came with the synthesizer, because they were wired together. With the exception of Ampeg's Patch 2000, which used a Hagstrom Swede as its guitar, most were just average Japanese guitars with no remarkable traits. Regardless of the guitar's value or utility, it added to the cost of the guitar synth. Prices ranged from $2,000 to $3,000.

Even those that let you use your own guitar were unreliable, monophonic (unless they had hexaphonic fuzz), and pretty limited. Some companies tried to provide polyphony for guitarists, only to run into maddening technical problems, even higher prices, and frightful unreliability (ARP built—but never marketed—a $15,000 synth that had an estimated time between servicing of only two hours). No matter what they tried, they couldn't make a guitar synth that offered what the standard guitar did: subtlety, predictability, reliability, and the forgiving qualities that make sloppiness part of the guitar's vocabulary.

ARP—the General Motors or Ford of the synth world—put too many eggs into its guitar synthesizer basket and eventually bankrupted itself. One by one, all of the smaller guitar synth makers and many of their keyboard counterparts went belly-up. Roland outlasted everyone else in the guitar synthesizer arena, eventually being saved by the explosion in digital technology in the late 1980s. Remarkably, the two biggest American guitar companies—Gibson and Fender—sat out the guitar synth debacle, even though Gibson could have collaborated with Moog, its fellow Norlin company.

Today the synthesizer has become a common instrument, used on pop hits, TV and movie soundtracks, and commercials, most often controlled by a keyboard. The guitar synthesizer has evolved into a MIDI controller, capable of driving synthesizers, linking with sequencers, and working as an educational and compositional tool with computers. And the standard guitar hasn't lost its appeal in any style of music. It's still the instrument at the center of the rock & roll universe, the heart of most country, and the soul of modern blues.

AC/DC's Angus Young didn't bring back short pants, but he kept the SG Standard in the spotlight.

Synthesizer threats had no effect on the rising blues scene that spawned George Thorogood, playing an obscure thinbody from the '50s, the ES-225.

Joe Walsh (top, right) with The Eagles, 1979.

Guitars—specifically Les Pauls—ruled Southern rock music at the 1984 Volunteer Jam. From left are Toy Caldwell, Tommy Crain, Dickey Betts, Billy Crain, and Charlie Daniels.

THE VINTAGE BACKLASH

BY GEORGE GRUHN

A formidable new competitor appeared during the folk music boom to challenge Gibson. The name of this newcomer was, ironically, Gibson, and the instruments that competed with new Gibsons were used and vintage models.

Prior to the mid '60s, the quality of new guitars was very high, designs for acoustic instruments were settling in, and electric guitars were still evolving, so most players considered new instruments to be better than older ones. The exception was in bluegrass music, where players had begun looking for vintage banjos and mandolins in the early 1950s. These were not collectors' items as they are today; they were simply good-sounding instruments. Bill Monroe played a 1923 Gibson F-5 mandolin because it gave him a sound he couldn't get from any new instrument. The most influential banjo players, Earl Scruggs and Don Reno, played early-'30s Mastertones with a "flathead" tone ring for the same reason. Players who wished to imitate them couldn't get their sound except on the old instruments.

The mainstream popularity of commercial folk music spawned interest in bluegrass, traditional old-time music, and acoustic blues, and folklore societies became very active on northern college campuses, bringing this music into areas where it had not been before. Consequently, for the first time, vintage guitars, banjos, and mandolins were actively sought by university-educated players. As is typical of university people, they also began to study and collect these instruments. Dealers emerged and prices began to escalate.

Bluegrass patriarch Bill Monroe with his Loar F-5 on **The Grand Ole Opry,** *1976.*

Les Leverett, courtesy Grand Ole Opry Archives

This phenomenon went unnoticed by Gibson and other guitar makers in the early '60s, as sales of new guitars boomed and demand far outstripped supply. However, for the first time, there were rumblings of discontent that the new instruments had slipped in quality. With the exception of adjustable-height bridges on flattops (a dubious improvement) and fancy pickguards on the Hummingbird, Dove, and Everly Brothers models, Gibson made no real advancements in flattop design after 1960. Furthermore, these new flattops simply were *not* better-suited to the music of the day than earlier designs. The contrast between new and vintage was even greater for the banjo and mandolin. The thin-rimmed Mastertone banjos and the mandolins of the 1960s were like soundless stage props next to older models.

The vintage phenomenon did not apply to the electric guitar in the early 1960s because designs were still rapidly evolving and the quality of new electrics remained high. Furthermore, the campus folklore societies, as well as most players of acoustic guitars, had no interest in electrics. In 1964 or '65, however, the University of Chicago Folklore Society discovered and started to promote "rhythm & blues" acts from the south side of Chicago, sponsoring concerts by Muddy Waters, Buddy Guy, and Little Richard (the term "blues" was reserved for acoustic, Delta-style players). Shortly thereafter, one of the first white blues groups appeared, the Butterfield Blues Band, featuring Michael Bloomfield on guitar. Bloomfield was the first player of vintage guitars to have a major influence on the market. In fact, there was virtually no market at all for used electric guitars before Mike Bloomfield.

Bloomfield's first electric was a 1952 Fender Telecaster. They could be had for $75 before he started playing one, $500–600 afterward. A year later, prices on used early-'50s Teles plummeted and goldtop Les Pauls (late 1953 to mid 1955 vintage) shot up. One did not have to attend a Bloomfield performance to know that he had switched to the goldtop Les Paul. As long as he played the goldtop, a cherry sunburst Les Paul

(1958–60, with humbucking pickups) could be bought for $250 because it was the "wrong" guitar to Bloomfield's followers. Suddenly, sunburst Les Pauls went up to $800 and goldtops dropped. Bloomfield had switched again.

The market for electrics emerged quickly, from nothing in early 1964 to dealers asking more for vintage Les Pauls than for new electric models by 1966 (there were no Les Pauls in the Gibson line at the time). By 1970, Eric Clapton had emerged as the most powerful influence on the vintage electric market, and his move from an early-'60s SG-style Les Paul to a Fender Strat brought the latter model into the vintage fold.

However, the most sweeping force of the era was Crosby, Stills, Nash and Young. Folk rock in the late '60s had brought acoustic and electric instruments together, and by 1970, CSN&Y had done the same in the vintage world, performing with a wide variety of high-grade vintage instruments. Moreover, they led the way for an infusion of

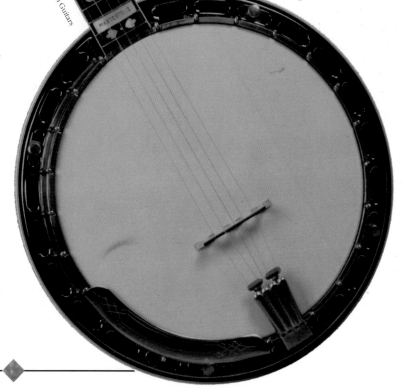

Dan Loftin, courtesy Gruhn Guitars

Gibson Granada RB, 1932, with one-piece flange and flathead tone ring—the Holy Grail for bluegrassers.

The "All American" Banjo

THE DREAM COLLECTION

BY GEORGE GRUHN

Gibson's diversity of instruments makes it impossible to single out any particular one as the ultimate or even the typical Gibson. For a collector, it's difficult to compare a Loar F-5 mandolin to an Orville Gibson original. They are both mandolins, but one represents the pinnacle of design, the other its genesis. Comparing either instrument to a Bella Voce banjo or a '59 Les Paul Standard is impossible. Therefore, the ultimate, representative Gibson collection would have to include a variety of instruments:

◆ Orville Gibson guitar and mandolin—the foundation of the Gibson name.

◆ Style O Artist guitar (scroll body) and F-4 mandolin, to represent the mandolin orchestra, plus a Style U harp guitar.

◆ F-5 mandolin and L-5 guitar signed by Lloyd Loar—the pinnacle of mandolin design and the first archtop f-hole guitar. Add a Loar-signed H-5 mandola and K-5 mandocello to complete the finest mandolin-family quartet possible.

◆ Florentine and Bella Voce banjos from the late '20s—a pair of highly ornate models from the Jazz Age, plus the most-ornate All American from the '30s.

◆ Mastertone five-string banjo from the '30s, with flathead tone ring and one-piece flange, preferably a Granada with hearts-and-flowers inlay—the bluegrass banjo equivalent of the sunburst Les Paul.

◆ Super 400, the first large-body archtop. Actually, the collection should have an early version (1934) and a cutaway (1939), plus examples of the advanced body L-5 and cutaway L-5P from the same years.

◆ Prewar Super Jumbo (J-200) and Advanced Jumbo— Gibson's best jumbo and dreadnought flattops, respectively, both with rosewood back and sides.

◆ EH-150 lap steel, ES-150 and ES-250 guitars—the first Gibson electrics, all with the "Charlie Christian" pickup.

◆ ES-5 Switchmaster, late-'50s version with three patent- applied-for humbucking pickups, and the electric Super

400CES and L-5CES from the early '50s (with single-coil pickups) and the late '50s (with humbuckers).

◆ EDS-1275 doubleneck six- and twelve-string, late-'50s version with carved top, hollow body, and no soundholes—a body style that existed only on doublenecks.

◆ Sunburst Les Paul Standard, 1958–60, with highly flamed top, of course.

◆ Flying V and Explorer, 1958–59. (If an original Moderne ever turns up, I'll need that, too.)

◆ ES-335, 1958, dot inlay, natural finish, the first semi- hollowbody electric.

◆ EB violin-shaped bass from the '50s, plus the early hollowbody version of the EB-2 and EB-6 basses.

◆ Firebirds and Thunderbird basses, 1963–64—not as radically modernistic as the V and Explorer and not as rare, but still in a class of their own. A Firebird VII and Thunderbird IV will do; custom colors would be preferable.

◆ Citation—one of precious few models of the post-McCarty period (1966 and after) worth talking to a collector about. The same applies to the Kalamazoo Award and the The Les Paul.

Many collectible models didn't make the list—no goldtop Les Paul or Les Paul Custom, no J-185 or Everly Brothers, no prewar Electraharp pedal steel—but we have to draw the line somewhere.

Price of the collection? Only about $20,000—if all the instruments had been bought new at their original list prices (save $10,000 by passing on the Citation, Kalamazoo Award, and The Les Paul). As of early 1994, this collection could be assembled—assuming the instruments could be found and the owners wanted to sell—for around $750,000.

rock and pop money into the acoustic vintage market, bringing in new dealers and elevating vintage instruments to the level of status symbols and collectors' items.

©John Bellissimo

Even though sales of new instruments remained strong, manufacturers felt the effect of the interest in vintage instruments as many influential musicians, who would normally be endorsing new models either formally or informally by appearing on stage with them, were instead using old instruments. In the meantime, higher production of new instruments had resulted in lower quality. By the 1970s, Gibson, Gretsch, Guild, and Fender were owned by corporations which typically were not managed by people who understood the market or were deeply concerned with quality control. They suffered further decline with musical and economic trends of the late 1970s and early '80s.

In the meantime, the vintage market found a life of its own with the emergence of an international clientele. Vintage guitars developed a reputation as good investments—more stable than the stock market and a lot more fun to play than a stock certificate.

In the 1990s, instrument makers have taken advantage of the strong demand for vintage models by reissuing the favorite models. Additionally, the vintage guitar industry has grown to the point that many vintage models no longer compete with new models: The most expensive new reissues of a sunburst Les Paul, a Flying V, an Advanced Jumbo, or a Loar F-5, for example, still bring only a fraction of the price of an original.

Bluesman Mike Bloomfield's use of older guitars helped spark the fire of the vintage market.

Stephen Stills, right, with a Firebird I; Graham Nash with a Les Paul Custom, 1977. Stills was a prime factor in bringing together the electric and acoustic vintage market.

©Beth Gwinn

B. B. AND LUCILLE

BY WALTER CARTER

B. B. King's powerful, lyrical, blues style has inspired generations of rock and roll guitarists. He had been playing Gibsons for more than 30 years when he and Gibson finally made the association official in 1980.

B. B. was born Riley B. King near Itta Bena and Indianola, Mississippi, in 1925. He made a name for himself on Memphis' 50,000-watt WDIA as the Pepticon Boy (Pepticon tonic was a competitor of Hadacol, which was promoted on a West Memphis station by Sonny Boy Williamson). The Pepticon Boy became the Beale St. Blues Boy, then Blues Boy King, and finally just B. B. King. He hit the big time in the early '50s with "Three O'Clock Blues,"

B. B. King works out

with Lucille, 1993.

the neck of it," he says. "I've always liked the neck. Even a Gibson that *you* played, the neck would be quite familiar with me. If I played yours I may not be as comfortable as I would mine, but it would be very similar."

In 1968, as B. B. was being discovered by mainstream white audiences, he immortalized Lucille by titling an album after his guitar. Two years later, he released his signature song, "The Thrill Is Gone."

By 1980, he was so closely identified with the ES-355 that he and Gibson got together to create a B. B. King model. His main complaint about the

Deryl Duer

which stayed at Number One on the rhythm & blues charts for 15 weeks.

B. B. recalls his first guitar as a "little black Gibson with the f-holes in it," an L-30 that he electrified with a DeArmond pickup. He lost it in 1949 at a club date in Twist, Arkansas, that gave rise to Lucille. Two men were fighting over a woman named Lucille, and they knocked over a lit barrel of kerosene. B. B. almost lost his life trying to save his guitar from the fire, and after that he called his guitars "Lucille" to remind himself never to be so foolish.

B. B. went through many Lucilles, including an ES-5 and then a Byrdland, before settling on an ES-355. Regardless of the guitar, as long as it was a Gibson, he felt comfortable. "There was something about

ES-355 had been a tendency to feed back, and he had stuffed paper inside his guitars to minimize it. The Gibson B. B. King model addressed that problem by eliminating the soundholes altogether. A TP-6 fine-tuner tailpiece was added; stereo output was achieved through two jacks rather than through the single jack and Y-cord of earlier 355s. B. B. also specified a thinner neck than the one he was playing at the time.

Two B. B. King models were introduced in 1980, the Standard (rosewood fingerboard, dot inlay, chrome-plated metal parts) and the Custom (ebony fingerboard, large blocks, gold-plated). In 1988, the Standard was dropped and the fancier model renamed the B. B. King Lucille. It reigns today, appropriately, as the king of the 335-style line.

CHET AND THE SOLID CLASSICAL

BY WALTER CARTER

The thousands of guitarists who slave away so they can play "just like Chet" are a testament to Chet Atkins's reputation as the most influential guitar player in the world. Equally important, though less heralded, are his accomplishments as a guitar designer.

Chet was born in 1924 in the tiny Tennessee mountain town of Luttrell, near Knoxville. Among his earliest influences were his older brother Jimmy and Jimmy's guitar-playing partner in Fred Waring's orchestra, Les Paul. Chet's own music found a direction in the early 1940s, when he tuned in WLW, the 50,000-watt clear channel station from Cincinnati, and heard the Drifting Pioneers, who featured the thumb-and-finger picking of Merle Travis.

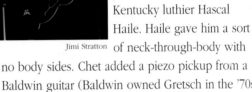

Jimi Stratton

Chet made his recording debut in 1945, playing guitar behind Wally Fowler and the Georgia Clodhoppers on a wartime novelty tune, "Propaganda Papa." (Fowler's group would eventually gain fame as the Oak Ridge Boys.) He began his long and successful solo career in 1947 with "Canned Heat."

By the late '40s, Chet was playing an acoustic archtop made by legendary luthier John D'Angelico, equipped with a homemade vibrato and a DeArmond pickup. In 1954, Gretsch offered him his own model. His only requirements were a metal bridge and nut (for greater sustain) and a vibrato tailpiece. Gretsch added the flash—Western trim and orange finish—but Chet later contributed more sustain-enhancing designs, such as closing the f-holes and extending the top braces all the way to the back. Gretsch's Chet Atkins models were the backbone of the company's success, but after Gretsch was sold to Baldwin in 1967, quality started falling. Chet and Gretsch parted ways in 1978.

A minor physical problem led him to a major innovation in guitar design: an electric classical guitar. "My nails aren't too good, and steel strings were bad for my nails," he explains, "so I always wanted an electric nylon. Years ago, I even got a patent on a nylon string, to put a little core of metal in the center of it so it would pick up. I tried to get Gretsch to build it. They weren't interested. When I went with Gibson I talked to Bruce Bolen and he went for the idea right away."

Chet had been working with Kentucky luthier Hascal Haile. Haile gave him a sort of neck-through-body with no body sides. Chet added a piezo pickup from a Baldwin guitar (Baldwin owned Gretsch in the '70s and had first used piezo pickups for pianos). Haile made a new prototype, and except for its 12-fret neck, it was essentially the same as the production model (which has a 14-fret neck).

The Chet Atkins CEC, for Cutaway Electric Classical, debuted in 1982. Rock musicians, including Mark Knopfler and Sting, have used them because the solidbodies can be turned up without feeding back. Expansion into an entire line began in 1987 with the steel-string Chet Atkins SST. With typical modesty, Chet says he never dreamed the guitar would appeal to anyone except classical players. "I just thought it would be easy on my nails."

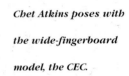

Chet Atkins poses with the wide-fingerboard model, the CEC.

Chet with a Chet Atkins Studio Classic at the Nashville NAMM show, summer 1993. Paul Yandell, behind Chet, plays a Gibson Chet Atkins Country Gentleman.

THE END OF NORLIN

B Y   T O M   M U L H E R N

The most pessimistic of pessimists believe that you start to die the moment you're born. While this fatalistic view may not sit too well with most people, it's an extremely apt description of what happened to Norlin, the company that acquired Gibson at its zenith and almost destroyed the guitar giant.

Norlin's poor judgment and inability to read the market, coupled with a failing economy, did result in the destruction of the manufacturing and distribution empire that had been the Chicago Musical Instrument Co. Norlin adopted a strategy of throwing ballast over the side to bail itself out of a sinking music market, and the casualties began piling up in the early 1970s:

Mick Jagger fronts the Rolling Stones with a '60s SG Standard.

Ironically, while Norlin was plunging ever downward, Gibson guitars maintained a strong presence on concert stages, thanks to loyal users like Chuck Berry.

©John Bellissimo

 Krauth & Benninghofen, a large manufacturer of music stands, was the first to go. Norlin needed money and sold the company around 1973.

 F. E. Olds band instruments peaked in the early 1970s at an annual sales level of about $18 million. Norlin management decided that that return on investment wasn't great enough, so they raised prices on Olds instruments. Not surprisingly, dealers had difficulty selling Olds products. Partly in protest to the Olds price increase, they started boycotting another Norlin product, Symmetricut reeds. Olds was liquidated at the end of the dedade and the tooling bought by Selmer,

reportedly for about $900,000. Symmetricut also withered and its equipment was eventually sold off to its competitor, Rico.

 William Lewis & Son, like most violin companies, imported instruments from Eastern Europe and then did the final setup in the States. Norlin set up a workshop at its main facility on Cicero Avenue in Lincolnwood, Illinois, but didn't build climate control into it. As a result, the violins had horrendous problems, resulting in a multitude of warranty returns. Eventually, Lewis was sold to a wholesaler and then rescued by Gemeinhardt, a respected company that straightened out the quality problems.

 Maestro effects, which lasted the last half of the 1960s and into the 1970s, wandered aimlessly and then disappeared. It was a truly innovative company, making fuzztones and wah-wahs as well as some hard-to-market devices such as a ring modulator and the Universal Synthesizer (a multi-effects unit for guitar). Maestro was the first company to successfully market a phase shifter—designed by Tom Oberheim, founder of Oberheim Electronics, the synthesizer company that, ironically, would later be acquired by Gibson.

 Buffet woodwind instruments and Armstrong flutes showed a lack of profitability and dim prospects for the future—at least that was the consensus of the Norlin board that met on January 19, 1979. Buffet and Armstrong followed Olds to

©1984 Jimi Stratton

©John Bellissimo

Jazz sounds are found in Pat Metheny's ES-175 (cameo) and Al DiMeola's Les Paul Standard.

the chopping block, ridding Norlin of all its band instrument companies.

◆ L. D. Heater, an important northwestern instrument distributor based in Oregon, and Turner Musical Instruments Limited, once the largest jobber of musical instrument products in Canada, were both destroyed. Heater suffered neglect and died a slow death. Turner was renamed Norlin Canada in the early 1980s and then went bust.

◆ Story & Clark pianos had its plug pulled by Norlin about 1982.

◆ Lowrey organs exemplified Norlin's poor judgment. During its heyday (around 1978), it was a $100 million company with a 300,000-square-foot facility in Romeoville, Illinois. Norlin decided that shopping malls would be the perfect place to sell Lowrey instruments, but dealers were reluctant, so Norlin leased the store space for them. One

©John Bellissimo

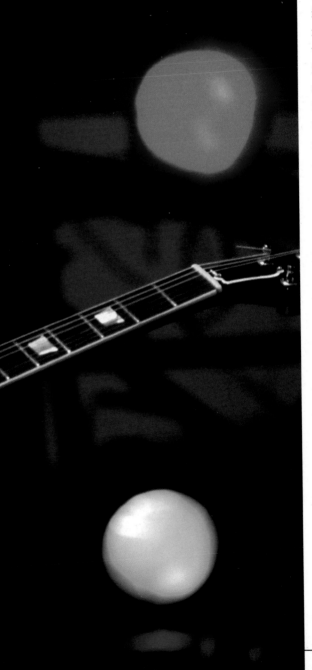

industry analyst describes the implications very succinctly: "If the dealer walked, went bad, or decided they didn't want to sell Lowrey organs anymore, the mall was Lowrey's problem, not the dealer's." Organ sales faltered at the end of the 1970s, and Lowrey—once a crown jewel in CMI's and Norlin's collection of companies—began bleeding to death at the rate of approximately $10 million a quarter. Norlin sold Lowrey in 1985.

(Lowrey's new owners got into financial hot water and sold to Kawai in February 1988.)

◆ Moog Music had the distinction of being the only music-related company Norlin ever acquired, but that didn't stop Norlin from unloading it. Norlin bought Moog in 1973 from an investor named Bill Weytana, who had purchased it from founder Robert Moog in 1971. (Mr. Moog stayed with the company through 1977.) With its high-tech inclinations, Norlin was always glad to show it off as its leading-edge venture in the music business, but as one ex-Moog employee sums it up, Moog was "a nice prestige thing. It was set up to be a $25 million-a-year company that never did more than $10 million."

Because of their electronics expertise, Moog engineers worked on amplifiers, including the Lab series, and active circuits for Gibson's RD guitars and basses. Moog even dabbled in signal processors (all excellent, but extremely expensive). Every aspect of Moog was bigger than reality. Moog's big seller, the Minimoog, was made from 1970 to 1981, yet only a few more than 12,000 were ever produced. The introduction of Sequential Circuits' Prophet pounded one stake through Moog's heart, and the Yamaha DX7 in 1982 hammered in another. In 1983, a Moog management group orchestrated a buyout from Norlin, but they eventually turned to non-musical electronic products in an unsuccessful attempt to save Moog.

Despite the ominous failure of Moog, Norlin put more of its eggs into the high-tech basket. In Norton Stevens's letter in the opening of the 1978 annual report, he noted, "One particularly

Norlin attempted to recapture the market with new versions of classic designs, but the original versions would probably have worked better.

The TP-6 tailpiece, with fine tuners, was one of few Norlin innovations with lasting power.

Steve Morse plays a Chet Atkins CEC.

gratifying accomplishment suggesting possibilities for the future was the successful operation of the Norlin-produced Ion Spectrometer that fed back reliable and, to some, surprising data from the Venus space shot completed successfully in November." Norlin Technology made carbide products, quartz crystals, electronic switching systems, and power supplies.

As Norlin gained speed on its roller-coaster ride toward oblivion, no division was safe—especially not a profitable division, not even one of the

Ecuadorian companies of Norton Stevens's old ECL empire. The Ecuadorian beer business—Norlin's only profitable business (sales of suds accounted for more than 40 percent of Norlin's 1981 total sales of $220.9 million)—was unloaded in September 1981 for $50 million.

In late 1983, Norlin took out a bank note for $55 million to purchase Ticor Print Network, Inc. Ticor's main business was printing stock certificates and other financial paper. In 1985, Value Line, virtually the stockbroker's bible, said, "This risky stock looks unappealing," and went on to say it would no longer report on Norlin due to the small number of shares publicly held and traded.

As CMI had been 14 years earlier, Norlin in 1983 was a sitting duck for a corporate takeover. According to *Businessweek's* August 27, 1984, issue, Rooney Pace, a New York brokerage house, paid $9 million for a 23.8 percent share of Norlin, "a troubled conglomerate that [Pat] Rooney believes has a breakup value far in excess of its market valuation." In the meantime, another company, Piezo Electric Products, Inc. (not related to musical instruments), bought another 23.8 percent share of Norlin. Then, Rooney Pace and Piezo wrested control of Norlin's board of directors.

From 1975 through 1984, Norlin had reported pre-tax losses attributable to the music business of approximately $145 million—an amount equal to twice the company's 1975 net worth. After a new board of directors was convened in 1984, they decided that Norlin was no longer to be in the music business.

Gibson, Norlin's last musical asset, was sold off in January 1986. It was good riddance, according to Rooney Pace chairman Patrick J. Rooney. In the annual report of April 14, 1986, Rooney wrote: "This is the last annual report from our company that you will read about music businesses. We estimate that the Company lost $158.0 million trying to be a leader in an industry that had been

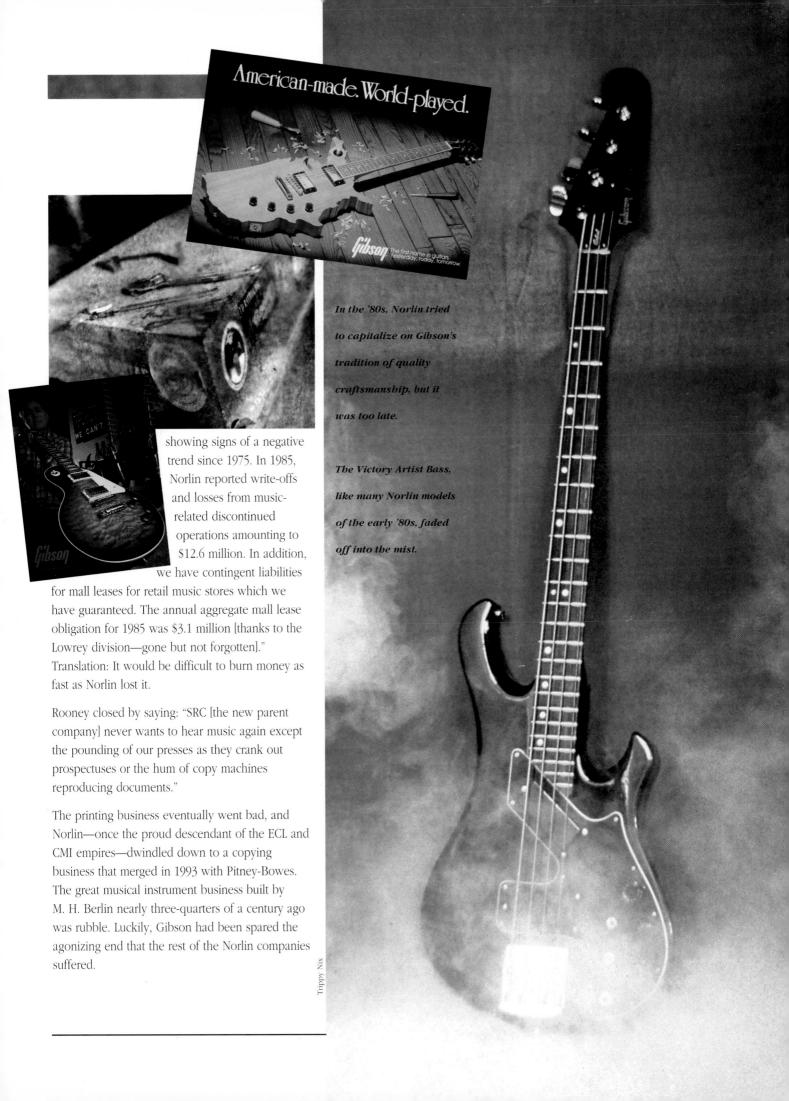

In the '80s, Norlin tried to capitalize on Gibson's tradition of quality craftsmanship, but it was too late.

The Victory Artist Bass, like many Norlin models of the early '80s, faded off into the mist.

showing signs of a negative trend since 1975. In 1985, Norlin reported write-offs and losses from music-related discontinued operations amounting to $12.6 million. In addition, we have contingent liabilities for mall leases for retail music stores which we have guaranteed. The annual aggregate mall lease obligation for 1985 was $3.1 million [thanks to the Lowrey division—gone but not forgotten]." Translation: It would be difficult to burn money as fast as Norlin lost it.

Rooney closed by saying: "SRC [the new parent company] never wants to hear music again except the pounding of our presses as they crank out prospectuses or the hum of copy machines reproducing documents."

The printing business eventually went bad, and Norlin—once the proud descendant of the ECL and CMI empires—dwindled down to a copying business that merged in 1993 with Pitney-Bowes. The great musical instrument business built by M. H. Berlin nearly three-quarters of a century ago was rubble. Luckily, Gibson had been spared the agonizing end that the rest of the Norlin companies suffered.

Trippy Nix

1986–1994

GIBSON
U. S. A.

HARVARD BOYS TO THE RESCUE

BY TOM MULHERN

When you think of power trios, chances are the names Cream, Jimi Hendrix Experience, Police, ZZ Top, or other musical movers and shakers come to mind. Pretty far down the list—if at all—would be three guys with MBAs from Harvard. But their impact on the guitar industry has been substantial.

If Henry Juszkiewicz, David Berryman, and Gary Zebrowski hadn't purchased Gibson in January 1986, there probably would be no new Gibson guitars today. The general consensus is that Gibson was about three months away from being liquidated, its equipment sold off piecemeal, and its name given to the highest bidder—regardless of whether they would put it on good instruments or bad.

Surprisingly, most major musical-equipment manufacturers and many distributors inspected the company and decided that the $15 million asking price was far out of line with what it was worth. Over the course of a few years, according to one Gibson insider, "There was an almost steady stream of people coming through the factory to check it out for possible purchase. Anybody who had a million bucks in the bank was pretty much fair game."

Indeed, Gibson was much like a nice-looking car, but with dismantled engine parts in the front seat,

transmission in the trunk, and four flat tires—a real "fixer-upper." After seven months of negotiations, Gibson was sold to Juszkiewicz, Berryman, and Zebrowski on January 15, 1986, for approximately $5 million. It was the trio's first foray into the music industry, and in less than a decade, it has proved to be the company's salvation.

Gary Zebrowski, the youngest of the three entrepreneurs, was born in Philadelphia, Pennsylvania, on October 3, 1955. Like so many other kids, he was drafted into piano lessons. Afterwards, he didn't play again. He attended Dartmouth College in New Hampshire, toiling under a double major in mathematics and economics. Rather than taking a break after earning his degree, he jumped right into the MBA program at Harvard, where Henry Juszkiewicz was his roommate.

David Berryman was born on January 7, 1952, in Buffalo, New York, and played guitar on and off as a kid. By the time he reached Boston College in 1970, he had almost quit playing and was concentrating on his studies in finance and accounting. After graduation in 1974, he went to work for Price Waterhouse as a certified public accountant. In 1977, he went to Harvard to work on his Masters of Business

Dave Berryman, left, and Gary Zebrowski revive Henry Juszkiewicz after a tough round in a negotiations course at Harvard business school.

Rolling Stones guitarist Keith Richards plays a custom single-pickup L-5S.

Administration degree. There he met Zebrowski and Juszkiewicz.

Born in San Nicolas, Argentina, on March 3, 1953, Henry Juszkiewicz emigrated to the States with his parents in 1958 and grew up in Rochester, New York. Hearing the Beatles and the other British Invasion bands inspired him to pick up the guitar. Throughout high school, he played in a variety of garage bands. He entered college at the General Motors Institute in Flint, Michigan, to pursue his other interest, engineering, but he brought his guitar along and played weddings and parties. "I was able to do gigs and get paid," he says. "I thought that was the most marvelous thing in the world. I couldn't believe that you got paid for doing something you liked."

GMI offered a co-op program, in which Henry was able to learn engineering while working at GM. After receiving his degree, he remained at GM for a couple of years in various engineering roles. When a recession hit, GM rescinded their offer to cover expenses for graduate courses, so Henry returned to Rochester, where he took courses at the University of Rochester toward an MBA degree. He applied and was accepted at both Stanford and Harvard, and after concerted soul-searching, opted for Harvard. While at Harvard, he decided that rather than work for a monolith like GM, he wanted to explore entrepreneurial avenues.

©Jimi Stratton

The three spread out after Harvard—Gary settled in Philadelphia, Henry in New York, and Dave in Reading, Pennsylvania—each pursuing his own career while keeping in touch with the others. None of their careers was even remotely related to music or musical equipment; instead, they were rooted in the financial world. In 1981, the trio worked out a deal to acquire Phi Technologies, a company in Oklahoma City that made specialized heavy-duty cassette recording units for data storage. Phi wasn't in the greatest shape, but they were sure they could turn it around, and by restaffing and restructuring, they were able to make the company profitable in a short period of time. (One of their customers was Muzak, the "elevator music"

©1992 Beth Gwinn

company, but their tape drives were also used for medical and broadcast applications.)

In 1985, with Phi Technologies running smoothly and profitably, Henry, Gary, and Dave started looking for other companies to put their money into, those with the growth potential that they felt was lacking at Phi. When they heard Gibson was available, the guitarist in Juszkiewicz was reawakened, and the three inspected the ailing (some might say dying) company. They endured seven months of negotiations, and on January 15, 1986, just in time for the annual National Association of Music Merchants winter show, they announced that they were the new owners of Gibson.

Neil Young, an influence on the vintage market of the early '70s, still rocks on a vintage Les Paul.

©John Bellissimo

MULTI-PLATINUM MUSIC

BY MICHAEL McCALL

Jazzman Larry Coryell holds a new L-5CES.

Clint Black led a new generation of country singers to new levels of record sales. His guitar is an extra-fancy Chet Atkins SST.

As the 1980s evolved, music got bigger, slicker, and more high-tech. In some circles, especially in the traditionally teen-oriented sphere of pop music, it also became more risque and, therefore, more controversial.

The introduction of the compact disc in 1982 proved revolutionary. At first, consumers reacted hesitantly to the availability of digitally encoded music, as the higher cost of CDs and the necessity of buying new playback equipment outweighed the audio advantages of cleaner, brighter sound. By the end of the decade, the CD had become the predominant format for playing music, a trend pushed along when record companies began phasing out vinyl albums and singles.

At about the same time, music fans started to concentrate their buying habits on select artists, making superstars of a few and short-lived flashes of others. Sales of the most popular artists skyrocketed, with Michael Jackson leading the way. The former child star's 1983 *Thriller* album set new sales standards for popular music. Jackson premiered Thriller's initial hit, "Billie Jean," as well as his famed "moonwalk" dance, on a network television special commemorating the 25th anniversary of Motown Records. He created an immediate sensation, and *Thriller* went on to sell more than 40 million albums while generating an unprecedented seven Top 10 hits.

Other artists also spiraled to newfound heights. Bruce Springsteen's *Born in the USA* lifted the popular blue-collar rocker to multi-platinum status. Madonna's *Like a Virgin* became the first album by a female artist to sell more than five million copies. Prince's *Purple Rain* movie soundtrack made his sexually suggestive urban pop music universally controversial.

©1992 Anthony Stroppa

Chuck Pulin, Star File

Jackson's followup, *Bad,* was the first album to feature five Number One pop hits. Newcomer Whitney Houston did him one better: she released seven consecutive Number One singles that stretched over her first two albums. Moreover, Houston's self-titled first album became the biggest-selling recording debut in history, topping the nine million plateau in its first two years and breaking the record set by the pop-rock band Boston nearly two decades earlier.

Hard rock also joined the fun, as brash upstarts Guns 'N Roses shot over five million with their debut, *Appetite for Destruction.* Def Leppard, veterans by comparison, sold several million copies of a few consecutive albums through the 1980s.

By the 1990s, even country music was getting into the act, as Garth Brooks sold more than 10 million copies of his *No Fences* album and another 20

million or so of three other albums. Several other country artists also went into the multiple-million sales category, including Randy Travis, Clint Black, Wynonna Judd, Reba McEntire, George Strait, Alan Jackson, Trisha Yearwood, and Brooks & Dunn.

Music video, virtually unknown prior to the 1980s, grew into an almost immediate force. MTV (for Music Television) premiered in 1982 and quickly blossomed into a multi-media sensation. At first, the all-music-video cable station helped popularize "new wave" bands, which took the fashion and ideas of punk music and put them behind age-old pop music concepts of repetitive melodic hooks. MTV helped make stars of such short-lived groups as Flock of Seagulls, the Human League, Duran Duran, Culture Club, Bananarama, Eurythmics, Men at Work, the Stray Cats, and other up-and-coming bands who exploited the potential of making high-

Even without the pickguard, the dove inlays on the bridge identify country star Alan Jackson's guitar as a Gibson Dove.

energy, highly stylized music videos. Before long it became standard for nearly every new album and single to come out with an accompanying music video promoting the songs shipped to radio. These same bands also helped bring the synthesizer into greater vogue.

Rap music was born in inner city neighborhoods, with impoverished teens making up brash, colorful rhymes over beat-heavy music snippets taken off of previously recorded albums spun on turntables by street-side disc jockeys. Grand Master Flash & the Furious Five and Afrika Bambaataa & the Soul Sonic Force emerged from the Bronx and Harlem neighborhoods of New York City to become rap's first national stars. By the mid '80s, acts like Run-DMC, Public Enemy, and the Beastie Boys were expanding rap's musical and lyrical boundaries. The form that was initially thought to be a short-lived trend became an influential and pervasively popular musical style.

The conservative climate of the 1980s, marked by the Republican presidencies of Ronald Reagan and George Bush, put some heat on the sexually and politically liberal attitudes put forth by pop and rock music. Tipper Gore, wife of then-Senator Al Gore of Tennessee, spearheaded an effort to try to get the music industry to create a rating code to warn parents of albums featuring potentially offensive material. The movement ended in a compromise with the record companies agreeing to put warning stickers on albums.

By the 1990s, most record companies had merged with larger media conglomerates, many of them based outside of the United States. Like many other industries, the record business was owned and managed by mammoth conglomerates and ruled by marketing strategies and heavy consumer analysis. The record industry had barely existed at the start of the century; now it was one of the most profitable and powerful businesses in the world.

Chris Hillman, left, and Herb Pedersen of the Desert Rose Band play the model now touted as "King of the Flat Tops," the J-200.

Slash's use of a Les Paul in Guns 'N Roses prompted a new surge of sunburst popularity.

THE RISE OF THE REISSUES

B Y   T O M   W H E E L E R

Frank Hannon of Tesla wears a 1956-style Les Paul goldtop reissue.

©1991 Anthony Stroppa

I got my first good guitar in 1962, a new SG/Les Paul Junior, and later traded it in on a Jazzmaster (hey, nobody's perfect). A few years ago, I realized how much I missed it and bought one just like it, and it's sitting here now as I write. It may not be the very same Junior I played in my first band, the Bonnevilles, but it's close enough. Not that I'm interested in reliving my adolescence, but when I pick it up, in some small way I'm at one with my past, at least subconsciously, experiencing a slice of Americana and playing a guitar with a history of its own. Anyway, it's a good thing I bought it when I did. These days, an original SG/Les Paul could cost me a bundle.

Nostalgia's expensive.

Until the 1960s, most players assumed new guitars were better than old ones. Companies had long prided themselves on innovation, and consumers responded with enthusiasm and cash. Maybe a few players revered their prewar flattops or jazz-age archtops, but for most people, this was America, where newer is better. After all, the manufacturer is one year older and one year smarter, its products presumably one year

better—like cars. Which would you rather have, a '56 Chevy or a '57? Get real, no comparison. Nostalgia has its place, sure, but otherwise the past is for chumps. In the razzle-dazzle of guitars and show biz, the future is where the action is.

Or was. Guitarists were primed to rethink old vs. new by the 1965 sale of Fender to CBS, which introduced a term that smacked of superiority and cool and shrouded Fender for years like a curse: pre-CBS. During the mid-'60s guitar boom, as manufacturers sold more new instruments than ever, superstars like Jimmy Page and Eric Clapton and Mike Bloomfield were playing Les Pauls from the previous decade. So what gives? These aren't the models in the crisp new catalog. They're old. Used. But these rock stars, who could afford any guitar, didn't look to the catalog for their instruments. They looked to a new place. They looked to the past. Single-cut Les Pauls apparently offered them something they couldn't get from new instruments, and light bulbs clicked on above heads everywhere. These guitar gods know something I don't.

Whatever secrets those old guitars held, everyone realized, as has been said many times in many fields, they don't make 'em like this anymore. Previously, any guitar on earth seemed available as long as you could cough up the dough. But as demand for certain oldies exceeded supply, results were inevitable. A sunburst Les Paul like Bloomfield's? Dream on, pal. You'll never afford it in a million years. Hell, if Bloomfield were still around, he couldn't afford it either.

Gibson reissued a Flying V in 1966. Unfortunately, it barely resembled the original. The goldtops of 1968, though, looked like the originals if you weren't paying attention. They sure weren't SGs.

Introduced without a lot of "returning to our roots" fanfare, they were early, wobbly steps toward the meticulously authentic reissues now offered for detail-obsessed aficionados with fat wallets.

Until the last couple of decades, collectors were a subcult scurrying about guitardom's fringes. They kept to themselves. But during the 1970s the vintage boom got underway, with "Rare Bird" columns in *Guitar Player* and expos devoted exclusively to classic instruments. Guitars weren't just bought and played and traded in and played some more, they were collected like wines, displayed in glass cases like coins, hoarded like bullion. Prices escalated to seemingly stratospheric heights for what used to be mere "used guitars."

I suppose the next step was inevitable, but when I walked into Ace Music on Santa Monica Blvd. in West L.A. and saw that Flying V, it dropped my jaw. It was in perfect condition, new, a genuine Rare Bird, or so I thought. As my eyes worked their way over the tailfins and up the neck I discovered an incomprehensible detail, the logo on the peghead: Ibanez. Pronouncing the first syllable as if it rhymed with "rib," I asked the salesman, "What's Ib-anez, and why are they making Gibson guitars?" ("E-bahn-yez," he corrected me.)

One unsettling fact about the Ibanez V: This knock-off looked much more like the original than Gibson's own reissue, which had its knobs in a triangle (another Gibson from '71 had that odd medallion). Gibson didn't get it, not yet, but these guys from Ibanez, whoever they were, did: If you can't even find an old Flying V, much less afford one, we'll sell you a new one. That's right—a new old guitar. All you have to do is accept our name on the peghead and you too can play a piece of history. Sort of.

Of course, Gibson knew its reissues differed from the original; it simply wanted to update the classic, to recall it rather than duplicate it. To actually replicate an old design seemed dangerous. Ibanez had nothing to risk; no one had heard of them anyway (with a name like that they must be from Spain or Mexico). But Gibson and Fender and others who saw the value of their old guitars rocketing past the new ones had plenty to risk. Would faithfully recreating a blast from the past be an admission that they were past their prime? Would they be throwing in the towel, resting on their laurels? Would authentic reissues dampen the dazzle of new models? Gibson's newer-is-better credo had gained momentum for decades. Would the company reverse course, proclaiming in the words of Emily Litella, never mind?

A reissue of Gibson's most highly respected bass, the Thunderbird IV, provides the bottom end for the Sleeze Beez.

Gibson realized that vintage buffs didn't want guitars that were kinda maybe sorta like the classics. They wanted the real thing—a real fake, not a fake fake. Not like, say, 1978's Les Paul 55/78, which although billed as a reissue sported a combo of features never seen on any classic. In what was now called the vintage market, such half-hearted reissues wouldn't cut it. The Kalamazoo company would have to pay attention to details that collectors had pondered for years, not just

general body shapes but also the height of pickup rings or even the covering on interior wire.

By the early 1980s Fender announced "We brought back the good old days" and Gibson invited players to "soar with a legend." Still, dilemmas remained. As an exec at a Gibson competitor confided, when we're recreating this great old guitar, do we recreate its shortcomings too? Take the Stratocaster. Leo Fender was aware of its limitations, but some parts were unavailable in 1954 so the guitar came with a three-way pickup selector. Years after players had been converting them to five-ways, Fender began installing five-ways as stock features. But what to do on an "authentic" reissue? Use the three-way, which hardly anyone ever liked, or the undeniably superior five-way, which would risk the wrath of purists? Fender's solution was nothing less than ingenious: They installed a five-way but tossed a freebie three-way in the case for players who wanted to move one inch closer to the original.

Manufacturers drew these lines at various places. Some of Gibson's early-'80s reissues were much more authentic than those medallion Flying V's, while at the other end of the spectrum the Flying V-II resembled its namesake in silhouette only and wasn't intended as a reissue anyway. Among recreations of sunbursts, black beauties, Explorers, Firebirds, and SGs, some were legitimate balances of old and new. They had their audiences, to be sure, but it became increasingly apparent that the real excitement was in reissues whose attention to detail gave new meaning to the word picky.

Fender's very-close vintage Strats, for example, are made in the U.S., feature nitrocellulose lacquer finishes and cloth-covered wire, and cost almost twice as much as the pretty-close imported reissues. John Page of Fender's Custom Shop explains, "Even on a recreation of a 1954 Strat, we'll use oblong string holes on the back plate rather than round ones ['54 Strats have round holes;

'55s have oblong], because we felt the round ones weren't functional. And on the U.S. Vintage guitars, we use a neck profile that people want rather than the original V neck or boat neck. If someone wants original specs in every detail, we can accommodate them in the Custom Shop."

The guitars of Gibson's early-'90s Historic Collection, the pride of Nashville, are esteemed, expensive, coveted, everything a manufacturer could hope for. While, say, the Heritage 80 reissue Les Paul (of 1980) looked a lot like the original, the Historic Collection version represents a quantum leap forward (or back) in authenticity. How did they do it? "We split hairs," explains Gibson's Tom Murphy. "We told the company it was going to take a lot of trouble to recreate, not just approximate, a '59 sunburst, but no one ever said no. At every stage they said, 'Just do it.'"

A few of the features that characterize the new reissue: a holly peghead veneer with a silkscreened logo (no decals, thank you), more accurate peghead dimensions, special attention to the inked serial numbers, a two-level unbeveled truss rod cover, a slight shoulder slope on the non-cutaway side, a "dish" top contour that was rendered by a form created by tracing 1959 guitars, short-shaft pots whose authenticity can be appreciated only by going inside the guitar, braided wire, a machined (not molded) pickguard, slightly increased rear pickup ring height, a one-degree shift in neck pitch, even a longer neck extension at the body joint. "The most hard-core buff can take the guitar apart and see that little line at the joint and know it's exactly like a '59," explains Murphy with unconcealed pride. The routs for interior wires match 1959 specs—even the slope of the floor inside the back body cavity. Folks, we're not just talkin' small details here, we're talkin' microscopic. "The earlier reissues were fine guitars," says

Murphy, "but this one has more. It has the magic."

How has Gibson addressed the dilemma of the superiority of certain parts vs. authenticity (for example, the Nashville tune-o-matic vs. older versions)? On a guitar that's billed as a vintage reissue, they stick with original specs. When Tom Murphy says, "It's not about sound or intonation, it's all about aesthetics," he doesn't mean that sound and intonation are unimportant. He means that such considerations are to be assumed in any fine Gibson, and that the Historic Collection begins where other guitars, even Gibson's earlier reissues, leave off.

As of 1994, the reissue market shows no signs of slowing down. Companies have reconciled their pasts and presents, discovering that it makes perfect sense to embrace their heritages (after all, everyone else has), and that the shine of authentic reissues reflects upon the entire line. Catalogs from Rickenbacker, Gretsch, Martin, and others offer scads of recreations of varying authenticity and quality, with labels like Vintage, Reissue, Historic, Classic, Anniversary, and the like. You can find reissues not just of Les Pauls but also the L-5, Tal Farlow, Super 400, and more. (The Les Paul Special has been reissued also—or at least its spirit has been revived—not by Gibson but by Hamer.) Fender has recreated not just several Strats, Teles, and Precision and Jazz Basses but also the Jazzmaster, Jaguar—even the Duo Sonic and others. Martin has revived '30s versions of the D-18 and D-28 and brought back herringbone purfling on models that didn't even exist when herringbone was phased out in the late '40s.

Several reissues on the market today are faithful recreations of their namesakes, down to the screws and wires and frets. If God is in the details, you can see why playing one of these guitars is a religious experience.

New York rocker Alan Stroppa sports a J-180, essentially a reissue of a '60s model except for the name: Everly Brothers.

Inspired by Gibson's fancy banjos, this '30s custom guitar features Venetian scenes.

Dean Dixon, courtesy Gruhn Guitars

CUSTOM SHOP AND ART GUITARS

BY WALTER CARTER

There has always been a custom shop at Gibson—at least in the sense that Gibson has always been willing to build custom-ordered instruments.

The very first catalog invited customers to send in their own wood if they wanted a special instrument made from it. The company was a little over a year old when a fancy harp guitar was made for the St. Louis Exposition of 1904. The "Artist" mandolins of the early years, with ornate fingerboards, never appeared in catalogs.

Guitarists of the '30s had their instruments outfitted with banjo-style fingerboards, made of pearloid with engraved and tinted artwork. Round holes showed up on what would normally be f-hole models, and vice versa. Doublenecks in the '60s were all special-order guitars, and any combination of necks was possible.

Gibson collectors have seen so many uniquely appointed instruments through the years that even the most outlandish creation hardly raises an eyebrow. They just shrug and say, "Gibson made at least one of everything."

Gibson has not been blind to the commercial appeal of guitars that started as special orders. Nick Lucas's custom-built guitar, with an extra-deep body and wider fingerboard, became a Gibson

catalog model in 1927. Ray Whitley's request for a fancy large-bodied flattop became the SJ-200. Herb Ellis's single-pickup ES-175 is now the Herb Ellis Model (ES-165).

In the early '80s, Custom Shop decals appeared on special guitars, but the Custom Shop was not a separate entity. Dealers could order virtually anything a customer was willing to pay for, and whatever was required in the way of engineering, luthiery, finishing, etc., was pulled together from the factory staff to fill the order. The market for special guitars was too small, too individualized to support a dedicated department. Or so it seemed.

A market for fancy, one-of-a-kind Gibsons was discovered almost by accident. As a Christmas bonus in 1987, factory supervisors were given an instrument. Jim Triggs, a mandolin builder, picked a Les Paul; Greg Rich,

Dan Loftin, courtesy Gruhn Guitars

Les Paul meets Venice on the first of the art guitars, shown at a Nashville vintage show in 1988.

Country star Travis Tritt plays a fancy 12-string version of the Chet Atkins SST.

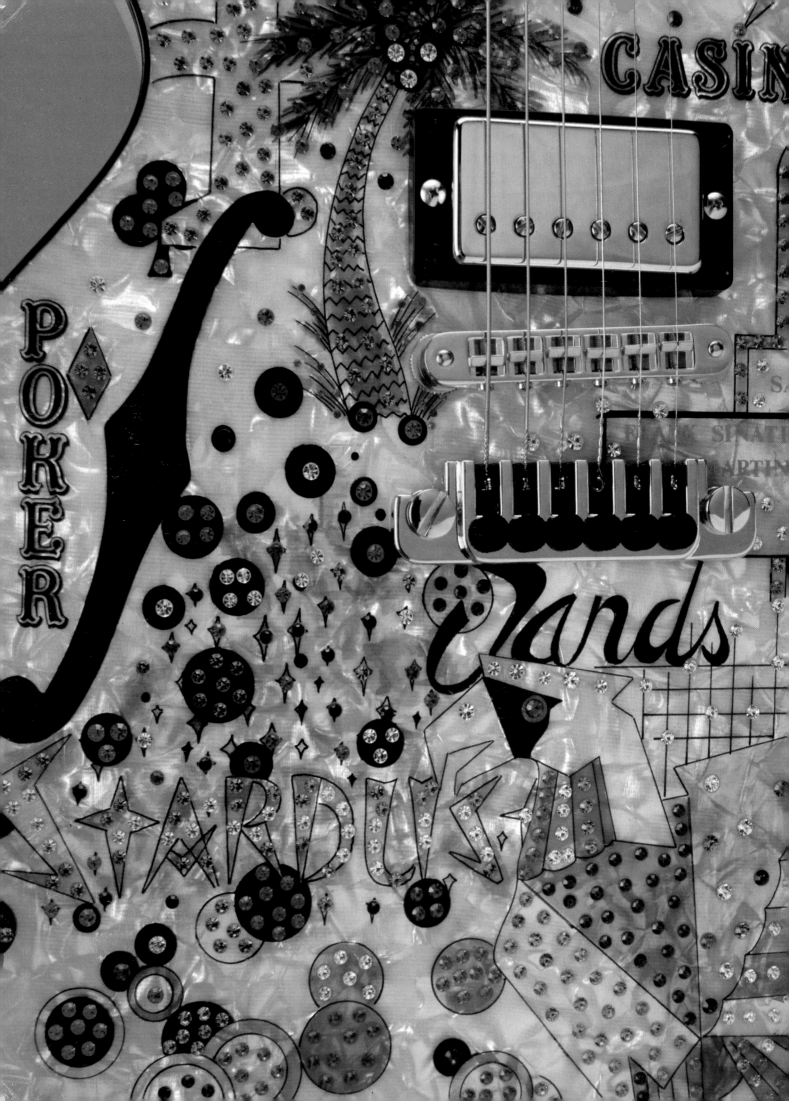

working in the banjo shop, picked an F-5 mandolin. They painted them white and then jazzed them up with lots of lavishly illustrated pearloid. In March 1988, these creations were unveiled at a vintage guitar show in Nashville—the toughest of audiences for new instruments, plain or fancy.

Although these instruments were perfectly playable, they were made on the speculation that someone might buy them as pieces of art. Someone did just that. Rich and Triggs went back to work and created four or five more instruments for the National Association of Music Merchants show in January 1989. A prominent Japanese collector bought them all and requested more. And a market was born.

In 1991, Gibson expanded the Custom Shop staff to accommodate dealer requests and to participate in various aspects of the Historic Collection, research and development, and the maintenance of specifications through the production line. Finally, in 1993, Gibson gave the Custom Shop its own facility with its own talent pool. Today the Custom Shop builds guitars to the custom specs of dealers and performing artists and also creates unique new guitars for collectors of fine art.

Horses from the Camptown Races adorn the fingerboard of this Stephen Foster banjo.

The Suroeste or Southwest series of art guitars, designed by Jim Landers, debuted at the 1994 NAMM show.

On ZZ Top's Recycler tour, Dusty Hill and Billy Gibbons sport balsa wood "Johnny Firesmith" models made in the Custom Shop by Matthew Klein.

Matt Barnes

Billy Mitchell, courtesy Gruhn Guitars

©1991 Anthony Stroppa

A market was born when this Rich/Triggs "Las Vegas" guitar hit the 1989 NAMM show.

GIBSON TODAY

BY TOM MULHERN

Henry Juszkiewicz, David Berryman, and Gary Zebrowski all agree that the acquisition of Gibson was probably the easiest part of the task ahead of them in early 1986. Straightening out the difficulties wrought by 17 years of Norlin's heavy-handed management was the first challenge that had to be addressed.

Zebrowski remained at Phi Technologies (which is now also the U.S. distributor of the famous Nagra tape recorders), while Berryman and Juszkiewicz took up residence in Nashville. (In 1991, Zebrowski and Phi Technologies split off from Gibson, leaving Berryman and Juszkiewicz as the company's primary partners, although Zebrowski owns some stock in Gibson.)

With Juszkiewicz in the role of chairman and chief

At the 1993 summer NAMM show in Nashville, Gibsons were showcased by such diverse artists as "The Last of the Full-Grown Men," Webb Wilder (top), jazz great Herb Ellis, and heavy rocker Zakk Wylde (right).

executive officer, and Berryman as president, they set about rescuing Gibson guitars. Entire levels of managers were fired, and even middle managers were replaced. One former employee recalls it as a purge, but a necessary one, adding, "The fact that Henry was a guitar player helped. Everybody wanted Gibson to succeed, so he was cut an enormous amount of slack."

Some experimentation went on in the design and production of new guitars, but as Juszkiewicz explains, "Every time we strayed from what consumers thought we should be, we failed. What they wanted were the classic, good

Photos by Jimi Stratton

guitars." A renewed emphasis on quality drove the factory, and toward that end production was actually cut—so that kinks in the processes and in the quality could be ironed out. It's generally acknowledged that the quality improved, and as a result production was again increased—all the time with as much attention paid to the instruments as to the bottom line.

Steinberger Sound, of New York, was the new Gibson's first acquisition, in 1987. The company that had started its own revolution at the dawn of the 1980s with Ned Steinberger's headless, small-bodied graphite-composite basses (and later, headless guitars) helped Gibson get its foot back into the bass business, an area in which Gibson had always stumbled. In late 1989, Steinberger was joined by Tobias, another well-regarded bass maker, which had been located in Burbank, California. Tobias basses were practically the antithesis of Steinbergers: laminated exotic woods,

Brett Michaels of Poison plays a customized Gibson Invader.

traditional headstock styling, and sculpted bodies. Today, they operate as a single division, pooling resources without pooling designs. "When you have two specialized lines that address a product niche," Berryman explains, "it's tough to be able to hire the right talent, in terms of general management, product and marketing management, and a separate financial person and a purchasing person. The infrastructure you need to do the business well is tough to do on a small revenue base. So that's why we put those two together. They're very specialized but at different ends of the spectrum. One's at the woody end and one's at the high-tech kind of space-age end."

Juszkiewicz affirms the need for specialization, saying, "We have Steinberger people working on Steinbergers and Tobias people working on Tobiases. We're giving them the benefit of our engineering, know-how, and better equipment, but they're still their own people. We won't make Tobiases that look like Les Pauls, though. We're very sensitive to maintaining the spirit of what's good there. Too many big companies buy smaller ones, and before you know it everything looks like Oreo cookies. We can truly say that we allow the freedom of the creative aspects of the instruments to maintain and grow."

According to Juszkiewicz, the Flatiron company, in Bozeman, Montana, was acquired in 1987 mostly because Gibson had lost the ability to produce mandolins ever since its move from Kalamazoo. It also meant that Gibson could get back into acoustic guitars in a big way. Part of that meant building a new factory for Flatiron in Bozeman in 1989 and bringing all flattop production to the Montana plant. Gibson also purchased Erika Banjos to get back into making banjos, once a staple of Gibson's fretted-instrument sales. Today, banjo resonators and necks are made in Bozeman and then shipped to Nashville for assembly and finish.

Gibson recently revived the Orange amplifier line, recreating the powerful, unique (the only orange Tolex-covered amps in regular production), 1970s-era amps right down to their knobs and face plates. In addition, Gibson acquired OMI (the Original Musical Instrument Co.), the renowned makers of Dobro resophonic guitars, bringing yet another dimension of guitar making into the company's fold.

Gibson also owns Oberheim (famous for its synthesizers) and Gibson Labs and has a partnership with Zeta Systems, all high-tech

©1992 Anthony Stroppa

electronics-based businesses that bring a non-guitar element to the company. Epiphone amps, made in Korea, and Dawn pro audio gear also fit into this end of the business. Gibson also distributes Mapex drums (it handled Pearl drums from the mid 1970s until the early '90s).

Dave Berryman stresses that although there are many pieces to the Gibson puzzle, each company is essentially autonomous, run by its own division manager. "We can't be involved in all the aspects of the business," he says. "Each division has to be able to flex to its own market, to their demand. We don't have a lot of centralized services, per se."

Imports, including Epiphone guitars, Mapex drums, and Orange amps, are handled through MCI (Music City International), for which Dave Berryman is responsible. The primary purpose of Epiphone guitars, in Juszkiewicz's estimation, is to let guitarists without the money for a Gibson buy a good-quality guitar. "Our Epiphone guitars are set up by the same people setting up Gibsons," he says. "We have a warranty on that product

that we stand behind." To that end, Gibson maintains offices with its own engineers to oversee design and production of its overseas operations, rather than simply importing equipment and sticking a label on it.

After pulling itself up by its bootstraps and rebuilding an empire that had eroded to almost nothing under Norlin's directorship, it might be fair to ask if Gibson has reached its apex. According to Henry Juszkiewicz, the company is still very much on the ascent. "We have a great commitment to the future and to the business, and there are a lot of things that can be done to get this industry into much healthier shape. By no means are we where we need to be in the fretted instrument area. The business is still fragmented. There are so many guitar companies— it seems like anyone who has anything to do in music has a guitar line. There are more than enough brands out there. Does the world need this? The fact is, the industry is too fragmented. Industries don't work that way. Any healthy industry is an oligopoly, where you have three or four major competitors who are fiercely competitive. When there are too many companies, nobody can make money, nobody can afford to do good things. In a healthy industry, you have some good guys beating each other's brains out, and then the consumer gets the best of a furiously competitive environment, and the companies have enough money to do development of new things. The industry is just starting to go in that direction. We're getting pretty healthy, and some other companies are doing well. It's a process that I see continuing to happen for another five years or so.

"At this point, we've established a leadership role once again. You can argue whether we're the leader, but you can't argue that we're not one of the top two or three companies. In many ways, we're already the leader in banjos and mandolins. Our objective is to become the largest fretted-instrument company and the recognized leader of guitars and other instruments."

THE NEXT HUNDRED YEARS

BY HENRY JUSZKIEWICZ

Tradition and innovation. Old-style craftsmanship applied to new ideas. That's the legacy of Orville Gibson, Lloyd Loar, Ted McCarty, and all those who made Gibson what it is today. It's also a blueprint for success for Gibson's next hundred years.

Tradition is the easier of the two parts to follow. Gibson has a wealth of tradition—a hundred years' worth that we've tapped quite profitably in continuing or reviving some of the Gibson's classic influential models. Our newly expanded Custom Shop ensures that the skills of artisans and craftsmen will not slip through the cracks of technological advances.

Innovation is the hard part. In recent years, advances in guitar design have been relatively minor or else not fully exploited. This is an industry of trends, of ups and downs, and we are due for another period of great innovation. It will take a bold, fearless spirit to move forward, however, because innovations of the future will probably not be immediately accepted. (They weren't during the last hundred years.) Fortunately, there's a spirit of innovation that has driven Gibson throughout its history. Orville himself set the standard for bold, fearless innovators. Fear of failure has never stopped Gibson from breaking new ground, and it won't stop Gibson in the next hundred years.

Innovations must be made on the business side as well as in instrument design. Early Gibson managers found new ways to make Gibsons available to musicians all across America; that challenge now is global. Even though Gibson has had great success in the international market, that success today is based largely on the appeal of Gibson as a piece of Americana. As the "global village" becomes a reality, I see Gibson integrating with all the cultures of the world, supplying instruments suited for each particular culture.

Advances in electronics revolutionized the music industry in the '30s, and the frontier today is still in electronics. We are out on that frontier, using state-of-the-art technology to explore the very essence of sound, to find out what makes instruments sound good, and to use that technology and knowledge to create new sounds. We won't be changing the creative end of musicianship. We'll be utilizing technology—like giving an author a word processor—to give a musician a more versatile instrument and a more efficient way to make sounds.

The casual observer in one of our electronics labs might see no sign that Gibson makes guitars. But Gibson is a guitar company, first and foremost, and will continue to be. Fortune-tellers have been predicting the end of the guitar since the late '70s, but I don't see that happening. The guitar has always been the instrument of the common people to have some fun with. Granted, over the last 40 years, with gifted players getting so much press, playing guitar has taken on a more esoteric image, but we're working to bring the guitar back to being an easy entrée into music.

Gibson makes a unique product—one that people buy to have fun with and yet one that has had a powerful influence on popular culture for the past 100 years. The next 100 years will be no different. With such an inspirational past, Gibson can look forward to an exciting future.

Gibson unveiled the ultimate Centennial guitar, a Les Paul Custom with solid gold hardware, at the summer 1994 NAMM show in Nashville.

ACKNOWLEDGMENTS AND CREDITS

The writers would like to thank the following people for their help in telling the Gibson story:

In Kalamazoo: Julius Bellson, John Broesamle, Jim Deurloo, Ted McCarty, Kate Harris, Alice Hughes, Jim Johnstone, Catherine Larson, J. P. Moats, Maudie Moore, and Dave Patrick.

And around the world: Chet Atkins, Walter K. Bauer, Jeff Beck, Dee Brown, André de Vekey, Dick Decosse, Jim Fisch, Robert Fripp, David Grisman, Jack Harvey, Steve Howe, John Huis, B. B. King, Les Paul, Mike Longworth, Stan Rendell, Alvino Rey, Greg Rich, Brian Majeski, Wilbur Marker, Earl Scruggs, Tim Shaw, and Gary Zebrowski.

Thanks to Gruhn Guitars for the use of photo equipment and access to the Gruhn collection of catalogs and photographs.

Thanks to Jim "Hutch" Hutchins and Terry Ryan for guidance around the Gibson factory.

SPECIAL PHOTO CREDITS

New photographs inside the Gibson factory by Matthew Barnes.

Thanks to the Tennessee Antiques Mall, Inc., for valuable help in researching and supplying props for period photographs.

Section opening spreads photographed by Matthew Barnes at the following locations:

Downtown Antique Mall, Nashville

Magic Memories, Franklin, Tennessee

Home of Mrs. Kathleen Wyatt

Home of Christie Carter

Truck of Ed Brook

Custom Car Motors, Nashville

Nashville Academy Theater

Masterfonics, Nashville

Downtown Antique Mall

Magic Memories

Home of Mrs. Kathleen Wyatt

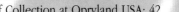

LITERATURE AND ARTIFACT OWNERS

Maps © Rand McNally: 60–65, 306–307

Walter Carter: all sheet music

Gibson Archives: 34–37, 39 (photo), 43–47, 50, 89, 98, 104, 138, 158, 170, 173, 187, 188, 195, 196, 198, 203–07, 219, 226, 228–29, 238, 268, 275, 277, 289

Gruhn Guitars: 20, 23, 25, 40, 41, 49, 51, 52–55, 56, 77, 78, 79, 82, 86, 87, 99, 102, 106, 111, 120, 123, 124, 125, 130, 131, 141, 146, 181, 222, 248

Dale Heintzelman, 120 (Hawaiians)

Home of Christie Carter

Truck of Ed Brook

INSTRUMENT OWNERS

Roy Acuff Collection at Opryland USA: 42

Clifford Antone: 208

Blackwell Brothers: 141

Gary Burnette: 156

Walter Carter: 66 (sax), 96, 159, 180

Bob Christopher: 211, 236, 237

Country Music Foundation: 150, 151

Danny Davenport: 188

Gibson Collection: 14, 15, 26, 28, 31, 32, 48, 66, 90–91, 109, 278, 295, 303

Gruhn Guitars: 44, 45, 51, 56, 113, 124, 125, 128, 134, 135, 136, 137 (Oriole), 144, 158, 161, 162, 164 (ES-250), 185, 188, 191, 198–99, 200, 201 (Les Paul Signature), 213, 217, 218–20, 238–39, 240, 261, 292, 300

Dave Hussong: 197

Mandolin Brothers: 28 (F mandolin)

Jim Reynolds: 201 (Les Paul Jumbo)

Greg Rich: 284, 293

Hank Risan: 147–49

Gary Roberts: 137 (Martelle)

Toby Ruckert: 196

Roger Siminoff: 30

Steve Soest: 106, 107, 111

Gil Southworth: 183

Thoroughbred Guitars: 46

Jimmy Wallace: 186

Crawford White: 164 (ES-300), 165, 174

Masterfonics

Custom Car Motors

Nashville Academy Theater

THE CONTRIBUTORS

TONY BACON

of London, England, is known in Europe as the Guitar Guru. He has been widely published in British periodicals and is the co-author of *The Ultimate Guitar Book, The Fender Book, The Les Paul Book,* and *The Guru's Guitar Guide*.

A. R. DUCHOSSOIR

is the author of *Gibson Electrics: The Classic Years, Guitar Identification,* and books on the Fender Stratocaster and Telecaster. He lives in Paris, France, and works as consultant for Barclay's Bank.

R. E. BRUNÉ

is an authority on European guitars. He has been a maker and dealer of classical and flamenco guitars since 1966. Based in Evanston, Illinois, he is working on a book of classical and flamenco makers.

THOMAS GOLDSMITH

is a city editor and former music reporter for *The Tennessean* in Nashville. He plays guitar in the Nashville Jug Band and has produced records by Dave Olney and Tracy Nelson.

Pat Casey Daley

GARY BURNETTE

is a bluegrass musician, vintage guitar dealer, and guitar show promoter who lives in Asheville, North Carolina. He owns the finest collection of prewar Gibson dreadnoughts in existence.

GEORGE GRUHN

is the proprietor of Gruhn Guitars in Nashville, one of the oldest vintage dealerships (founded in 1970). He is the author of numerous magazine articles on vintage fretted instruments and the co-author of *Gruhn's Guide to Vintage Guitars* and *Acoustic Guitars and Other Fretted Instruments: A Photographic History*.

WALTER CARTER

is the author of *The Songwriter's Guide to Collaboration* and the co-author of *Gruhn's Guide to Vintage Guitars* and *Acoustic Guitars and Other Fretted Instruments: A Photographic History*. He is also a songwriter and former music reporter for *The Tennessean* daily newspaper.

Christie Carter

SCOTT HAMBLY, PH.D.,

researched the mandolin as a Predoctoral Fellow at the Smithsonian Institution and wrote his doctoral dissertation on the mandolin at the University of Pennsylvania in 1977. He is now Publications Editor and Research Project Editor in the Clinical Investigation Department and manager of the Institutional Review Board at the Naval Medical Center in Oakland, California.

Sandy Rothman

MICHAEL I. HOLMES is the founder of *Mugwumps,* one of the earliest publications dealing with vintage instruments. He has been compiling information for an encyclopedia of American guitar makers for the past 20 years. He is the head of Wamsutta Software, based in New Bedford, Massachusetts.

TOM MULHERN of Campbell, California, is the former managing editor of *Guitar Player* magazine. He is now the head of Tom Mulhern and Associates and is an independent consultant to the music industry.

Brian Tramontana

HENRY JUSZKIEWICZ has been the chief executive officer of Gibson Guitar Corp. since January 1986 and is the driving force behind Gibson's recovery and reemergence as a leading guitar maker.

MARY SHAUGHNESSY has covered music for *People* magazine since 1984 and is the author of *Les Paul: An American Original.* She lives in New Jersey.

DR. ELIAS J. KAUFMAN is Associate Professor at the State University of New York at Buffalo and Senior Research Fellow in the Center for American Studies at SUNY at Buffalo. He and his spouse, Dr. Madeleine Kaufman, have been the editors of the American Banjo Fraternity's *Five-Stringer* since 1973.

ROGER SIMINOFF founded *Pickin'* magazine and was later editor of *Frets* magazine. He was one of the first to research in depth the lives and work of Orville Gibson and Lloyd Loar. He works for the Radius company in Los Gatos, California.

MICHAEL McCALL is a music columnist for the *Nashville Scene* weekly newspaper. He is a former music reporter for the *Nashville Banner* and has contributed numerous articles to music-related publications.

Catherine McCall

THOMAS A. VAN HOOSE is a clinical psychologist in Dallas, Texas, and the author of *The Gibson Super 400: The Art of the Fine Guitar.* He is currently working on a book about independent builders of archtop guitars.

Jimi Stratton

TOM WHEELER is the former editor of *Guitar Player.* His two books, *The Guitar Book* and *American Guitars,* are the earliest comprehensive treatments of guitars and guitar makers. He is a journalism professor at the University of Oregon.

FOR FURTHER READING

Gibson's 100-year history has provided material and inspiration for many writers and photographers. For detailed discussions of various Gibson models or for wider photographic treatment, the following books are recommended:

Bacon, Tony, and Paul Day. *The Gibson Les Paul Book.* San Francisco: GPI Books, 1993.
Thorough history of Gibson's Les Paul line with a reference section for all guitars with "Les Paul" in the model name. All color (15 spreads). 96 pages.

Bacon, Tony, and Paul Day. *The Ultimate Guitar Book.* New York: Alfred A. Knopf, 1991.
All-color coffee-table history and overview of the guitar, including photos of many important Gibson models. 192 pages.

Bellson, Julius. *The Gibson Story.* Kalamazoo: Julius Bellson, 1973.
The first history of the company, lovingly written by an employee with 38 years of Gibson service. Includes many black-and-white photos of instruments and employees. 96 pages.

Duchossoir, A. R. *Gibson Electrics: The Classic Years.* Milwaukee, WI: Hal Leonard, 1994.
Detailed model histories, specs, and production totals for Gibson electric guitars from the ES-150 (Charlie Christian) through the Firebirds in the mid '60s. Many black-and-white photos, 32 pages of color. 256 pages.

Duchossoir, A. R. *Guitar Identification.* 3rd ed. Milwaukee, WI: Hal Leonard Publishing Corporation (distributor), 1981.
Dating information for four major brands including Gibson. Details changes in logo, labels, etc., and includes serial number and factory order number lists. 48 pages.

Fisher, Don, and Mike Longworth. *Mastertones.* (publisher unavailable)
A detailed history of Gibson Mastertone banjos, scheduled for spring 1995 publication.

Gruhn, George, and Walter Carter. *Acoustic Guitars and Other Fretted Instruments: A Photographic History.* San Francisco: GPI Books, 1993.
Coffee-table size, includes color photos of important Gibson acoustic archtops and flattops, from Orville Gibson's creations to current models.

Gruhn, George, and Walter Carter. *Electric Guitars and Basses: A Photographic History.* San Francisco: GPI Books, 1994.
Coffee-table size, includes color photos of important Gibson electrics, from the first metalbody lap steel to Custom Shop creations.

Gruhn, George, and Walter Carter. *Gruhn's Guide to Vintage Guitars.* San Francisco: GPI Books, 1991.
Portable reference with descriptions and dates of all Gibson guitars, harp guitars, basses, mandolins and steel guitars (over 600 models); serial numbers and other dating information; a few black-and-white photos; keys for quick model identifcation.

Howe, Steve, with Tony Bacon. *The Steve Howe Guitar Collection.* **San Francisco: GPI Books, 1993.**
The Yes guitarist has an extensive collection, almost half of which are Gibsons and Epiphones. All color, with comments from Howe. 88 pages.

Rich, Bill, and Rick Nielsen. *Guitars of the Stars: Rick Nielsen.* **Gots Publishing, Ltd., 1993.**
The collection of Cheap Trick's lead guitarist includes lots of Gibsons—64 pages' worth, mostly vintage electrics, some vintage flattops and a couple of Custom Shop jobs. All color, 181 pages.

Scott, Jay, and Vic Da Pra. *'Burst: 1958–60 Les Paul.* **Hauppauge, NY: Seventh String Press, Inc., 1994.**
The sunburst Les Paul Standard—a whole book about it. Lots of black-and-white photos, 16 color pages. 120 pages.

Shaughnessy, Mary Alice. *Les Paul: An American Original.* **New York: William Morrow & Co., 1993.**
Biography of the man whose name graces the headstocks of thousands of Gibsons.

Tsumura, Akira. *Banjos: The Tsumura Collection.* **New York: Kodansha International Ltd., 1984.**
Tsumura's first book on his banjo collection focuses on Jazz Age (tenor) banjos, with some Gibsons featured. Limited edition, out of print, but copies turn up occasionally. 168 pages.

Tsumura, Akira. *Guitars: The Tsumura Collection.* **New York: Kodansha International Ltd., 1987.**
Tsumura's taste in guitars runs to high-end archtops. Includes more Citations (11) in one place than anywhere else in the world, and some flattops. Limited edition, out of print, but copies turn up occasionally. 192 pages, all in color, with 50 pages of Gibsons, 11 pages of Epis.

Tsumura, Akira. *One Thousand and One Banjos: The Tsumura Collection.* **New York: Kodansha International Ltd., 1993.**
Tsumura's limited-run tome weighs in at over 15 pounds. All Gibson prewar banjo styles are represented but especially the high-end. Only 88 of the 903 pages are devoted to Gibson. Pricey at $500-plus, but where else can you find 10 original All Americans in one place?

Van Hoose, Thomas A. *The Super 400: Art of the Fine Guitar.* **San Francisco: Miller Freeman, 1991.**
Everything about Super 400s, acoustic and electric, down to the manufacturer of the case latches. Includes production figures for each variation and also a lengthy discussion of the Gibson L-5.

Wheeler, Tom. *American Guitars.* **New York: HarperCollins, 1990.**
Gibson takes up over 100 of the 373 pages in this seminal work, an illustrated encyclopedia of American makers. The Gibson entry includes an overview of the company and its models, plus some interviews and detailed accounts of the Les Paul and Korina models, and selected production totals from the '50s, '60s, and '70s.

Whitford, Eldon, David Vinopal, and Dan Erlewine. *Gibson's Fabulous Flat-Top Guitars.* **San Francisco: Miller Freeman, 1994.**
Detailed model histories, specs, and production totals for all Gibson flattop guitars. Black-and-white photos throughout, 16 color pages of standard models plus 16 color pages of fancy custom creations. 207 pages.

INDEX